Men'sHealth.

TODAY 2008

THE POWER OF FOOD REMEDIES

Men's Health.

TODAY 2008

THE POWER OF FOOD REMEDIES

RODALE

Printed in the United States of America
Rodale Inc. makes every effort to use acid-free ♾, recycled paper ♻

Book design by Christina Gaugler

ISBN-13 978–1–59486–872–6
ISBN-10 1–59486–872–7

2   4   6   8   10   9   7   5   3   1   hardcover

We inspire and enable people to improve their lives and the world around them

For more of our products visit **rodalestore.com** or call 800-848-4735

Contents

Introduction

Nearly every day, researchers announce more exciting discoveries that show how the foods we eat help fight disease. There is now no doubt that Mother Nature's most powerful foods—from apples and apricots to wheat and wine—can be your best medicine for cutting cholesterol, losing weight, preventing cancer, reversing heart disease, and managing scores of other conditions.

Thanks to the constant deluge of new studies, we now know that it's the remarkable microscopic substances in plants called *phytonutrients* that act in any number of ways to help us prevent illness and achieve optimal health. Quercetin, lycopene, resveratrol, ellagic acid, alpha- and beta-carotene . . . these are just a few of the powerful phytonutrients you'll read about in this book. Some stimulate your body's immune cells and infection-fighting enzymes, preventing colds and flu and combating environmental toxins. Others help to balance hormone levels, thus reducing the risk of hormone-related conditions, such as prostate cancer. And still other phytonutrients function as antioxidants, neutralizing the harmful free radicals (unstable oxygen molecules) that are believed to play a role in the onset of so many degenerative diseases.

Today more than 9,000 phytonutrients have been documented, and this is just the tip of the iceberg. These discoveries have changed everything we thought we knew about foods! Oats, for example, have long been known to lower cholesterol because of the dietary fiber they contain. But that's not the only reason they protect the heart. Scientists now know that oats contain natural chemicals called tocotrienols that are 50 percent more powerful than even vitamin E in reducing the risk of heart disease.

Apples are another food that may surprise you. They've always been thought to be healthy, mostly because they are chock-full of vitamins and fiber. But it turns out that it's the phytonutrients in apples (found mainly in the skin) that are the powerhouses. In addition, one of those phytonutrients, quercetin, has been shown to help improve lung function, reducing the risk of asthma and obstructive pulmonary disease.

Or take red wine. We all know a glass with dinner can be a great relaxer, but who could have predicted that the resveratrol present in red wine could help make bad low-density lipoprotein (LDL) cholesterol less likely to stick to artery walls. Or that wine might even play a role in preventing diabetes.

One of the most exciting discoveries is that some foods can literally stop the chemical changes that can lead to cancer. Beans, for example, contain lignans, isoflavones, saponins, and other compounds that have been shown to inhibit cancer cell growth. And strawberries, and other berries that contain ellagic acid, have been found to block the harmful effects of cancer-causing chemicals in the body.

And as if all this isn't enough to make you head for the produce aisle, scientists have also discovered ways to make the foods that we eat even more powerful. You may know, for instance, that beta-carotene (found in dark orange and dark green vegetables and fruits) is good for your heart. But scientists have learned that the body can't readily absorb beta-carotene unless you eat it with a little fat. That's why a drizzle of olive oil on your veggies or a dab of yogurt on your fresh fruit can vastly increase their healing powers. Garlic, used in a number of the recipes in this book, also needs a little help. Chop whole cloves fine and suddenly the protective compound allicin is released. It quickly breaks down into a cascade of other healthful compounds, which can help lower triglycerides and cholesterol, reduce the risk of stomach and colon cancers, and much more.

And the list of foods and their seemingly magical healing powers goes on and on.

At *Men's Health*, we've reviewed the latest scientific journals and talked with hundreds of the country's top doctors and nutrition experts in order to bring you the most current information on a range of food remedies. We want to be sure you are armed with the best and most recent advice and information on how to take advantage of something we all love to do (eat) and avoid something we all fear (disease). The new science we've tapped into amazes us—and surely it will amaze you, too.

So grab an apple, or a glass of wine if you like, and start reading—and eating to your health's content!

Apples

THEIR BENEFITS ARE SKIN DEEP

John Chapman, a Massachusetts resident who liked to travel, isn't remembered for his groundbreaking efforts to prevent heart disease and cancer and improve Americans' overall health. But he certainly did his part. As he wandered around the eastern states and the Midwest for the first half of the 1800s, he planted apple seeds, transplanted seedlings, and established apple orchards to help supply pioneers with the tasty fruit.

He's now remembered as Johnny Appleseed, and nowadays, chemists, doctors, and other researchers are expanding his legacy as they discover new reasons why apples are so good to have around.

Apples are more than just a wholesome snack. Studies suggest that eating apples can help reduce the risk of heart disease, and they may also help protect you from lung cancer. In addition, they may lower your risk of asthma and improve your overall lung function. Indeed, it appears that having an apple or two a day really can help keep the doctor away.

Filled with Antioxidants

Some of the most powerful disease-fighting components in apples are phenolics, and they've been getting a lot of research attention lately. Phenolics are a type of phytochemical that can act as powerful antioxidants, neutralizing free radicals before they have the chance to harm your DNA and other important components within your body.

Research conducted by scientists at Cornell University in Ithaca, New York, and Seoul University in South Korea found that these phenolics, rather than the vitamin C in the fruit, may provide the bulk of apples' antioxidant power.

Other research from Cornell set out to rank the total phenolic content in many popular fruits. Apples came in second place, behind the cranberry, and beat out other favorites such as the red grape, strawberry, pineapple, banana, peach, lemon, orange, pear, and grapefruit.

This study also found that apples had the second highest total antioxidant activity of these fruits (again, the cranberry beat it). Finally, the study also measured the ability of extracts of these fruits to inhibit liver-cancer cells in the lab. Apples came in third place, behind cranberries and lemons.

If you factor in their tastiness, easy preparation time, and versatility, apples are hard to beat as an easy way to get a quick dose of antioxidants—after all, have you ever grabbed a handful of cranberries or a lemon and eaten them?

Getting to the Heart of the Matter

The phytochemicals lurking in apples may make them useful tools in warding off heart disease.

Research have found that intake of flavonoids—particularly catechin and epicatechin (both flavonoids found in apples)—may be associated with a lower risk of death from coronary heart disease.

Even though many people favor the flesh, much of an apple's healing power resides in the skin, which contains large amounts—about 4 milligrams—of an antioxidant compound known as quercetin. Like vitamin C and beta-carotene, this antioxidant can help prevent harmful oxygen molecules from damaging individual cells.

Even in the healing world of antioxidants, quercetin is thought to be exceptional. In a Finnish study that followed more than 10,000 adults, it was found that the people who ate the most quercetin had a 20 percent lower risk of dying from coronary heart disease than those who ate the least.

"So eating an apple a day is not a bad idea," says Lawrence H. Kushi, ScD, associate director for etiology and prevention research at Kaiser Permanente's division of research in Oakland, California.

Keeping Cancer Away

Apples may also be helpful in warding off the dreaded disease of lung cancer. A Hawaiian study looking at the diet history of 582 people who had lung cancer and 582 without the disease found that the people who ate the most apples, onions, and white grapefruit had roughly half the risk of lung cancer than those who ate the least amounts of these foods. Apples and onions are both high in quercetin. In another study, Finnish researchers found that men who consumed more quercetin were 60 percent less likely to have lung cancer than men with lower quercetin intakes.

"When you subject cells to a carcinogen and then put in the quercetin, you prevent mutation from occurring—you prevent the carcinogen from acting," says Dr. Kushi.

Apples' Effect on Lung Problems

Apples may also help reduce your risk of asthma and improve your lung health. An Australian study involving 1,600 adults associated apple and pear consumption with a lower risk of asthma. Finnish researchers—who seem to be pretty busy when it comes to studying apples—found fewer cases of asthma among people with high levels of quercetin in their diets.

And a study of more than 13,000 adults in the Netherlands found that those who ate more apples and pears had better lung function and less chronic obstructive pulmonary disease.

Maintaining Digestive Health with Apple Fiber

Recent discoveries aside, apples are also excellent sources of fiber. They contain both soluble and insoluble fiber, including pectin. A 5-ounce apple with the skin has about 3 grams of fiber. "They're a good source," says Chang Lee, PhD, professor of food science and technology at the Cornell University–New York State Agricultural Experimental Station in Geneva.

Insoluble fiber, found mostly in the skin, is the kind that we used to call roughage, which has long been recommended for relieving constipation. More is at stake, though, than just comfort. Studies show that a smoothly operating digestive tract can help prevent diverticulosis, a condition in which small pouches form in the large intestine, and also cancer of the colon. Plus, insoluble fiber is filling, which is why apples are such an excellent weight-control food for people who want to lose weight without feeling hungry.

The soluble fiber in apples, which is the same kind that is found in oat bran, acts differently from the insoluble kind. Rather than passing through the digestive tract more or less unchanged, soluble fiber forms a gel-like material in the digestive tract that helps lower cholesterol and, with it, the risk of heart disease and stroke.

It's not just the soluble fiber that's so helpful, but a particular type of soluble fiber called pectin. The same ingredient used to thicken jellies and jams, pectin appears to reduce the amount of cholesterol produced in the liver. An average-size apple contains 0.7 gram of pectin, more than the amount in strawberries and bananas.

GETTING THE MOST

Store them cold. If you're buying more apples than you can eat quickly, store them in a plastic bag or a produce drawer in your refrigerator.

Protect their color. If you're serving apple slices, dip them in a citrus juice—such as lemon or grapefruit juice—after you cut them to help preserve their bright color.

Don't count on processed apples. Although apple juice contains a little iron and potassium, it's no great shakes compared with the whole fruit. By the time apples wind up as juice, they've given up most of their fiber and quercetin. In

In the Kitchen

There are 2,500 kinds of apples in the United States alone. Even if you can't sample all of the world's apples, you can try some of the more notable varieties. Here are a few types to look for.

Braeburn. Ranging in color from greenish gold to almost solid red, Braeburn apples combine sweetness and tartness. A great eating apple.

Fuji. Available year-round, Fuji apples are crisp and sweet, with just a hint of spice. They are wonderful eating apples. The Fuji actually becomes more flavorful while you store it.

Gala. These apples have distinctive red stripes running down yellow-orange skin. Both crisp and sweet, they are used for munching and also for making applesauce.

Golden Delicious. The most commonly grown apple in many countries, it's firm, sweet, and crisp. It's a good choice for recipes

that require baking or cooking, since it retains its shape.

Granny Smith. Probably best known for its bright green color, even when ripe, this apple is crisp and tart, and good for baking and sautéing.

Jonagold. Tangy and sweet, Jonagold apples are used both for eating and baking.

Liberty. A favorite of organic growers, Liberty apples are resistant to many diseases and don't require large amounts of pesticides. They're excellent for eating and cooking.

Northern Spy. Greenish yellow with red stripes, these apples have a tart taste that's wonderful for cooking and baking.

Rome. These apples are firm and crisp, and they're great for baking.

Winesap. Spicy and tart, these are often used for ciders and also for baking and adding to salads.

addition, the antioxidant-rich peel is discarded when producers make applesauce and canned apples. If you have a choice, eat a whole fresh apple rather than the processed versions.

Of course, if you're choosing between sugary soda and apple juice, by all means choose the juice. But don't use juice as a substitute for the real thing.

Apple Crumble with Toasted-Oat Topping

- 6 medium Jonagold apples
- ½ cup unsweetened applesauce
- ¾ cup old-fashioned or quick-cooking rolled oats
- 3 tablespoons toasted wheat germ
- 3 tablespoons packed light brown sugar
- 1 teaspoon ground cinnamon
- 1 tablespoon canola oil
- 1 tablespoon unsalted butter, cut into small pieces

Preheat the oven to 350°F. Coat a 12- × 8-inch baking dish with cooking spray.

Cut the apples in half lengthwise. Remove the cores and stems and discard. Cut the apples into thin slices.

Place the apples and the applesauce in the prepared baking dish. Toss to coat the apples evenly with the applesauce, and spread the apples out evenly in the baking dish.

In a small bowl, mix the oats, wheat germ, brown sugar, and cinnamon. Drizzle with the oil. Add the butter. Mix with your fingers to work the oil and butter into the dry ingredients.

Sprinkle the oat mixture evenly over the apples. Bake for 30 to 35 minutes, or until the topping is golden and the apples are bubbling. Serve warm.

Makes 6 servings

PER SERVING

Calories: 197
Total fat: 5.7 g
Saturated fat: 1.6 g

Cholesterol: 5 mg
Sodium: 3 mg
Dietary fiber: 4.7 g

Apricots

A BOUNTY OF BETA-CAROTENE

When you think of Chinese food, apricots might not be the first item that comes to mind. But food historians think that apricots were first cultivated in China more than 4,000 years ago! The tasty fruit spread through the Middle East and the Mediterranean in ancient times, and now it's grown in Europe, Africa, Australia, and America, too.

Not only is this sweet, velvety fruit a delicious treat, but it's also loaded with a variety of compounds that research shows can fight infections, blindness, and heart disease.

Most of apricots' health benefits are due to their copious and exceptionally diverse carotenoid content. Carotenoids are the pigments in plants that paint many of our favorite fruits and vegetables red, orange, and yellow. In humans, they have a wide range of health-protecting properties. Researchers have identified more than 600 different carotenoids, with some of the most powerful, including beta-carotene, being found in apricots.

"Apricots are one of the best foods to look to for carotenoids," says Ritva Butrum, PhD, senior science advisor at the American Institute for Cancer Research in Washington, D.C.

Fruit for the Heart

The apricot's unique mix of healing compounds makes this food a powerful ally in fighting heart disease. Along with beta-carotene, apricots contain another carotenoid called lycopene, and both compounds have been shown in studies to fight the process by which the dangerous low-density lipoprotein (LDL) form of cholesterol becomes oxidized, or altered by free radicals. This is important because experts consider oxidized LDL to be a major player in atherosclerosis, which stiffens and narrows arteries, such as the ones supplying your heart.

A Japanese study that followed more than 3,000 adults for nearly 12 years found that those with high levels of carotenoids, such as beta-carotene and lycopene, were less likely to die of cardiovascular disease. Yet another study, this time following

nearly 5,000 Dutch adults for 4 years, found that those with the most beta-carotene in their diets had a significantly lower risk of heart attack.

Potential Cancer Fighter

Although tomatoes (more specifically, processed tomato products) seem to provide more than 85 percent of the lycopene in Americans' diets, apricots are another source of this carotenoid. Lycopene is one of the most potent antioxidants that experts know about. It could help prevent cancer by protecting your cells' DNA from free-radical attacks. (Its antioxidant properties explain why it might also be helpful in preventing the atherosclerosis involved in cardiovascular disease.)

Research looking at the possible role of lycopene in cancer prevention has focused on tomatoes and prostate cancer. A meta-analysis—which synthesizes research results from a number of studies—found that men who ate a lot of cooked tomato products had 19 percent less risk of prostate cancer than men who seldom ate tomato products. So what does this have to do with apricots?

Researchers point out that the protective effects from tomatoes could come from other components in them. If you enjoy the taste of apricots anyway, the knowledge

In the Kitchen

Although most of us eat apricots straight from the fruit bin, there are many other ways to prepare—and enjoy—these little golden gems.

Grill them. Grilled apricots take on a smoky, slightly sweet flavor as the sugars caramelize. Simply thread whole or halved fresh apricots on skewers, brush with honey, and cook for 7 to 10 minutes, turning frequently.

Broil them. To cook apricots indoors, cut the fruit in half, brush with honey, and broil in the oven, cut side up.

Poach them. Poached apricots are a great way to warm up a cool evening. Put fruit juice and whole cloves or a cinnamon stick in a small saucepan, and bring to a simmer. Add whole or halved apricots, and cook for 6 to 8 minutes. Remove the apricots, and continue cooking the sauce until it thickens. Then use it as topping for the apricots.

Slip them into a recipe. Health-savvy cooks know that they can use applesauce in some baked goods in place of some of the oil called for in the recipe. The next time you reach for the applesauce in one of these instances, use apricot purée instead. Just run some canned apricots through a food processor or blender until they're smooth.

You don't have to seek out fresh apricots to enjoy their benefits—dried or canned versions are quite nutritious, too, says Adel Kader, PhD, professor of post-harvest physiology in the department of plant science at University of California, Davis. According to the USDA, five raw apricots contain 3,370 IU of vitamin A and 1,915 micrograms of beta-carotene. A half-cup of canned apricots contains 2,063 IU of vitamin A, and 1,232 micrograms of beta-carotene. And 10 dried apricot halves contain 1,261 IU of vitamin A and 757 micrograms of beta-carotene.

that the lycopene within them might be helpful for fighting cancer makes them even sweeter.

Good for the Eyes

You can also get lots of vitamin A by eating apricots. (The beta-carotene in apricots is converted to vitamin A in the body.) This nutrient helps protect the eyes, and as it turns out, the eyes need all the help they can get.

Every time light passes through the eyes, it triggers the release of tissue-damaging free radicals. Left unchecked, these destructive oxygen molecules attack and damage the lenses of the eyes, possibly setting the stage for cataracts. Free radicals can also attack blood vessels supplying the central portions of the retinas, called the maculas. If the blood supply gets cut off, the result can be macular degeneration, the leading cause of vision loss in older adults.

Vitamin A has been shown in studies to be a powerful antioxidant—that is, it helps block the effects of free radicals. Three apricots provide 2,769 IU of vitamin A, 55 percent of the Daily Value (DV) for this vitamin.

Help from Fiber

It's almost impossible to exaggerate the benefits of getting enough fiber in your diet. High-fiber foods can help you lose weight, control high blood sugar, and lower cholesterol levels. They're also essential for keeping digestion regular.

So here's another reason to add apricots to your fruit bowl. Three fruits contain 3 grams of fiber, 12 percent of the DV. Better yet, that's at a minimal calorie cost—just 51 calories for all three. When you're eating apricots for fiber, however, be sure to eat the skin, which contains a substantial amount of the fruit's fiber.

GETTING THE MOST

Eat them firm. Even if you enjoy your fruit nice and soft, it's best to eat apricots while they're still slightly firm. Apricots contain the most nutrients when they're at their peak of ripeness; once they start getting soft, these compounds quickly begin to break down.

Shop for color. Unlike most fruits, apricots can be yellow or orange and still be ripe. Both colors are acceptable when you're trying to get the most healing benefits. However, apricots that have green in them were picked early and may never ripen, which means that you lose out on much of their healing goodness.

Store them carefully. It's important to keep apricots cool to prevent them from getting overripe. Unless you're going to eat them within a day or two, it's best to store them in the fruit bin in the refrigerator, where they'll keep for about a week.

Here's another storage tip. Because apricots are such a soft, delicate fruit, they readily pick up flavors—from other fruits they're stored with, for example, or even from refrigerator smells. It's a good idea to store them in the refrigerator bin in a paper or plastic bag.

FOOD ALERT
Dangerous Claims

The idea that apricot pits could be used as medicine dates back to the 1920s, when Dr. Ernst T. Krebs put forth a theory that amygdalin, a compound found in apricot pits that is converted to cyanide in the body, could destroy cancer cells.

Some 30 years later, his son reformulated the extract and named it Laetrile. By the 1970s, people with cancer who felt that they couldn't be helped by modern medicine were traveling to obscure clinics and paying exorbitant prices for this new "miracle" cure. So popular was Laetrile that at one time, it was available in health food stores in 27 states.

Today, Laetrile is not approved by the FDA, although it's readily available in Mexico and other countries. Actor Steve McQueen was treated with the drug in a Mexican clinic shortly before he died of cancer. Does Laetrile work? According to most experts, the answer is an emphatic no.

"Laetrile is not only useless but also potentially fatal," says Maurie Markman, MD, vice president of clinical research at the M. D. Anderson Cancer Center in Houston. Indeed, a study at the Mayo Clinic in Rochester, Minnesota, found that Laetrile frequently caused nausea, vomiting, headache, and other symptoms of cyanide poisoning.

Laetrile is dangerous for another reason, Dr. Markman adds. Some people depend on it instead of turning to a safer and more effective cancer therapy.

Apricot-Mango Smoothie

6 apricots, peeled, pitted, and chopped (about 2 cups)

2 ripe mangoes, 10 to 12 ounces each, peeled and chopped (about 2 cups)

1 cup reduced-fat milk or plain low-fat yogurt

4 teaspoons fresh lemon juice

¼ teaspoon vanilla extract

6–8 ice cubes

Lemon peel twists (garnish)

Place the apricots, mangoes, milk or yogurt, lemon juice, and vanilla extract in a blender. Process for 8 seconds. Add the ice cubes, and process 6 to 8 seconds longer, or until smooth.

Pour into tall glasses, garnish with lemon twists, if desired, and serve immediately.

Makes 2 servings (12 ounces each)

PER SERVING

Calories: 213
Total fat: 1.7 g
Saturated fat: 0.9 g

Cholesterol: 6 mg
Sodium: 84 mg
Dietary fiber: 5.5 g

Arthritis

FOODS TO EAT (AND AVOID)
FOR JOINT PAIN

Although there isn't a specific food that will help relieve arthritis in all people, doctors today recognize that what you eat—or, in some cases, don't eat—can help ease discomfort and even slow the progression of the disease.

Joints Out of Joint

Arthritis, which causes pain, stiffness, and swelling in and around the joints, isn't just one disease, but many. The most common form of arthritis is osteoarthritis, which is caused by wear and tear on cartilage, the shock-absorbing material between the joints. When cartilage wears away, bone grinds against bone, causing pain and stiffness in the fingers, knees, feet, hips, and back.

A more serious form of the disease is rheumatoid arthritis. It occurs when the immune system, instead of protecting the body, begins attacking it. These attacks cause swelling of the membrane that lines the joints, which eventually eats away at the joints' cartilage. It is the form of arthritis most affected by diet.

The Fat Connection

These days, it's difficult to think of an illness that isn't made worse by a diet high in saturated fats. Arthritis, it appears, is no exception.

A diet low in saturated fats reduces the body's production of prostaglandins, hormonelike substances that contribute to inflammation. In addition, a low-fat diet may hinder communications sent by the immune system, thereby interrupting the body's inflammatory response and helping the joints heal.

Some doctors recommend limiting dietary fat to no more than 25 percent of total calories, with no more than 7 percent of these calories coming from saturated fats. "There's a very simple way to reduce your intake of saturated fats—just don't add them to food," says David Pisetsky, MD, PhD, director of the Duke University Arthritis Center in Durham, North Carolina. "When you have a sandwich, for example, use low-fat mayonnaise instead of the real thing."

Replacing butter, sour cream, and cheese with their lower-fat or fat-free counterparts can also lower your intake of saturated fats. Even if you don't cut them out of your diet completely, just cutting back can make a difference.

Eating a diet that's largely vegetarian can also help reduce the amount of saturated fat that you eat, plus provide other arthritis-relieving benefits, as you'll see later in this chapter.

Fish for Relief

Even though it's generally a good idea to cut back on fats, there is one type of fat that you should consider including in an antiarthritis diet. The omega-3 fatty acids, found primarily in cold-water fish like Spanish mackerel, trout, and salmon, reduce the body's production of prostaglandins and leukotrienes, both substances that contribute to inflammation.

A number of studies have found that fish oil offers benefits to people with rheumatoid arthritis, including less morning stiffness, fewer painful joints, more strength in the hands, and less need for anti-inflammatory drugs.

Scientific studies often require the use of fish oil supplements in order to provide high enough doses of omega-3s. Some experts recommend getting a daily dose of 3 grams of EPA and DHA, which are types of omega-3s, in supplement form. (You'd likely need a very large serving of fish to get an equivalent amount.)

However, you can still get healing benefits from fish oil by eating fish two or three times a week. In addition to the fish mentioned above, bluefin tuna, rainbow trout, halibut, and pollack are also good sources of omega-3 fatty acids. Canned fish such as salmon, herring, sardines, and chunk light tuna are also high in omega-3s.

Nutritional Triggers

Since there's evidence that rheumatoid arthritis is triggered by a faulty immune system, and the immune system is affected by what we eat, it makes sense that, for some people, diet can make a difference in how they feel.

"Diet is critical in the treatment of this form of arthritis," says Joel Fuhrman, MD, a specialist in nutritional medicine at Hunterdon Medical Center in Flemington, New Jersey, and author of *Eat to Live*. "In populations that consume natural diets of mostly unprocessed fruits, vegetables, and grains, autoimmune diseases are almost nonexistent."

For people with rheumatoid arthritis, Dr. Fuhrman recommends a vegan diet—which means no meat or other animal products—that also minimizes the use of wheat, salt, and oils. Instead, you'd eat lots of leafy green vegetables in salads, vegetable-rich soups, and vegetable juice. Dr. Fuhrman also suggests making room for plenty of cruciferous vegetables, such as broccoli and cabbage.

In a study at Norway's University of Oslo, 27 people with rheumatoid arthritis followed a vegetarian diet for 1 year. (After the first 3 to 5 months, they could eat dairy products if they wished.) They also avoided gluten (a protein found in wheat), refined sugar, salt, alcohol, and caffeine. After a month, their joints were less swollen and tender, and they had less morning stiffness and a stronger grip than people who followed their usual diets.

But more may be involved in an arthritis-treating diet than just getting more fruits and vegetables. Some people are sensitive to certain foods—like wheat, dairy foods, corn, citrus fruits, tomatoes, and eggs—which can switch on the body's inflammatory response. For the most part, food sensitivities are rarely involved in arthritis flare-ups, says Dr. Pisetsky. Since there are so many things that can exacerbate the pain of rheumatoid arthritis, knowing which foods, if any, to avoid can be difficult. He recommends starting a food diary so that you can keep track of what you were eating around the time a flare-up occurred. If you discover a pattern—for example, you remember eating tomatoes shortly before an attack—you'll have an idea of what to avoid in the future. Once you've identified a possible culprit, stop eating that food (or foods) for at least 5 days, says Dr. Pisetsky. Then try the food again and see if your symptoms return.

> ## Doctor's Top Tip
>
> If you have rheumatoid arthritis, cut animal protein from your diet, recommends Joel Fuhrman, MD, a specialist in nutritional medicine. A vegetable-based diet can make significant improvements in many cases of arthritis. When you eat meat and other animal foods, the proteins they contain can slip through the walls of your digestive tract and get into your blood circulation, he says. Your body's reaction to these proteins can contribute to autoimmune diseases like rheumatoid arthritis. A diet free of animal protein won't help everyone, but it's a standard part of his approach to treating his patients with this type of arthritis.

Help for Wear and Tear

For years, doctors didn't suspect that there could be a link between diet and osteoarthritis. After all, they reasoned, this condition is a "natural" result of wear and tear on the joints. What could diet possibly do?

According to a preliminary study, however, what you eat can make a difference. Researchers at Boston University School of Medicine studied the eating habits of people with osteoarthritis of the knee. They found that those getting the most vitamin C—more than 200 milligrams a day—were three times less likely to have the disease get worse than those who got the least vitamin C (less than 120 milligrams a day).

Since vitamin C is an antioxidant, it may protect the joints from the damaging effects of free radicals, unstable oxygen molecules that can cause joint inflammation.

"Vitamin C may also help generate collagen, which enhances the body's ability to repair damage to the cartilage," says study leader Timothy McAlindon, MD, MPH, who's now an associate professor of medicine at Tufts University School of Medicine in Boston.

Dr. McAlindon recommends that people get at least 120 milligrams of vitamin C a day in their diets, twice the Daily Value. "That's the amount in a couple of oranges," he says. Other fruits and vegetables rich in vitamin C include cantaloupe, broccoli, strawberries, peppers, and cranberry juice.

But it's not only what you eat that can affect osteoarthritis. It's also how much you weigh.

"There's good evidence that people who are overweight are at increased risk for developing osteoarthritis in weight-bearing joints like the knee," says Dr. Pisetsky. Research also suggests that overweight people are at higher risk for developing osteoarthritis in non-weight-bearing joints, such as those in the hands. "Losing weight leads to less pain and improved mobility," he says.

Bananas

A BUNCH OF POTASSIUM

We seem to take bananas for granted. They're a commonly accepted punch line, guaranteed for a laugh when someone slips on a banana peel. We say we're "going bananas" when we feel out-of-sorts. Harry Belafonte is famous for singing about them.

And bananas make few demands on our attention. They're simple to eat—they don't get your hands messy or dribble juice as you eat them—and they're extremely portable. The average American eats about 30 pounds of the fruit each year. And, according to the American Diabetes Association, they outsell apples, which are as American as, well, apple pie.

It's time to honor the banana instead of laughing at it, or stripping its peel and eating it without a second thought! Studies have shown that the fruit beneath that slippery skin can do wonders for our health.

Bananas for the Heart

If the needle on the blood pressure cuff has been inching up in recent years, it may be time for a tropical vacation. If the sun and surf don't bring your pressure down, the bananas sure will.

Bananas are one of nature's best sources of potassium, with a large banana providing about 487 milligrams, or 14 percent of the Daily Value (DV) for this essential mineral. Study after study shows that people who eat foods rich in potassium have a significantly lower risk of high blood pressure and related diseases like heart attack and stroke.

According to the National Institutes of Health, by adopting its DASH diet—which is rich in fruits and vegetables that provide potassium—you can lower your systolic blood pressure (the top number) by 8 to 14 millimeters of mercury.

Even if you already have high blood pressure, eating plenty of bananas may significantly reduce or even eliminate your need for blood pressure medication, according to scientists at the University of Naples in Italy. Researchers believe that one of the ways that bananas keep blood pressure down is by helping to prevent plaque from

Doctor's Top Tip

Morning is a great time to get the benefits of an easy-to-eat banana, according to the National Heart, Lung, and Blood Institute. Some statistics say that more than 35 percent of Americans don't eat breakfast, most likely because they're in a rush. The NHLBI offers meal plans to show people how to eat a low-sodium diet to maintain good blood pressure. By combining a medium banana with a bowl of bran flakes, low-fat milk, a slice of whole-wheat bread with trans-fat-free margarine, and a cup of orange juice, you get a quick breakfast that's high in fiber and potassium and low in sodium.

sticking to artery walls. They do this by keeping the bad low-density lipoprotein cholesterol from oxidizing, a chemical process that makes it more likely to accumulate. That's why bananas may be a good defense against atherosclerosis, or hardening of the arteries, another contributor to high blood pressure, heart attack, and stroke.

And the best part is that you don't have to eat a boatload of bananas to get these benefits, says David B. Young, PhD, professor emeritus of physiology and biophysics at the University of Mississippi Medical Center in Jackson.

"Studies show that you can get a significant impact from relatively small changes," says Dr. Young. "My advice would be to think of potassium-rich foods like love and money: You can never get too much."

Stomach Relief

According to the National Library of Medicine, bananas can help relieve heartburn and upset stomach. They do this by encouraging your stomach to produce more of the mucus that naturally protects it from the acidic digestive fluid it contains. And as you'll see below, bananas can soothe and encourage the normal function of other digestive organs, too!

Restoring Balance

When you've been run ragged by a case of the runs, it's important that you replenish all the vital fluids and nutrients that diarrhea depletes. And a banana is just the food to do it, says William Ruderman, MD, a gastroenterologist in Orlando, Florida.

"Bananas are a very good source of electrolytes, like potassium, which you lose when you become dehydrated," he explains. Electrolytes are minerals that turn into electrically charged particles in the body, helping to control almost everything that happens inside, from muscle contractions and fluid balance to the beating of the heart.

Bananas are also the bland type of food that the National Institute of Diabetes and Digestive and Kidney Diseases recommends as you're recuperating from a bout of diarrhea. Along with bananas, they suggest centering your recovery meals around rice, toast, crackers, baked skinless chicken, and cooked carrots.

Bananas also contain some pectin, a soluble fiber that acts like a sponge in the digestive tract, absorbing fluids and helping to keep diarrhea in check.

Promote Digestive Health

Though bananas may not "feel" like a food that's high in fiber as you're eating them, the yellow fruit is actually a decent source of fiber. One large banana contains 3.5 grams of fiber, or 14 percent of the DV for fiber.

A diet rich in fiber may help protect you from a variety of diseases ranging from potentially fatal conditions like heart disease and cancer to problems in the digestive organs, like appendicitis, diverticulosis, and hemorrhoids.

GETTING THE MOST

Buy a bunch. One reason that some people may avoid bananas is that they tend to get soft and mushy if you don't eat them quickly enough. Here's a trick for keeping them fresh. When bananas are getting soft too quickly, put them in the refrigerator. This will quickly stop the ripening process. (Don't be alarmed when the cold turns the skin black—the fruit inside will still be fresh and tasty.) On the other hand, when you're waiting for that bunch of green bananas to ripen, it's easy to speed up the process. Put them in a brown paper bag at room temperature. The ethylene gas that bananas produce naturally will speed up the ripening.

Beans

SMALL BUT MIGHTY

HEALING POWER

Can Help:

Lower cholesterol

Stabilize blood sugar levels

Reduce the risk of cancer

Prevent heart disease in people with diabetes

In the annals of the International Federation of Competitive Eating—where men and women stuff their bellies with shocking amounts of food at one sitting—several bean-related records have been set. One man ate 6 pounds of baked beans in less than 2 minutes. Another eater scarfed down more than 5 pounds of pork and beans in less than 2 minutes.

Although gulping this many beans at one time might not be the wisest activity, at least these competitors had *sort* of the right idea: Beans are a superb addition to a healthy diet.

Despite their small size, beans pack a surprisingly rich and varied array of substances that are vital for good health. Take fiber, for example. "What's so good about beans, I think, is the high fiber in particular. They're one of the better sources of dietary fiber there is," says Joe Hughes, PhD, assistant professor in the nutrition and food sciences program at California State University in San Bernardino, whose research is centered on beans.

What's especially nice is that they're high in soluble and insoluble fiber, which have different effects in the body. Oats are one of the few other foods high in both types of fiber, but beans can be used in many more types of dishes than oats, and it's easier to eat a hearty portion of beans, he points out.

Beans are also a good source of minerals, protein, and, you may be surprised to learn, antioxidants.

Sending Cholesterol South

While beans aren't the only food that can help lower cholesterol, they're certainly one of the best. The soluble fiber in beans is the same gummy stuff found in apples, barley, and oat bran. In the digestive tract, soluble fiber traps cholesterol-containing bile, removing it from the body before it's absorbed.

"Eating a cup of cooked beans a day can lower total cholesterol about 10 percent in 6 weeks," says Patti Bazel Geil, MS, RD, a diabetes educator and nutrition author in Lexington, Kentucky, who's written about the benefits of beans. While 10 percent may not seem like much, keep in mind that every 1 percent reduction in total cholesterol means a 2 percent decrease in your risk for heart disease.

Beans can lower cholesterol in just about anyone, but the higher your cholesterol, the better they work. In a study at the University of Kentucky, 20 men with high cholesterol (more than 260 milligrams per deciliter of blood) were given about ¾ cup of pinto and navy beans a day. The men's total cholesterol dropped an average of 19 percent in 3 weeks, possibly reducing their heart attack risk by almost 40 percent. Even more remarkable, the dangerous low-density lipoprotein (LDL) cholesterol—that's the artery-plugging stuff—plunged by 24 percent.

It appears that all beans can help lower cholesterol, even canned baked beans. In another University of Kentucky study, 24 men with high cholesterol ate 1 cup of canned beans in tomato sauce every day for 3 weeks. Their total cholesterol dropped 10.4 percent, and their triglycerides (another blood fat that contributes to heart disease) fell 10.8 percent.

In further research into the cholesterol-lowering effects of beans and other legumes, authors of a report in the *British Journal of Nutrition* compiled the findings of 11 studies that looked at the relationship between cholesterol and different types of legumes, such as pinto beans, chickpeas, white beans, and mixed beans (but not soybeans). They found that the beans in these studies lowered total cholesterol by 7.2 percent, LDL (bad) cholesterol by 6.2 percent, and triglycerides by 16.6 percent. The soluble fiber in these foods appeared to be the most important factor responsible for their cholesterol-lowering effect.

Beans play another, less direct role in keeping cholesterol levels down. They're extremely filling, so when you eat beans, you'll have less appetite for other, fattier foods. And eating less fat is critical for keeping cholesterol levels low.

Keeping Blood Sugar Steady

Keeping blood sugar levels steady is the key to keeping diabetes under control. "Many people don't realize how good beans are for people with diabetes," says Geil. In fact, eating between ½ and ¾ cup of beans a day has been shown to significantly improve blood sugar control. And beans provide yet another benefit for people with diabetes, she says. "People with diabetes are four to six times more likely to develop heart

> **Doctor's Top Tip**
>
> Even though he sings the praises of beans, Joe Hughes, PhD, of California State University, acknowledges that it takes time to work your way up to being a regular bean aficionado. If you suddenly start eating them daily, you're likely to develop gas and bloating. Start out having beans with a meal once a week. After a month, go to twice a week. Keep building gradually. Your digestive tract, and the gas-producing bacteria it contains, will adapt better to this routine.

In the Kitchen

If you roll right by the dried beans at the supermarket because you don't have time for all the soaking and boiling and waiting around, put on the brakes. Cooking beans from scratch doesn't have to be a daylong project, says Patti Bazel Geil, MS, R.D. With the quick-soaking method, you can shave hours off the cooking time. Here's how to do it:

Rinse the beans in a colander, put them in a large pot, and cover with 2 inches of water. Bring to a boil, reduce the heat to medium, and simmer for 10 minutes. Drain the beans, and cover with 2 inches of fresh water. ("Discarding the water that the beans were cooked in gets rid of most of their gas-producing sugars," Geil explains.) Soak for 30 minutes. Then rinse, drain, and cover with fresh water again. Simmer for 2 hours or until the beans are tender.

---

disease," she says. "Eating more beans will help keep their cholesterol low, thereby reducing their risk."

Beans are rich in complex carbohydrates. Unlike sugary foods, which dump sugar (glucose) into the bloodstream all at once, complex carbohydrates are digested more slowly. This means that glucose enters your bloodstream a little at a time, helping to keep blood sugar levels steady, says Geil.

Foods' effect on blood sugar is commonly measured on a scale called the glycemic index, or GI, and beans are a "very good low-GI food" because of their soluble fiber, says Dr. Hughes. This should be good news for the approximately 21 million Americans with diabetes, and the 54 million with "prediabetes," a condition that causes a rise in blood sugar and usually occurs in people before they develop diabetes.

Unfortunately, Americans on average only eat 17 grams of fiber daily—and people with diabetes only eat 16 grams—according to a survey from the federal government. The American Dietetic Association recommends 25 grams daily.

In a small study from the University of Texas, researchers had 13 people with diabetes follow two diets for 6 weeks each. One diet had 24 grams of daily fiber (8 grams were soluble fiber), and the other diet provided a whopping 50 grams of fiber, half of which was soluble. Compared with when they ate the regular-fiber diet, the people eating the high-fiber diet had better control over their blood sugar and lower insulin. Perhaps the best news is that the subjects were eating regular foods—not taking fiber supplements or eating foods specially fortified with fiber. (Experts had previously declared that it's difficult to consume a lot of soluble fiber each day without the use of supplements or fiber-fortified foods.)

A nice quality about beans is that they're available in so many varieties—and you can prepare them in so many ways—that it's easy to eat beans even several times a day in relatively large quantities to reap their fiber-giving benefits, says Dr. Hughes.

Cancer-Licking Legumes

Fruits and vegetables tend to get the spotlight during discussions of foods rich in antioxidants. Indeed, when USDA researchers compiled the antioxidant capacities of hundreds of foods in the American diet, many of these foods stood out. The Granny Smith apple, for example, scored a 5,381 on the measurement of total antioxidant capacity per serving. The artichoke scored 7,904. And the lowbush blueberry got a whopping 13,427.

But several beans more than held their own, too. The pinto bean scored 11,864. And the red kidney bean scored 13,259!

Beans are rich sources of phytochemicals, which are plant components that have antioxidant and other disease-fighting properties, says Dr. Hughes. Beans may contain hundreds of types of antioxidant chemicals. Remember that antioxidants help protect you from cancer by limiting damaging attacks on your cells from free radicals. Plus, unlike some antioxidant-rich plant foods like blueberries, you can put lots of different beans on your plate meal after meal without getting bored or overwhelmed by the flavor.

Some other compounds in beans—like lignans, isoflavones, saponins, phytic acid, and protease inhibitors—have been shown to inhibit cancer-cell growth. These compounds appear to keep normal cells from turning cancerous and prevent cancer cells from growing.

The Healthy Alternative to Meat

Beans used to be called the "poor man's meat." But a more accurate name would be the healthy man's meat. Like red meat, beans are loaded with protein. Unlike meat, they're light in fat, particularly dangerous, artery-clogging saturated fat.

For example, a cup of black beans contains less than 1 gram of fat. Less than 1 percent of that comes from saturated fat. Three ounces of lean, broiled ground beef, on the other hand, has 15 grams of fat, 22 percent of which is the saturated kind.

Beans are also a great source of essential vitamins and minerals. A half-cup of black beans contains 128 micrograms, or 32 percent of the Daily Value (DV) for folate, a B vitamin that may lower risk of heart disease. That same cup has 2 milligrams of iron, 11 percent of the DV, and 305 milligrams of potassium, or 9 percent of the DV. Potassium is a mineral that has been shown to help control blood pressure.

GETTING THE MOST

Go for the fiber. While virtually all dried beans are good sources of fiber, some varieties stand out from the pack. Black beans, for example, contain 6 grams of fiber in a half-cup serving. Chickpeas, kidney beans, and lima beans all weigh in at about 7 grams of fiber, and black-eyed peas are among the best, with about 8 grams of fiber.

Enjoy them canned. In general, the dry beans that you cook for yourself have a slight edge over canned beans in terms of retaining nutrients, says Dr. Hughes. However, the average American these days just doesn't have the time needed to cook dry beans (even with the expedited method featured in the sidebar). If you only have time for canned beans, then by all means eat canned beans, he says. However, canned beans may be higher in sodium, so if that's a concern, drain and rinse canned beans before using them.

Use gas-deflating spices. Has the fear of uncomfortable and embarrassing gas kept you from reaping beans' nutritional benefits? Try spicing them with a pinch of summer savory or a teaspoon of ground ginger. According to some university studies, these spices may help reduce beans' gas-producing effects.

Read the label. Some canned refried beans contain a lot of fat, and some contain little to none, says Dr. Hughes. Be sure to pick a kind that's low in fat—they still taste great.

Go dark. Buy darker beans for more disease protection. In general, the darker the beans, the more powerful the antioxidants they contain, says Dr. Hughes.

Cannellini Seafood Pouches

2 **cans (15 ounces each) cannellini beans, rinsed and drained**

12 **ounces sea scallops (halved if very large)**

8 **ounces large shrimp, peeled and deveined**

1 **cup diced plum tomatoes (¾-inch dice)**

1 **jar (6 ounces) marinated artichoke hearts, drained**

1 **tablespoon extra-virgin olive oil**

2 **teaspoons chopped fresh rosemary**

1 **teaspoon finely chopped garlic**

½ **teaspoon salt (optional)**

¼ **teaspoon crushed red pepper flakes**

Preheat the oven to 425°F. Tear off 4 pieces of parchment paper, each about 15 inches long. Fold each sheet in half lengthwise, and then open it up so you can see the crease.

In a large bowl, combine all of the ingredients; toss well.

To make each pouch: Mound 1½ cups of the bean mixture on 1 side of the crease. Lift the other side of the parchment over the filling, and fold the edges together around the filling to seal. Repeat with remaining ingredients to make 3 more pouches, then place them on a baking sheet.

Bake until the scallops and shrimp are slightly opaque in the centers, 10 to 12 minutes. To serve, cut an "X" in each pouch, and tear the paper back to reveal the filling.

Makes 4 servings

Cook's Note: *You can use any canned white beans you prefer in this recipe.*

PER SERVING

Calories: 430
Total fat: 12 g
Saturated fat: 2 g

Cholesterol: 140 mg
Sodium: 655 mg
Dietary fiber: 9 g

Edamame and Escarole Salad

1 cup shelled frozen edamame

1 tablespoon fresh lemon juice

1 tablespoon minced shallot

2 tablespoons extra-virgin olive oil

  Sea salt and freshly ground black pepper

1 head escarole (5 pounds), torn into bite-size pieces

2 teaspoons chopped fresh mint

2 teaspoons chopped flat-leaf parsley

¼ pound Pecorino Romano cheese

Bring a large pot of salted water to a boil. Add the edamame, and cook for 2 minutes. Drain well.

In a small bowl, whisk together the lemon juice and shallot; slowly whisk in the olive oil. Season to taste with salt and pepper.

In a large serving bowl, combine the edamame, escarole, mint, parsley, and the dressing; season to taste with salt and pepper. Shave the cheese over the salad.

Makes 4 servings

Cook's Notes: *If you like, use arugula or mixed greens instead of escarole. You can also shell and steam fresh edamame for this recipe if you have time.*

PER SERVING

Calories: 318	Cholesterol: 28 mg
Total fat: 18 g	Sodium: 583 mg
Saturated fat: 7 g	Dietary fiber: 13 g

Gingered Lentils

1¼ **cups lentils**

2 **teaspoons canola oil**

2 **tablespoons grated fresh ginger**

2 **cloves garlic, minced**

1¼ **teaspoons curry powder**

¼ **teaspoon salt**

1 **lemon, halved**

Place the lentils in a colander and rinse with cold water, then drain. Transfer the lentils to a large saucepan, and add 4 cups water. Bring to a boil over high heat. Reduce the heat to low. Partially cover, and cook until the lentils are tender but not mushy, about 30 to 35 minutes.

Drain the lentils, and set aside. Wipe the pan dry. Add the oil and heat over medium heat. Add the ginger, garlic, curry powder, and salt. Stir for a few seconds, until fragrant. Add the lentils, and stir well to reheat. Remove from the heat.

Squeeze the juice from one half of the lemon, and stir it into the lentils. Cut the remaining half into 4 wedges. Serve the lentils with the lemon wedges.

Makes 4 servings

Cook's Note: *This makes a great meatless meal. Serve it with bread or rice and a steamed vegetable.*

PER SERVING

Calories: 208
Total fat: 3 g
Saturated fat: 0.3 g

Cholesterol: 0 mg
Sodium: 137 mg
Dietary fiber: 7.4 g

Berries

MORE THAN JUST DESSERT

The Romans believed that strawberries could cure everything from loose teeth to gastritis. Raspberries, according to folklore, had the ability to soothe inflamed tonsils.

While long-ago folk healers may have somewhat exaggerated the curative powers of berries, these small colorful fruits do still have a reputation for their beneficial effects in the body. Researchers around the world are analyzing a wide variety of substances in berries that show promise for preventing such serious problems as cataracts and cancer.

Filled With Healing Components

More than 9,000 phytochemicals have been identified in plant foods, with many more still to be named, scientists say. These are chemicals in the plants that have a variety of beneficial health effects. And berries, despite their diminutive size, can be powerful sources of phytochemicals.

One such phytochemical is a compound called ellagic acid, which is believed to help prevent cellular changes that can lead to cancer. All berries contain some ellagic acid, with raspberries and strawberries ranking among the top providers. "Ellagic acid is a good friend to us, helping fight the cancer process," says Hasan Mukhtar, PhD, vice chairman for research in the department of dermatology and professor of cancer research at the University of Wisconsin in Madison.

In fact, berries—and the ellagic acid they contain—may help fight cancer on several fronts, says Gary Stoner, PhD, professor and cancer researcher at Ohio State University in Columbus, who has worked on a number of studies involving blackberries. Ellagic acid is a powerful antioxidant, meaning that it can reduce damage caused by free radicals, harmful oxygen molecules that can literally punch holes in healthy cells and kick off the cancerous process. "It also detoxifies carcinogens," says Dr. Stoner.

But ellagic acid is just one of a host of cancer fighters in berries. They also contain flavonoids, tannins, phenolic acid, and lignans, which may help keep you cancer-free through a variety of mechanisms, including their antioxidant power.

A Cornell University study found that extracts from eight different types of

Dangerous Pickings

Even though elderberries are a treasure trove of nutrients, you don't want to pick them in the wild. Before they get ripe, they may contain compounds called cyanogenic glycosides, which can be poisonous, says Ara DerMarderosian, PhD, professor of pharmacognosy and director of the Complementary and Alternative Medicine Institute at the University of the Sciences in Philadelphia.

It's not only the berries that are dangerous, he adds. The leaves and bark of the tree also contain the poisonous compounds. In fact, there have been a number of cases of poisoning in children who carved elderberry branches, used them as peashooters, and didn't even eat the berries.

You don't have to avoid elderberries to be safe, however. Just treat them as you would wild mushrooms—a tasty food that's best picked at your favorite fruit stand instead of in the woods. It's also a good idea to cook the berries, because heat destroys the dangerous compounds, Dr. DerMarderosian notes.

strawberries significantly inhibited liver-cancer cell growth in a lab study.

A University of Georgia lab study found that phenolic compounds extracted from blueberries could limit colon cancer cells' ability to multiply and also trigger these renegade cells to die. Cancer cells can develop into tumors when they multiply too fast and stubbornly refuse to die—and even a little pressure to keep these cells in line can decrease the chance that a cancer will progress, the study authors write. Thus, their findings "suggest that blueberry intake may reduce colon cancer risk."

Need more tantalizing clues that a bowl of berries may help keep you cancer free? Okay, here's some more data. Some berries may have an ingredient that can help "starve" cancer. Louisiana State University researchers found that an extract from black raspberry can inhibit the growth of new blood vessels. Tumors coax your body to grow new blood vessels to feed them nutrients, and they can't grow beyond a few millimeters in size without this food supply. The researchers found that a compound called gallic acid in the black raspberries was partially responsible for this potentially cancer-starving activity.

Help for the Eyes and More

Berries are also very high in vitamin C, which is a powerful antioxidant. Getting a lot of vitamin C in your diet may help reduce your risk of heart disease, cancer, and infections. Vitamin C seems particularly important in preventing cataracts, which are thought to be caused by the oxidation of the protein that forms the lenses of the eyes.

All berries contain large amounts of vitamin C. A half-cup of strawberries, for example, has 42 milligrams, or 70 percent of the Daily Value (DV) for this vitamin. (That's more vitamin C than you'll get in a similar amount of grapefruit.) A half-cup of elderberries has 26 milligrams of vitamin C, or 43 percent of the DV, and a half-cup of blackberries has 15 milligrams, or 25 percent of the DV.

Berry Full of Fiber

One of the pleasant things about berries is that they're a sweet solution to a distinctly unpleasant problem: constipation. Berries contain large amounts of insoluble fiber, which is incredibly absorbent. It draws rivers of water into the intestine, which makes stools heavier. Heavy stools travel through the intestine faster, which means that you're less likely to become constipated.

The fiber in berries is helpful in yet another way. It helps prevent bile acid (a chemical that the body uses for digestion) from being transformed into a more dangerous, potentially cancer-causing form.

Elderberries are an incredible source of fiber, with a half-cup containing 5 grams. A half-cup of blackberries has more than 3 grams of fiber, while a half-cup of raspberries has 4 grams.

Keep a Youthful Brain

According to researchers from the USDA, your brain is particularly vulnerable to free-radical damage as you go through life. It uses 20 percent of the oxygen you breathe (cells produce free radicals from oxygen). Its natural antioxidant system to

---

FOOD ALERT

Cranberry Juice and Warfarin

The medical literature contains several reports about possible interactions between warfarin—an anticlotting drug also known as Coumadin—and cranberry juice. Drinking cranberry juice if you're taking warfarin could possibly lead to bleeding or excessively "thin" blood. Until more is known about their possible interactions, it's prudent to limit your consumption of cranberry juice if you're taking warfarin, a team of researchers advised in the *British Medical Journal*.

protect it from free radicals is not particularly robust, and long-living neurons in your brain tend to be exposed to lots of damage from free radicals during your lifetime. Oxidative stress—which is a term for free-radical damage—probably plays a role in some of the cognitive (a fancy word for thinking) declines that occur with age, researchers say.

However, antioxidant polyphenols, such as those found in blueberries, cranberries, and strawberries, may help preserve brain function. One of the research-ers' studies in rats found that a long-term diet that included strawberry extracts helped prevent age-related cognitive declines. Another found that feeding older rats strawberry or blueberry extracts reversed age-related effects on neurons and cognitive function—and the blueberry extracts helped improve the rats' balance and coordination.

These studies are still a long way from proving that berries will offer specific protections to humans, but since berries taste so good and offer so many other health benefits, it's nice to know that brain health is yet one more potential benefit you may enjoy years down the road.

GETTING THE MOST

Shop by color. To get the most nutrients in each bite, it's important to buy (or pick) berries that are at their peak of freshness. Perhaps the easiest way to tell is by checking the color. Blackberries should be jet black; raspberries should be black, golden, or red; blueberries, a powdery blue; and strawberries, a bold red.

In the Kitchen

Fresh berries are highly perishable and need special handling to maintain peak freshness.

Look for leakage. Berries that are leaking from the bottom of the package are either old or have been crushed and are giving up their juice. Look for a fresher, drier batch.

Give them room. When storing berries at home, don't crowd them together, which will cause them to deteriorate rapidly. It's best to store them, unwashed and uncovered, in a large bowl in the refrigerator or spread out on a platter.

Eat them fresh. Cooking destroys large amounts of vitamin C in berries. In fact, even slicing strawberries, for example, can cause vitamin C levels to decline because it causes the release of an enzyme that quickly destroys the vitamin. So to get the most vitamin C from strawberries, it's best to buy those that are still wearing their little green caps and slice them just before serving.

Double-Berry Sundaes

½ pint raspberries

12 ounces blueberries

2 tablespoons fresh orange juice

1 tablespoon honey

1 teaspoon vanilla extract

¼ teaspoon almond extract

1 pint fat-free vanilla frozen yogurt

Place half of the raspberries in a medium glass bowl. Mash lightly with a fork. Add the blueberries, orange juice, honey, vanilla and almond extracts, and the remaining raspberries. Stir well to mix. Cover and let stand for at least 30 minutes to allow the flavors to blend.

Scoop the frozen yogurt into 4 dessert dishes. Stir the berry mixture and spoon over the yogurt.

Makes 4 servings

PER SERVING

Calories: 170	Cholesterol: 0 mg
Total fat: 0.6 g	Sodium: 45 mg
Saturated fat: 0 g	Dietary fiber: 4 g

Strawberry Tart with Oat-Cinnamon Crust

CRUST

- ⅔ cup old-fashioned or quick-cooking rolled oats
- ½ cup all-purpose flour
- 1 tablespoon sugar
- 1 teaspoon ground cinnamon
- ¼ teaspoon baking soda
- 2 tablespoons canola oil
- 2–3 tablespoons fat-free plain yogurt

STRAWBERRY FILLING

- 1½ pints strawberries
- ¼ cup all-fruit strawberry spread
- ½ teaspoon vanilla extract

To make the crust: Preheat the oven to 375°F. Coat a baking sheet with cooking spray.

In a medium bowl, combine the oats, flour, sugar, cinnamon, and baking soda. Mix with a fork until blended. Stir in the oil and 2 tablespoons of the yogurt to make a soft, slightly sticky dough. If the dough is too stiff, add the remaining 1 tablespoon yogurt.

Place the dough on the prepared baking sheet, and pat evenly into a 10-inch circle. If the dough sticks to your hands, coat them lightly with cooking spray. Place a 9-inch cake pan on the dough, and trace around it with a sharp knife. With your fingers, push up and pinch the dough around the outside of the circle to make a 9-inch circle with a rim ¼ inch high.

Bake for 15 minutes, or until firm and golden. Remove from the oven, and set aside to cool. With a pancake turner, gently ease the crust onto a large, flat serving plate.

To make the strawberry filling: Wash the strawberries, and pat dry with paper towels. Slice off the stem ends and discard.

In a small microwaveable bowl, combine the strawberry spread and vanilla. Microwave on high for 10 to 15 seconds, or until melted.

Brush or dab a generous tablespoon evenly over the crust. Arrange the strawberries, cut side down, evenly over the crust. Brush or dab the remaining spread evenly over the strawberries, making sure that you get some of the spread between the strawberries to secure them.

Refrigerate for at least 30 minutes, or until the spread has jelled. Cut into wedges.

Makes 6 servings

Cook's Note: *You can serve the tart with a scoop of fat-free vanilla frozen yogurt on the side.*

PER SERVING

Calories: 161	Cholesterol: 0 mg
Total fat: 5.5 g	Sodium: 73 mg
Saturated fat: 0.5 g	Dietary fiber: 2.6 g

Blood Pressure Control

GETTING THE NUMBERS DOWN

High blood pressure quietly sneaks around your body, causing damage here and wreaking havoc there. It can cause so much strain on your heart that the organ fails from working so hard. It can make arteries in your brain rupture or develop blockages, potentially leaving you disabled. It can hurt your kidneys so badly that you need to use a dialysis machine, and your eyes so much that you become blind.

If you think that's bad, here's the *really* scary part: Since high blood pressure usually causes no symptoms, you might not even know you have it until you develop a serious health problem.

But while high blood pressure works quietly, it's frequently deadly (for this reason, high blood pressure is often called the silent killer). "High blood pressure is just a reflection of a cardiovascular system that's about to burst internally," says John A. McDougall, MD, medical director of the McDougall Program in Santa Rosa, California, and author of *The McDougall Program for a Healthy Heart*. "But if you eat a good diet—lots of fruits and vegetables and whole grains versus rich foods—you can help change all that," he says.

According to the National Institutes of Health, nearly one in three adults has high blood pressure. By eating a healthy diet, you can help ensure that you won't be one of them.

The How of Hypertension

Everyone has blood pressure, and it can go up or down frequently during the course of a day, and even from minute to minute. Your heart pumps blood throughout your body through a system of arteries. Each time your heart beats, it sends out a new wave of blood, and your blood pressure goes up. This is your systolic blood pressure. Between beats, your heart briefly relaxes and the pressure subsides. This is your diastolic blood pressure. When you have your blood pressure tested, you're given two numbers, one over the other (your systolic over your diastolic), measured in millimeters of mercury, or mm Hg. A sample blood pressure might be 135/86 mm Hg.

Your heart, brain, kidneys, eyes, and other organs depend on a reliable flow of blood that courses through your delicate "plumbing." When you develop chronic high blood pressure, or hypertension, trouble follows.

High-pressure blood whooshes through the arteries with damaging force. Your heart has to struggle harder to push out the blood, and it may grow enlarged and unable to bear the extra strain. Your arteries, which should be elastic and flexible, may more rapidly grow stiff and narrow. They may deliver less blood to your organs, and a blood clot can more readily get "stuck" and totally block the flow, causing a heart attack.

In most cases, doctors don't know the exact cause of high blood pressure. But they do know the preventable lifestyle factors that increase your risk of the problem: being overweight or obese, excessive alcohol use, a diet that provides too much salt or too little potassium, smoking, a sedentary lifestyle, chronic stress, and taking certain medications. Other risk factors can't be changed: your age (high blood pressure is more common in middle age and after), your race (it's more common in African Americans than Caucasians), and family history of high blood pressure.

The National Institutes of Health (NIH) and the American Heart Association use the following classifications to identify normal and high blood pressure:

Blood Pressure Classification	Systolic Blood Pressure (in mm Hg)		Diastolic Blood Pressure (in mm Hg)
Normal	Less than 120	and	Less than 80
Prehypertension	120 to 139	or	80 to 89
Stage 1 hypertension	140 to 159	or	90 to 99
Stage 2 hypertension	More than 160	or	More than 100

Even if your blood pressure falls into the normal or "prehypertension" categories, it's not time to breathe a sigh of relief. Your risk of death from heart disease or stroke rises progressively as your blood pressure goes up, and according to the NIH, the risk starts going up in these early stages. In other words—you need to start getting concerned well before you have a diagnosis of hypertension.

Research from the major, long-running Framingham Heart Study shows that having systolic blood pressure between 130 and 139 or diastolic blood pressure between 85 and 89 may more than double your risk of cardiovascular disease versus having blood pressure in the "normal" range.

According to the NIH, people in the prehypertension category should be "firmly and unambiguously advised to practice lifestyle modifications in order to reduce their risk of developing hypertension in the future."

Mild high blood pressure responds well to nondrug therapies. If you feed and exercise your body well, you may be able to avoid blood pressure drugs (and their often troublesome side effects) and calm your rushing blood. Don't be misled by the "mild" label, though. "Most heart attacks and strokes that occur do so in people with stage 1 high blood pressure," says Norman Kaplan, MD, professor of internal medicine and hypertension specialist at the University of Texas Southwestern Medical Center at Dallas.

A major study published in the *Journal of the American Medical Association* measured the effects of lifestyle changes on 810 adults with "above optimal" blood pressure. They were divided into three groups. One received many counseling sessions on how to reduce blood pressure with lifestyle measures such as weight loss, physical activity, and a low-sodium diet. Another got counseling, plus lots of information on the DASH diet for lowering blood pressure, which is rich in fruits and vegetables (more on that later). The third group received a single 30-minute counseling session covering these basics on lowering blood pressure.

After 6 months, the first group reduced their systolic blood pressure by an average of 3.7 mm Hg, and the DASH diet group reduced theirs by 4.3 mm Hg. The third group had less impressive changes in their blood pressure. At the beginning of the experiment, 38 percent of the subjects had hypertension, but after 6 months, only 17 percent in the first group had it, and only 12 percent in the DASH group. This contrasted with a considerably higher 26 percent in the advice-only group.

Giving Your Heart a Break

Losing weight—even just 10 pounds—can reduce your blood pressure or prevent you from developing hypertension.

What's the connection between excess weight and hypertension? The more tissue you have in your body, the harder your heart has to pump to feed it. And that work exerts more pressure on artery walls.

Everybody knows that losing weight is no piece of cake. But exercise makes it easier. And the best weight-loss diet is the same as the best diet for controlling blood pressure: low-fat foods and lots of fruits and vegetables.

"We really emphasize following a low-fat, high-fruit-and-vegetable diet. It's almost certain to lower your blood pressure because it lowers sodium and increases all the good stuff that's hypothesized to lower blood pressure—fiber, calcium, and potassium—and it's an effective avenue to weight loss," says Pao-Hwa Lin, PhD, assistant research professor of medicine at Duke University in Durham, North Carolina, and coauthor of *The DASH Diet for Hypertension*.

A diet low in fat won't include large amounts of red meat, which is packed with saturated fat. Nor will it include many processed foods, because they're high-fat minefields. Processed foods also tend to be high in salt and low in potassium, so when you get rid of them, you wipe out three bad birds with one dietary stone.

The Story of Salt

Experts believe that many people with high blood pressure are salt "responders," meaning that their blood pressure levels depend on the amount of salt they eat. "But there is some controversy about the issue," says Lawrence Appel, MD, professor of medicine and epidemiology at Johns Hopkins University School of Medicine in Baltimore. "Some people have a greater response than others. Older people tend to be more sensitive to salt, as are African Americans." Some research shows that roughly 26 percent of Americans with normal blood pressure—and about 58 percent of those with hypertension—are salt sensitive.

Here's what happens. When you eat the typical American's ration of sodium—3,000 to 6,000 milligrams or more a day, compared with the recommended 2,400-milligram limit—your blood pressure rises. If you're sensitive to salt, the sodium it contains makes your body attract water like a sponge. You soak it up, and your blood vessels expand with it, producing higher pressure.

Some experts feel that you shouldn't worry much about whether you're salt sensitive. It's hard to determine an individual's sensitivity to salt—you're better off just reducing your salt intake to the recommended limits to be safe.

"If you have high blood pressure, your sodium needs to be reduced by half," says Dr. Kaplan. "Don't put salt on the table or in the food you cook. Avoid most processed foods, which is where 80 percent of the sodium in American diets comes from. If that doesn't bring your blood pressure down, then sodium isn't the culprit," he says.

According to the NIH, reducing sodium in your diet to no more than 2,400 milligrams daily (equal to about a teaspoon of table salt) will lower your systolic blood pressure by 2 to 8 mm Hg. An even better goal is to reduce daily sodium to 1,500 milligrams, or ⅔ teaspoon of table salt, to lower your blood pressure even further.

Mining for Minerals

Potassium and calcium are two minerals that act like a massage on a tense body. They help the blood vessels relax. When arteries relax, they dilate, or open up, and give blood the room it needs to move calmly.

"You can think of potassium as the opposite of sodium," says Harvey B. Simon, MD, associate professor of medicine at Harvard Medical School. Potassium helps the body excrete sodium, so the more potassium you get in your diet, the more sodium you get rid of. In fact, the landmark INTERSALT study looked at more than 10,000 people from 32 countries and found that people with the highest amounts of potassium in their blood had the lowest blood pressures, and those with the lowest amounts had the highest.

"Fruits and vegetables are naturally low in sodium and high in potassium," says Dr. Lin. "A diet high in vegetables and fruits almost mimics a vegetarian diet, which is known to be linked to lower blood pressure," she says. Foods that are especially rich in potassium include beans, potatoes, avocados, steamed clams, lima beans, bananas, and apricots.

Calcium has shown similar ties to blood pressure in studies. Some have found that low intake is actually a risk factor for developing high blood pressure. The landmark Framingham Heart Study looked at the calcium intakes of 432 men. Those who ate the most (between 322 and 1,118 milligrams a day) had a 20 percent lower risk of developing high blood pressure than those who ate the least (8 to 109 milligrams a day).

A study in the journal *Hypertension* that analyzed the diet habits of nearly 5,000 people found that as they consumed more dairy, they became less likely to have hypertension. In fact, the people who consumed the most dairy were nearly 40 percent less likely to have hypertension as the people who consumed the least. However, this association was mainly seen in people whose diets were relatively low in saturated fat. Since regular dairy foods contain saturated fat, it's wise to make sure that you get your calcium from low-fat or fat-free dairy products.

A cup of fat-free yogurt contains about 415 milligrams of calcium and a glass of fat-free milk has about 352. Besides low-fat and fat-free dairy products, your best sources of calcium include tofu, calcium-fortified orange juice, kale, broccoli, and collard greens.

The government-promoted DASH diet—for Dietary Approaches to Stop Hypertension—is heavy on whole grains (six to eight daily servings) and fruits and vegetables (eight to 10 servings). It calls for two or three servings of low-fat dairy; moderate amounts of lean meat, nuts, and seeds; and limited amounts of fats and oils and sweets. It urges you to eat processed foods sparingly, since these are the main source of sodium in the American diet.

Adopting the DASH plan can lower your systolic blood pressure by 8 to 14 mm Hg. As you can see, by cutting out the salt and sodium and boosting fruits, vegetables, and other plant foods, the blood pressure reductions really add up.

Eating Right

For starters, you should practice what Dr. Appel calls active shopping. In other words, read the nutrition labels and be sure to glance at the sodium content. One 8-ounce can of stewed tomatoes can contain more than 800 milligrams of sodium, while another can might have only 70. "You often have to look hard for low-sodium cereals," he adds. "Shredded wheat is one of the low-salt ones."

Sodium-free is a good phrase to look for on a label. So is *low-sodium*. The word *light*, however, is not as conclusive. Light soy sauce, for instance, can still have 605 milligrams of sodium per tablespoon. *No salt added* doesn't mean a food is sodium-free, either. In the Nutrition Facts box on a food label, also look to see how the sodium in the food relates to the Daily Value (DV). Go for foods containing less than 5 percent of the DV. If the product contains 20 percent or more of the DV, it's high in sodium.

While bread is often a nutritious, wholesome food, it too is occasionally high in salt. If you buy bread fresh at a bakery where it isn't labeled, don't be shy about asking how much salt is in each loaf.

When you're buying canned foods, like the tomatoes mentioned above, salt can be a real problem. In many cases, however, rinsing the food will eliminate a good percentage of the salt. If you don't have a can of beans that states it's low-sodium, for example, you can rinse off at least half the salt the food was packed in, says Neva Cochran, RD, a nutrition consultant in Dallas.

Since produce is the cornerstone of a diet for healthy blood pressure, you should always be looking for ways to eat more fruits and vegetables. Here are a few of Dr. Lin's suggestions:

- Buy prepackaged salads for busy days (best to rinse it before using, however).
- Order a fruit plate as an appetizer before your meal in a restaurant.
- Eat two vegetarian dinners a week.

When you're picking up produce, be sure to grab some apples, pears, and oranges. These three fruits are fiber kings. And heart researchers are starting to find that not only does fiber decrease dangerous cholesterol, it may also lower blood pressure. Fruit fiber made a strong showing in a study at Harvard Medical School, where scientists tracked more than 30,000 men. The men in the study who ate less than 12 grams of fruit fiber a day (about four oranges or three apples or

STAY OUT OF THE SALT MINES

If you're sodium savvy and watching your blood pressure, you already know to say no thanks to foods such as chips and salty pickles. Yet sodium appears in many foods in which you might not expect it. Baking soda and baking powder, for instance, are both sodium bicarbonate. Dried fruit contains sodium sulfite, and ice cream often has sodium caseinate and sodium alginate.

Even a sharp-eyed sodium detective can miss a few salt mines. Here are some to watch out for:

Instant chocolate-flavored pudding. A half-cup contains 470 milligrams of sodium, more than the amount in two slices of bacon.

Ketchup. One tablespoon contains 156 milligrams of sodium.

Pastries. A fruit Danish has 333 milligrams of sodium, while a cheese Danish has 319. Scones and baking-powder biscuits also tend to be high in sodium.

Cheese. Most types are high in sodium. This includes cottage cheese, which has 425 milligrams in a half-cup serving.

---

pears) were 60 percent more likely to develop high blood pressure. The DASH diet is particularly high in fiber, given the amount of grain foods, fruits, and vegetables it recommends.

Finally, it's essential to reduce the amount of fat in your diet. You don't have to be fanatical, however. Instead of cutting out fat with a cleaver, start by slicing it off with a scalpel, bit by bit. Dr. Lin recommends making small, gradual changes that will cut the total amount of fat you use in half. Buy butter substitutes and trans-fat-free versions of margarine. For sautéing, use olive oil cooking spray instead of liquid oils or butter. Use mustard instead of mayonnaise, and snack on low-salt pretzels instead of potato chips.

Keep Drinks to a Minimum

Research has found that 16 percent of hypertensive disease worldwide is due to alcohol use.

The NIH recommends that men drink no more than two drinks daily. A drink is the equivalent of a 12-ounce beer, 5 ounces of wine, or 1½ ounces of 80-proof liquor.

By staying moderate with your alcohol use, you can reduce your systolic blood pressure by 2 to 4 mm Hg.

Brussels Sprouts

GOOD THINGS IN SMALL PACKAGES

If you've never seen Brussels sprouts growing on a farm, you might wonder how farmers harvest them. Do they walk down the rows, bending down to pluck the tiny vegetables, which look like miniature cabbages, off the ground? Do they drive little harvesters across the fields?

Actually, Brussels sprouts grow in bunches of 20 to 40 up and down the sides of a central stalk that's several feet tall—they don't pop up individually. Surprised? It's possible that you may harbor some other, more common misconceptions about Brussels sprouts, too. When many people hear the words "Brussels sprouts," they remember those piles of bitter, overcooked blobs from childhood dinners.

It's time to reevaluate this vegetable with an undeserved bad reputation. Today's Brussels sprouts taste better than those of bygone days, and researchers have uncovered that they may contain great disease-stopping power.

New Taste in the Marketplace

Brussels sprouts are related to cabbage, cauliflower, and broccoli . . . none of which are famous for their pleasing taste. However, while the Brussels sprouts of yore were often strong and bitter, today their taste has changed.

In recent years, Brussels sprouts growers have shifted to growing varieties that are sweeter and milder than those you may remember from your childhood. Plus, if you take care to store and cook them properly, you can maximize their tastiness. So now you'll be smacking your lips instead of holding your nose when you spoon these health-saving leafy nuggets onto your plate.

Belgium's Can-Do Cancer Beaters

Like other cruciferous vegetables, Brussels sprouts are chock-full of natural plant compounds called phytonutrients, which may help protect against cancer. These compounds may be particularly effective against common cancers, like those of the colon.

One of the key protective compounds in Brussels sprouts is sulforaphane.

Research from test tubes to lab animals to humans shows that this component can interfere with cancer at many stages of its development. It can keep cancer-causing chemicals from becoming activated in your body; it may trigger cancer cells to spontaneously die; it can prevent new blood vessels from growing to a tumor to feed it; and it may help prevent cancer from metastasizing, or spreading to new locations.

In one study looking at the effects of vegetables on cancer, researchers from the Fred Hutchinson Cancer Research Center in Seattle compared the diet history of more than 600 men with newly diagnosed prostate cancer with the diet history of more than 600 men without prostate cancer. Although a diet that is rich in vegetables reduced the risk of cancer, cruciferous vegetables—such as Brussels sprouts—were particularly helpful. Men who ate three or more servings of crucifers a week were 41 percent less likely to have prostate cancer than those who ate less than one serving a week.

Another study, which reviewed 80 studies looking at the relationship between consumption of brassica vegetables (such as Brussels sprouts), found that most showed a link between higher consumption of these vegetables and a lower risk of cancer. The results were most consistent with cancer of the lung, stomach, colon, and rectum.

Brussels sprouts contain another protective phytonutrient called indole-3-carbinol, or I3C. This compound works as an antiestrogen, meaning it helps break down your body's estrogens before they contribute to the growth of cancer cells. It also helps boost the production of certain enzymes that help clear cancer-causing toxins from the body.

Lab tests have shown that I3C inhibits the growth of a variety of types of cancer cells, including prostate, endometrial, colon, and leukemia.

In one small study, researchers in the Netherlands found that people who ate more than 10 ounces of Brussels sprouts (about 14 sprouts) a day for 1 week had levels of protective cancer-fighting enzymes in their colon that were, on average, 23 percent higher than people who did not eat Brussels sprouts.

In the Kitchen

For such tiny vegetables, Brussels sprouts sure cause some large culinary conundrums. Not only is it challenging to cook them just so, but it's also likely that you'll smell up the house while you do it.

It doesn't have to be this way. If you follow these tips, you'll get the health benefits of Brussels sprouts without the hassles:

Mark the spot. To allow the stems to cook as quickly as the leaves, make an "X" on the bottom of each stem, using a sharp knife. Then steam them for 7 to 14 minutes, until they're just tender enough to poke with a fork.

Quell the smell. The big sulfur smell thrown off by these little cabbages discourages some people from taking advantage of their healing power. Try tossing a stalk of celery in the cooking water. It will help neutralize the smell.

Use them fast. Although Brussels sprouts will keep for a week or more in the refrigerator, they start getting bitter after about 3 days, which may discourage you and your family from eating them and reaping their benefits. Buy only as many as you'll use in the next few days.

Brussels for Your Bowels

Aside from all the "sciency" compounds in Brussels sprouts, there are also plenty of good old-fashioned vitamins, minerals, and other substances that can help fight off cancer, heart disease, high cholesterol, and a host of other health problems.

Topping this list is fiber. Brussels sprouts are a decent source of fiber, with about 3 grams in a half-cup serving. That's more than you'd get in a slice of whole-grain bread.

Eating your daily fill of Brussels sprouts can help you avoid all the conditions that a diet rich in fiber is known to prevent, like constipation, hemorrhoids, and other digestive complaints.

A half-cup of Brussels sprouts also provides 48 milligrams of immunity-building vitamin C, more than 80 percent of the Daily Value (DV) for this vitamin. It also provides 47 micrograms of the B vitamin folate, about 12 percent of the DV. Folate is essential for normal tissue growth, and studies show that it may protect against cancer and heart disease.

Glazed Brussels Sprouts

1 pound small Brussels sprouts

1 teaspoon unsalted butter

2 tablespoons all-fruit apricot spread

¼ teaspoon salt

¼ teaspoon dry mustard

Trim the bottoms of the Brussels sprouts and cut them in half lengthwise. Place in a large saucepan and add 2 tablespoons water. Bring to a boil over high heat, then cover, and reduce the heat to medium-high. Cook, stirring once, for 5 to 7 minutes, or until the sprouts are crisp-tender. If the sprouts start to dry out, add another 1 to 2 tablespoons water.

If any water remains in the pan, drain the sprouts in a colander. Transfer to a medium bowl.

Add the butter to the pan and melt over medium heat. Stir in the apricot spread, salt, and mustard. Cook for 30 seconds, or until bubbly and hot. Add the Brussels sprouts to the pan, and toss to coat with the glaze.

Makes 4 servings

PER SERVING

Calories: 83	Cholesterol: 3 mg
Total fat: 1.7 g	Sodium: 164 mg
Saturated fat: 0.7 g	Dietary fiber: 5.7 g

Bulgur
A WHOLE-GRAIN HEALER

Despite its unfamiliar name, bulgur is simply wheat in its whole form. And as you would expect, this wholesome grain is one of the healthiest foods you can eat.

Research shows that bulgur may play a role in preventing colon and breast cancers as well as heart disease and diabetes. In addition, it's extremely high in fiber, which means it can help prevent and treat a variety of digestive problems, including constipation and diverticular disease.

Chemical Repair

No matter how carefully you watch your diet, you're probably being exposed to dangerous chemicals nearly every day. Two of the most common are nitrates and nitrites. Nitrates occur naturally in lots of vegetables, including beets, celery, and lettuce. Nitrites are common ingredients in processed foods such as cured fish, poultry, and meat.

These compounds themselves aren't harmful. But when you get them from food, your body transforms them into related compounds called nitrosamines, which have been linked to cancer.

While it's difficult to avoid nitrates and nitrites, a diet high in bulgur can help reduce the potentially dangerous effects. Bulgur contains a compound called ferulic acid, which helps prevent these compounds from making the troublesome conversion into nitrosamines.

Bulgur protects against cancer in yet another way because it contains lignans. According to Lilian Thompson, PhD, professor of nutritional sciences at the University of Toronto, "Lignans are potent cancer warriors, especially against colon cancer in both men and women (and breast cancer in women)."

Lignans have antioxidant properties, which means that they gobble up dangerous oxygen molecules (free radicals) before they damage individual cells. "Lignans also subdue cancerous changes once they've occurred, rendering them less likely to race out of control," says Dr. Thompson.

Help for the Heart

We've seen that free radicals can contribute to cancer. The same vicious molecules can also damage blood vessels, setting the stage for heart disease.

Somewhat paradoxically, the lignans in bulgur can help protect the heart by protecting cholesterol. Why would you want to protect a bad guy? Because when cholesterol is damaged by free-radical molecules, it is more likely to stick to artery walls, contributing to the development of heart disease.

Bulgur can help in yet another way. This grain has a low glycemic index, meaning that the sugars it contains are released relatively slowly into the bloodstream, says David J. A. Jenkins, MD, DSc, PhD, professor of nutritional sciences at the University of Toronto. Not only does this help keep blood sugar levels stable, which is important for people with diabetes, it also may play a role in reducing the risk of heart disease.

Rich in Fiber

Getting more fiber in your diet helps lower cholesterol, reduces cancer and diabetes risk, and helps treat or prevent many digestive complaints, from constipation to hemorrhoids. Bulgur is a good fiber source, with 1 cup of cooked bulgur providing over 8 grams, almost a third of the Daily Value (DV) for fiber. Compare that to a cup of cooked oatmeal, which has 4 grams of fiber, or a cup of cooked white rice, which has a measly 0.8 gram.

Many of bulgur's benefits come from insoluble fiber. This type of fiber doesn't break down in the body. Instead, it stays in the intestine, soaking up large amounts

In the Kitchen

Even if you've never cooked bulgur, don't let the exotic name put you off. It's extremely easy to prepare. Here's how:

Choose the right kind. Bulgur comes in three grinds, each of which is recommended for different types of recipes.

- The **coarse grind,** which has a consistency similar to rice, is recommended for making pilaf or when using bulgur in any rice recipe.

- The **medium grind** is used when making breakfast cereal or bulgur filling.
- The **fine grind** is usually used for making tabbouleh.

Start it hot. You don't have to cook—and cook and cook—bulgur the way you do other grains. Just cover it with about 2 cups of boiling water for each cup of bulgur. Then let it stand, covered, for 15 to 20 minutes for "al dente," or longer if you like it softer.

of water. This makes wastes heavier, so they move through the digestive system faster. Potential cancer-causing substances are ushered out of the body more quickly, giving them less time to create problems.

In a 4-year study at the New York Hospital–Cornell Medical Center in New York City, researchers studied 58 adults with histories of intestinal polyps. (While polyps themselves aren't dangerous, over time, they may become cancerous.) In the study, those given bran cereal containing 22 grams of insoluble fiber were more likely to have their polyps shrink or disappear entirely than were those who were given a low-fiber look-alike.

Insoluble fiber has also been shown to prevent (and relieve) constipation. This isn't just a matter of comfort. Moving wastes more quickly through the digestive tract reduces the time that harmful substances are in contact with the intestine. In addition, preventing constipation also helps relieve conditions such as hemorrhoids and diverticular disease.

Minerals for Health

Finally, bulgur is a virtual metal warehouse, rich in minerals essential to health. In addition to iron, phosphorus, and zinc, 1 cup of cooked bulgur contains the following minerals:

- 1 milligram of manganese, or half the DV for this mineral. Manganese is needed to ensure healthy bones, nerves, and reproduction.
- 15 micrograms of selenium, or 21 percent of the DV for this mineral. Selenium is needed to help protect the heart and immune system.
- 58 milligrams of magnesium, or 15 percent of the DV for this mineral. Magnesium helps keep your heart beating, nerves functioning, muscles contracting, and bones forming.

GETTING THE MOST

Have it with hot dogs. Since bulgur can help block the process that converts the nitrites in processed foods into cancer-causing substances, it's a good idea to combine it with these foods whenever possible. Tabbouleh, which is made from cooked bulgur mixed with chopped tomatoes, onions, parsley, and mint, and flavored with olive oil and lemon juice, makes a wonderfully fresh salad that goes well with any meal.

Buy it in bulk. Unlike many whole grains, which can be extremely slow-cooking, bulgur is steamed, dried, and crushed before it gets to the store. Essentially, it's precooked, meaning that it's ready to go in about 15 minutes. If you always have it on hand, you'll find out how easy it is to get more of this healthful grain into your diet.

Keep it cold. Since bulgur is cracked open during processing, the fatty portion of the germ is exposed to air and tends to go rancid. To keep bulgur fresh and ready to eat, be sure to keep it refrigerated until you're ready to use it.

Bulgur Salad with Currants

1 cup fine bulgur

3 cups cold water

¼ cup dried currants

¼ cup minced parsley

¼ cup chopped scallions or onions

2 tablespoons fresh lemon juice

1 tablespoon extra-virgin olive oil

⅛ teaspoon salt (optional)

In a medium bowl, combine the bulgur and water; stir to mix. Let stand for 30 minutes, or until the bulgur has absorbed the water. If the bulgur is tender but has not completely absorbed the water, drain through a fine sieve and return to the bowl.

Add the currants, parsley, scallions, lemon juice, oil, and salt (if using). Toss to combine. Serve at room temperature.

Makes 4 servings

PER SERVING

Calories: 180	Cholesterol: 0 mg
Total fat: 3.9 g	Sodium: 77 mg
Saturated fat: 0.5 g	Dietary fiber: 7.4 g

Cancer

FOODS AS THE ULTIMATE PROTECTOR

According to the American Cancer Society, cancer is the leading killer of Americans under age 85, causing about 25 percent of all deaths. Thankfully, when it comes to cancer prevention, food is powerful medicine. Study after study shows that a healthful diet—eating less fat and getting more fruits, vegetables, whole grains, and legumes—can vastly reduce the risk of cancer. In fact, research indicates that if we all ate more of the right foods and less of the wrong ones, the incidence of all cancers would be reduced by at least 30 percent.

"Food goes beyond being crude fuel, as we once believed," says Keith Block, MD, medical director of the Block Center for Integrative Cancer Care in Evanston, Illinois. "Our experience over the past 2 decades indicates that diet plays an important role when dealing with cancer. We're discovering that there are compounds in foods that can actually both prevent and help fight cancer at the cellular level."

Protection from the Garden

Researchers have known for a long time that people who eat the most fruits, vegetables, and other plant foods are less likely to get cancer than those who fill up on other, less wholesome foods. Recent research suggests that eating five servings of fruits and vegetables each day reduces cancer deaths by 35 percent. One study in particular found that a diet rich in fruits and vegetables slashes the risk of pancreatic cancer—a particularly deadly kind—in half.

But it's only recently that researchers have discovered the reason why plant foods offer such powerful cancer protection. Certain substances found only in plant foods and known collectively as phytonutrients (*phyto* is a Greek word meaning "plant") have the ability to stop cancer.

Research has shown, for example, that eating just one serving of watermelon or pink grapefruit a day can reduce a man's risk of developing prostate cancer by 82 percent! Watermelon and pink grapefruit are high in a phytonutrient called lycopene. In fact, watermelon contains about 40 percent more lycopene than do fresh tomatoes—the produce most people probably think of when they think of lycopene.

When processed into sauce, juice, or ketchup, however, tomatoes do yield more usable lycopene. Interestingly, a recent study found that organic ketchup has up to three times more lycopene than ordinary kinds. Why? Perhaps because organic ketchups are made with riper tomatoes than other types of ketchup. The darker red a ketchup is, the greater its lycopene content.

Another common garden dweller, garlic, has a long tradition as a healing food, and it turns out it is also very rich in phytonutrients. Some of the most impressive are called allyl sulfides, which appear to help destroy cancer-causing substances in the body.

The Power of Antioxidants

Every day, your body is attacked, again and again, by a barrage of harmful molecules called free radicals. These are oxygen molecules that have lost an electron, and they careen around your body looking for replacements. In the process of pilfering electrons, they damage healthy cells, possibly kicking off the cancer process.

Nature anticipated this threat by packing fruits, vegetables, and other foods with antioxidants, protective compounds that either stop the formation of free radicals or disable them before they do harm.

There are many compounds in foods that act as antioxidants in the body, but two of the best studied and most powerful are beta-carotene and vitamin C.

Beta-carotene is the pigment that gives many fruits and vegetables their lush, deep orange to red hues. It's more than nature's palette, however. Beta-carotene has been shown to stimulate the release of natural killer cells, which hunt down and destroy cancer cells before they have a chance to cause damage.

Literally dozens of studies have shown that people who get a lot of beta-carotene in their diets can reduce their risks of certain cancers, especially those of the lungs, intestinal tract, mouth, and gums.

It doesn't take a lot of beta-carotene to get the benefits. Evidence suggests that getting 15 to 30 milligrams a day—the amount provided by one or two large carrots—is probably all it takes. Cantaloupes, sweet potatoes, spinach, and bok choy all are excellent sources of beta-carotene.

Another antioxidant is vitamin C, which has been shown to help prevent cancer-causing compounds from forming in the digestive tract. In one large study, Gladys Block, PhD, professor of epidemiology and public health nutrition at the University of California, Berkeley, analyzed dozens of smaller studies that looked at the relationship between vitamin C and cancer. Of the 46 studies she examined, 33 showed that people who consumed the most vitamin C had the lowest risk of cancer.

The DV for vitamin C is 60 milligrams, an amount that's very easy to get in foods. One green bell pepper, for example, contains 66 milligrams of vitamin C, while a half-cup of broccoli has 41 milligrams.

Beans, Beans, They're Good for . . . Fighting Cancer

They may not be glamorous, but beans are showing their stuff as cancer fighters thanks to their high magnesium content. Just a half-cup of beans provides 43 milligrams of magnesium, almost 11 percent of the 400-milligram DV. The optimum intake is 310 to 420 milligrams per day.

In a study from the M. D. Anderson Cancer Center in Houston, found that people who ate the most foods containing phytoestrogens, such as beans, were the least likely to get lung cancer. Interestingly, men reduced their risk more than women—by 72 percent compared with 41 percent.

Drink Some Protection

Drinking a 4-ounce glass of red wine a day may cut a man's prostate cancer risk in half, according to a study of more than 1,400 men by the Fred Hutchinson Cancer Research Center in Seattle. Which wine is best? Order a Pinot Noir from California. Researchers at the University of Mississippi tested 11 red wines and found that Pinot Noirs from California have the most resveratrol, an antioxidant that can help ward off cancer and even heart attacks.

Although the Fred Hutchinson researchers didn't find an association between beer and prostate cancer in their study, researchers in Italy found that an antioxidant in hops called xanthohumol inhibits the growth of cancer cells. The results have been shown only in test tubes so far, but studies in humans are planned.

The world's second most popular beverage (next to water) is tea, which has long had a reputation as a cancer fighter. It was known to defeat cancer cells in test tubes, but now it's been shown to fight cancer in people, too.

Yet one more beverage, milk, really does do a body good. Researchers reviewed 63 studies and revealed that high levels of vitamin D cut the risk of colon cancer by up to 50 percent. The researchers recommend getting 1,000 IU of vitamin D per day. One cup of milk contains 100 IU. However, the FDA recently changed its vitamin D fortification guidelines so that food manufacturers can now add nearly three times more vitamin D to dairy products.

The Fiber Solution

For a long time, no one took dietary fiber seriously. It's not a nutrient. It isn't absorbed by the body. In fact, it doesn't seem to do much of anything.

As it turns out, fiber does more than anyone ever imagined. "Consuming a high-fiber diet is essential for reducing the risk of certain types of cancer, particularly colon cancer," says Daniel W. Nixon, MD, a scientific counselor with the Cancer

Treatment Research Foundation in Schaumburg, Illinois.

Fiber works against cancer in several ways, he explains. Since fiber is absorbent, it soaks up water as it moves through the digestive tract. This makes stools larger, which causes the intestine to move them along more quickly. And the more quickly stools move, the less time there is for any harmful substances they contain to damage the cells lining the intestine. In addition, fiber helps trap cancer-causing substances in the colon. And since the fiber itself isn't absorbed, it exits the body in the stool, taking the harmful substances with it.

According to doctors at the National Cancer Institute, you need between 20 and 35 grams of fiber a day to keep your risk of cancer low. That may sound like a lot, and it would be if you ate it all at once. (And truth be told, most people get only 11 grams of fiber per day.) But since many foods contain at least some fiber, it's fairly easy to get enough if you pick the right foods. Simply make it a point to eat more fruits and vegetables—raw, when possible, and with their skins rather than peeled—than you're currently eating. If you do this regularly, you'll soon find that you're getting most of the fiber you need, says Dr. Keith Block.

Beans and certain vegetables are among the best sources of fiber you can find. Eating one of them a few times a day will automatically bring your fiber intake into the comfort zone. A half-cup of kidney beans, for example, contains 7 grams of fiber, while the same amount of chickpeas contains 5 grams. As for vegetables, a half-cup of cooked okra contains 3 grams of fiber, while the same amount of Brussels sprouts has 3 grams.

Whether you're eating whole-wheat toast (2 grams of fiber per slice) for breakfast or a bowl of kasha (about 3 grams per half-cup, cooked), whole grains are also great sources of fiber. If you can, get 6 to 11 servings of whole grains a day.

Carpal Tunnel Syndrome
MORE FLEX WITH FLAX

Just as highways go through tunnels in order to get around (or under) obstacles, some structures in your body, such as nerves and ligaments, also use tunnels to get where they're going. One of the busiest tunnels is the carpal tunnel, which allows a nerve, blood vessels, and ligaments to pass through the wrist and into the fingers.

There's usually a lot of room inside the carpal tunnel. But when you use your hands and wrists a lot while typing, knitting, or doing other repetitive motions, tissues inside the tunnel may become inflamed and swollen, causing them to press against the nerve. This can cause pain in the wrist as well as tingling or numbness in the fingers, says James L. Napier Jr., MD, assistant clinical professor of neurology at Case Western Reserve University School of Medicine in Cleveland. Doctors call this condition carpal tunnel syndrome. It affects about 3 out of every 100 people in the United States, and it's one of the most common causes of partial disability.

One of the best remedies for carpal tunnel syndrome is simply to give your wrists a rest. It may also help to keep your hands warm. Pain and stiffness are more likely to occur if your hands are cold. In addition, there's some evidence that eating flaxseed may help reduce inflammation in the body, including in the wrists, says Jack Carter, PhD, professor emeritus of plant science at North Dakota State University in Fargo and president of the Flax Institute.

Flaxseed contains a compound called alpha-linolenic acid, which has been shown to reduce levels of prostaglandins, chemicals in the body that contribute to inflammation, says Dr. Carter. It also contains other compounds called lignans, which have antioxidant properties that can block the effects of harmful oxygen molecules called free radicals. This is important because free radicals are produced in large amounts whenever there's inflammation, and unless they're stopped, they make the inflammation even worse.

So far, researchers haven't put flaxseed to the test against carpal tunnel syndrome, so there's no way to know for sure how much you might need to get the benefits, says Dr. Carter. Some evidence suggests, however, that getting 25 to 30 grams (about 3 tablespoons) of ground flaxseed or 1 to 3 tablespoons of flaxseed oil might be enough to help ease the symptoms.

Since the body can't digest whole flaxseed, be sure to buy flaxseed that's ground, or grind it yourself. You can add the ground seed to hot cereals or mix it into flour when you bake. Refrigerate any leftover ground seeds in an airtight container. Once the oils in flaxseed are exposed to air, they quickly become rancid.

A Weighty Problem

While you're thinking about ways to get more flaxseed into your diet, you should also be thinking about how to get extra calories out. There's scientific evidence that people who are overweight are more likely to get carpal tunnel syndrome than those who are lean, says Peter A. Nathan, MD, hand surgeon and carpal tunnel researcher at the Portland Hand Surgery and Rehabilitation Center in Oregon. In fact, research by Dr. Nathan suggests that people who are overweight have greater risks of getting carpal tunnel syndrome than typists, cashiers, or other folks who use their hands and wrists a lot on the job.

"Heavy people have a tendency to accumulate more fluid in the soft tissues, including in the wrist," Dr. Nathan explains. As fluids accumulate, they may begin putting pressure on the nerve inside the carpal tunnel, while also reducing the amount of oxygen it receives. Losing weight isn't necessarily a "cure" for carpal tunnel syndrome, Dr. Nathan adds. But if you are overweight and having problems, losing even a few pounds might take some pressure off this vulnerable nerve.

Perhaps the best way to lose weight if you have carpal tunnel syndrome is through exercise. In addition to the weight-loss benefit, a study conducted by Dr. Nathan at the Portland Hand Surgery and Rehabilitation Center found that exercise relieved the carpal tunnel syndrome symptoms of pain, tightness, and clumsiness.

Too Much of a Good Thing

One thing you might want to eliminate from your diet if you have carpal tunnel syndrome is the artificial sweetener aspartame. A study found that heavy users of aspartame have developed symptoms of carpal tunnel syndrome. After eliminating aspartame from their diets, symptoms subsided within 2 weeks, even though no changes were made in work habits.

Celery

STALKS OF PROTECTION

The ancient Romans, notorious party animals that they were, wore wreaths of celery to protect them from hangovers, which may explain the practice of putting celery sticks in Bloody Marys.

While there's no evidence that donning a celery chapeau will save you from the consequences of having one too many, celery does have other healing properties. This member of the parsley family contains compounds that may help lower blood pressure and perhaps help prevent cancer. Celery is also a good source of insoluble fiber as well as a number of essential nutrients, including potassium, vitamin C, and calcium.

Clobber Cholesterol with Celery

The humble, pale celery stalk seems like an unlikely warrior in the battle against high cholesterol. Yet, studies of animals have shown celery's cholesterol-lowering activity. In one study, conducted at the National University of Singapore, researchers fed laboratory animals a high-fat diet, plumping them up for 8 weeks and raising their cholesterol. Then they gave some of the animals celery juice. The animals that drank the celery juice had significantly lower total cholesterol and LDL (bad) cholesterol than the animals that weren't given any celery juice.

In a later study, also conducted at the National University of Singapore, researchers gave celery juice for 8 weeks to animals that were bred to have high cholesterol. The researchers found that the celery juice significantly lowered the animals' total cholesterol. Granted, these studies were on rats, so it's not clear whether eating celery will help lower a human's cholesterol or not, but it's certainly not going to hurt.

Chomp Down on Blood Pressure

Celery has been used for centuries in Asia as a folk remedy for high blood pressure. In the United States, it took one man with high blood pressure and persistence to persuade researchers at the University of Chicago Medical Center to put this remedy to the scientific test.

The story began when a man named Mr. Le was diagnosed with mild high blood pressure. Rather than cutting back on salt as his doctor advised, he began eating a quarter-pound (about four stalks) of celery per day. Within a week, his blood pressure had dropped from 158/96 to 118/82.

William J. Elliott, MD, PhD, who was then assistant professor of medicine and pharmacological and physiological science at the University of Chicago, decided to put celery to the test. Researchers injected test animals with a small amount of 3-n-butyl phthalide, a chemical compound that is found in celery. Within a week, the animals' blood pressures dropped an average of 12 to 14 percent.

"Phthalide was found to relax the muscles of the arteries that regulate blood pressure, allowing the vessels to dilate," says Dr. Elliott, who is now an associate professor of preventive medicine at the Rush University Medical Center in Chicago. In addition, the chemical reduced the amount of "stress hormones," called catecholamines, in the blood. This may be helpful because stress hormones typically raise blood pressure by causing blood vessels to constrict.

If you have high blood pressure and would like to give celery a try, employ this strategy recommended by Asian folk practitioners. Eat four to five stalks every day for a week, then stop for 3 weeks. Then start over, and eat celery for another week.

But don't overdo it and start eating celery by the pound, Dr. Elliott warns. Each stalk of celery contains 35 milligrams of sodium, and for some people, this can cause blood pressure to go up rather than down. "Eating a ton of celery can be dangerous if you have salt-sensitive hypertension," he says.

Blocking Cancer Cells

Who'd have thought that crunching celery might help prevent cancer? Celery contains a number of compounds that researchers believe may help prevent cancer cells from spreading.

For starters, celery contains compounds called acetylenics, which have been shown to stop the growth of tumor cells.

In addition, celery contains compounds called phenolic acids, which block the action of hormonelike substances called prostaglandins. Some prostaglandins are thought to encourage the growth of tumor cells.

Also, celery contains compounds called coumarins, which help prevent free radicals from damaging cells. That gives celery a one-two-*three* punch against cancer.

> ### Doctor's Top Tip
>
> While it's tempting to cut up celery ahead of time to eat later, resist! Best to eat it soon after you cut it. After only 24 hours in the fridge, the flavonoids in cut-up celery are considerably decreased, according to researchers in Buenos Aires, Argentina.

GETTING THE MOST

Snap to it. Choose a bunch of celery that looks crisp and snaps easily when pulled apart. Look for celery that's relatively tight and compact, not splayed out.

Leave on the leaves. Celery leaves should be pale to bright green and free from yellow or brown patches. While celery stalks are certainly a healthful snack, it's the leaves that contain the most potassium, vitamin C, and calcium.

Eat it the way you like it. While many foods lose nutrients during cooking, most of the compounds in celery hold up well during cooking. Eating a cup of celery, raw or cooked, provides about 9 milligrams of vitamin C, or 15 percent of the Daily Value (DV); 426 milligrams of potassium, or 12 percent of the DV; and 60 milligrams of calcium, or 6 percent of the DV.

Chile Peppers
RED-HOT HEALERS

HEALING POWER
Can Help:

Reduce weight

Prevent the spread of cancer

Clear sinuses and relieve congestion

Stop ulcers

Reduce the risk of heart disease and stroke

According to an old saying, "Whatever doesn't kill you makes you stronger." This might be the perfect motto for the chile pepper. Not only can many people withstand the heat, they actually enjoy it. Chile pepper fans savor the heat at every opportunity, not just in traditional favorites like tacos and burritos but also in foods such as omelets, stews, and even salads.

More is involved than just a little culinary spice. These thermogenic morsels are prized around the globe for their healing power as well as their firepower. Hot chiles have long been used as natural remedies for coughs, colds, sinusitis, and bronchitis, says Irwin Ziment, MD, professor emeritus at the University of California, Los Angeles. There's some evidence that they can help lower low-density lipoprotein (LDL) cholesterol, the type associated with stroke, high blood pressure, and heart disease. There's also some evidence that chiles can help prevent—of all things—stomach ulcers. And research suggests that chile peppers might help you win the battle of the bulge and prevent cancer.

Burn Off Pounds

Historically, chile peppers were used to stimulate appetite. But ironically, they may actually do just the opposite. In fact, chile peppers seem to provide a three-pronged attack against obesity. First, eating chile peppers may help fight off cravings. Some experts believe that eating sharp-tasting foods such as hot peppers, pickles, and tomato juice can overwhelm taste buds, cutting off cravings.

Second, chile peppers may help you eat less. Researchers in the Netherlands gave 12 men 0.9 gram of ground chile pepper, either as a pill or mixed into a tomato juice beverage. Thirty minutes later, they turned the men loose at an all-you-can-eat buffet. Compared with men who were given a placebo, the men who had chile pepper reduced their food intake by 10 to 16 percent.

And third, it actually *requires* energy to eat chile peppers. That's right, it burns calories to eat them! That's because the heat you feel when you eat chile peppers takes energy to produce.

Protect Against Cancer

Compounds in chile peppers show promise against cancer. For example, researchers at the University of Pittsburgh discovered that the capsaicin, the compound that gives chile peppers their heat, caused pancreatic cancer cells that had been implanted in mice to die through a process called apoptosis. Pancreatic cancer, one of the most aggressive cancers, is the fifth-leading cause of cancer death in the United States.

Another study, this one by researchers at the University of California, Los Angeles, School of Medicine, found that capsaicin stops the spread of prostate cancer cells. Researchers found it does that in several ways, including causing cancer cells to commit suicide. Researchers gave animals capsaicin three times a week. After a month, the animals' prostate cancer tumor growth and size had decreased significantly.

Heat Up a Cold

Chile lovers have long asserted that hot peppers, from serranos to jalapeños, are the ultimate decongestant, clearing a stuffy nose in the time it takes to gasp "Yow!" In fact, the fiery bite of hot chiles (or chile-based condiments like Tabasco sauce) can work as well as over-the-counter cold remedies, says Dr. Ziment. "Some of the foods used to fight respiratory diseases for centuries, including hot peppers, are very similar to the drugs we now use."

The stuff that makes hot peppers so nose-clearing good is capsaicin, a plant chemical that gives hot peppers their sting. Chemically, capsaicin is similar to a drug called guaifenesin, which is used in many over-the-counter and prescription cold remedies such as Robitussin, says Dr. Ziment.

Of course, eating a chile pepper has more of an immediate impact than taking a spoonful of medicine. When hot pepper meets the tongue, the brain is slammed with an onslaught of nerve messages. The brain responds to this "Ow!" message by stimulating secretion-producing glands that line the airways. The result is a flood of fluids that makes your eyes water, your nose run, and the mucus in your lungs loosen, says Dr. Ziment. In other words, chile peppers are a natural decongestant and expectorant.

Even beyond that, though, researchers in Korea found that capsaicin actually affects the immune system. In one study, mice were given a daily dose of capsaicin and had nearly three times more antibody-producing cells after 3 weeks than other mice that weren't given any capsaicin. What does this mean for humans? More antibodies equals fewer colds and infections.

It doesn't take a lot of pepper to get the healing benefits. Adding 10 drops of hot pepper sauce to a bowl of chicken soup can be very effective, says Paul Bosland, PhD, professor in the department of horticulture at New Mexico State University in Las Cruces and founder of the Chile Pepper Institute at the university. "Most of us here in New Mexico do this when we're sick," he says. "We all feel better after we've had a little bit of chile pepper."

Dr. Ziment recommends treating a cold with a warm-water gargle to which you've added 10 drops of Tabasco sauce. "This remedy can be quite effective, particularly if you want to clear your sinuses," he says.

Help for Heart and Stomach

"Consuming peppers may lower your risk for heart disease," says Rallie McAllister, MD, MPH, a board-certified family physician at Nathaniel Mission Clinic in Lexington, Kentucky, and author of *Healthy Lunchbox: The Working Mom's Guide to*

In the Kitchen

Cooking with hot peppers is like riding a Harley. You have to do it very carefully.

"Approach hot peppers with respect," says Bill Hufnagle, author of *Biker Billy Cooks with Fire*. "People tell me the most unusual stories about their experiences with hot peppers—where they touched, whom they touched, and what happened," says Hufnagle.

To enjoy the heat of peppers without getting burned, follow these Hufnagle tips:

Protect your hands. When you're cooking with very hot peppers—"anything hotter than a jalapeño," Hufnagle says—put on a pair of disposable plastic gloves. (If you have sensitive hands, you may want to wear gloves even when working with milder peppers.) When you're done, thoroughly rinse the tips of the gloves with soapy water before taking them off to avoid transferring the pepper oil to your fingers. Then immediately wash your hands, says Hufnagle.

Use plenty of soap. Chile oil sticks to the skin, and water alone won't get it off. You need to use plenty of soap as well. "You might want to wash your hands more than once, depending on the kind of pepper you were working with and how much of it you handled," says Hufnagle.

Protect against pepper dust. When grinding or crushing dried hot peppers, wear a dust mask and goggles. "The dust can get in your throat and eyes," says Hufnagle.

Crush them by hand. It may be convenient to grind dried hot peppers in a blender or coffee grinder—but you won't appreciate the aftershocks. "How thoroughly can you wash a coffee grinder or blender, anyway?" says Hufnagle. "If you use them to grind peppers, you're going to have some nice hot coffee—or milk shakes." At the very least, you may want to consider getting a separate grinder to use on dried hot peppers only.

Keeping You and Your Kids Trim. Capsaicin not only improves circulation, but it also decreases the clotting potential of your blood, preventing blockages in the arteries of the heart and brain that can lead to heart attacks and strokes.

In experiments at the Bristol-Myers Squibb Pharmaceutical Research Institute, capsaicin was found to reduce the occurrence of dangerous heart-rhythm disturbances, lower blood pressure, and improve bloodflow to the heart. It seems to function in these roles as a natural calcium channel blocker, analogous to some prescription heart drugs, says Dr. McAllister.

Interestingly, capsaicin has been shown to lower cholesterol levels in turkeys eating high-cholesterol diets. Like humans, turkeys are known to develop hardening of the arteries that can lead to heart disease.

> ## Doctor's Top Tip
>
> The heat source and beneficial compound in chile peppers is called capsaicin. Capsaicin is produced by the pepper membranes, and then drawn into the seeds, says Rallie McAllister, MD, MPH, a family physician in Lexington, Kentucky. Eating the entire pepper—seeds and all—gives you the highest concentration of this healing compound and the most heat.

For years, doctors advised people prone to ulcers to abstain from spicy foods. Research now suggests the opposite—that chile peppers may help prevent ulcers from occurring.

Capsaicin appears to shield the stomach lining from ulcer-causing bacteria by stimulating the flow of protective digestive juices. Researchers at National University Hospital in Singapore found that people who consumed the most chili powder had the fewest ulcers, leading them to speculate that chile, or capsaicin, was the protective factor.

Red-Hot Vitamins

Getting more hot chiles into your diet may strengthen your personal antiaging arsenal. That's because they're a rich source of the antioxidants vitamin C and beta-carotene (which is converted into vitamin A in the body).

These antioxidants help protect the body by "neutralizing" free radicals, harmful oxygen molecules that naturally accumulate in the body and cause cell damage. Upping your intake of antioxidant vitamins, researchers believe, may help prevent damage that can lead to cancer, heart disease, and stroke as well as arthritis and a weakened immune system.

One red chile packs 3 milligrams of beta-carotene, between 30 and 50 percent of the amount recommended by most experts. Studies show that people who consume more beta-carotene-rich foods are not as prone to cancer and heart disease.

GETTING THE MOST

Choose with care. Buy fresh chile peppers that have vivid, deep colors. Their skin should be glossy, firm, and taut, and their stems should be hardy and fresh. Look for dried chile peppers with vivid colors as well. Drab chile peppers offer drab flavor.

Go for paper over plastic. Storing peppers in plastic bags isn't a great idea because the moisture accumulation can cause them to spoil more quickly. Instead, keep them in paper bags, or wrap them in paper towels. They should last for a week in the vegetable drawer of the fridge.

Enjoy them raw. Although raw chiles can be uncomfortably hot for some people, that's the best way to get the most vitamin C; cooking destroys the stores of this vitamin, says Dr. Bosland. On the other hand, capsaicin isn't affected by heating, so if that's what you're after—to help relieve congestion, for example—cook the peppers to your taste.

Preserve the powder. Storing chili powder at room temperature will eventually deplete its beta-carotene. "Keep chili powder in a dark, cool place, like in the freezer," says Dr. Bosland.

Eat for comfort. The hottest chile pepper isn't necessarily the most healing, so don't make yourself suffer unnecessarily. From wild to mild, here are a few chiles you may want to try:

- Habanero peppers and Scotch bonnets are among the most mouth-blistering peppers.
- Jalapeño and Fresno peppers weigh in at 50 percent firepower, compared to the habanero.
- Hungarian cherry and Anaheim peppers emit more of a glow than a flame and are a good choice for tamer palates.

Fiery Chile Pepper Salsa

2 medium tomatoes, coarsely chopped

2 small jalapeño peppers, cut in half lengthwise and very thinly sliced (wear plastic gloves when handling)

¼ cup finely chopped red onion

2 tablespoons chopped fresh cilantro

2 tablespoons fresh lime juice

⅛ teaspoon salt

In a small bowl, combine the tomatoes, peppers, onion, cilantro, lime juice, and salt. Mix well. Let the salsa stand for at least 30 minutes to allow the flavors to blend.

Makes 1⅓ cups

Cook's Notes: *The salsa can be covered and stored in the refrigerator for several days. Also, serve with fat-free corn chips or as a condiment for baked potatoes or grilled poultry or meat.*

PER ⅓ CUP

Calories: 29

Total fat: 0.2 g

Saturated fat: 0 g

Cholesterol: 0 mg

Sodium: 74 mg

Dietary fiber: 0.8 g

Cholesterol Control

KEEP YOUR ARTERIES CLEAN

When you consider that haggis, a favorite food in Scotland, is made of the innards of various animals mixed with animal fat and that many of the people there never eat vegetables, it's easy to understand why the Scots still have one of the highest mortality rates from cardiovascular disease in the world. Of course, Americans are more likely to eat hamburgers than haggis, but when it comes to cardiovascular health, we're only a few chest-clutching steps behind the Scots.

The reason, to a large extent, is high cholesterol. Having high cholesterol levels is one of the primary risk factors for heart attack, stroke, and other vascular diseases. Almost 100 million American adults have cholesterol levels over 200. Of these, about 34.5 million have cholesterol levels of 240 or above.

If there's any good news in these statistics, it's this: While elevated cholesterol puts you at higher risk for heart disease, it's a risk that you can control every day. Eating foods that are low in saturated fats and cholesterol is an efficient way to reduce the amount of cholesterol in your blood. Moreover, making even small reductions in cholesterol can add up to big health benefits. For each 1 percent that you lower your total cholesterol, you lower your risk of having a heart attack by 2 percent.

Understanding Cholesterol

By itself, cholesterol isn't the toxic sludge that people think it is. Indeed, the body uses cholesterol, which is produced in the liver, to make cell membranes, sex hormones, bile acids, and vitamin D. You couldn't live without it. In large amounts, however, this essential substance, which is found in animal foods such as meats, milk, eggs, and butter, quickly becomes dangerous. This is particularly true of a form of cholesterol called low-density lipoprotein (LDL), the bad cholesterol.

As LDL cholesterol circulates in the bloodstream, it undergoes a process called oxidation. Essentially, this means that it spoils and turns rancid. Your immune system quickly spots the decaying LDL and reacts to it as it would to any other invader. Immune cells gobble up the cholesterol molecules. Once engorged, they stick to the walls of arteries, hardening into a dense, fatty layer called plaque. When enough plaque accumulates, there's less room for blood to flow. Eventually, bloodflow may slow or even stop. When this occurs in arteries supplying the heart, the result is a heart attack. When it occurs in arteries supplying the brain, the result is a stroke.

Your body has a mechanism for dealing with this threat. A second form of cholesterol, called high-density lipoprotein (HDL), transports the dangerous cholesterol out of the blood and to the liver for disposal. Normally, it does a good job. (In fact, one study found that every one-point rise in HDL cholesterol protects the heart at least as much as a one-point drop in LDL cholesterol, reducing risk of a fatal heart attack by 2 percent.) But when cholesterol levels get too high, the HDL cholesterol can't keep up, and LDL gradually rises to dangerous levels.

Ideally, you want to have high levels of HDL and low levels of the dangerous LDL. The National Cholesterol Education Program recommends keeping total cholesterol below 200 milligrams per deciliter of blood. More specifically, LDL should be below 130, and HDL should be above 40. Even better, they say that an HDL above 60 is protective against disease.

One way to help keep your blood cholesterol within healthy limits is to eat no more than 300 milligrams of dietary cholesterol a day (a little more than the amount in 1½ egg yolks). But as mentioned, the body makes cholesterol on its own. That's why limiting the amount of cholesterol in your diet is only part of the solution.

Nuts to You

Not long ago, nuts were generally regarded as "fat pills," and people were urged to eat less of them. But that has changed in recent years. One of the many health benefits of nuts is their cholesterol-fighting ability.

Scientists at the USDA found that nuts contain significant levels of nutrients called plant sterols. These nutrients can lower LDL cholesterol, possibly by keeping your digestive system from absorbing the cholesterol in the foods you eat. Researchers in Canada found that when people with high cholesterol ate 1.8 grams of plant sterols a day, their cholesterol levels dropped by 8 percent.

You can buy sterol-fortified foods, such as margarine and juices, that contain extra sterols. Or you can eat them the way Mother Nature intended—in sesame seeds, sunflower seeds, and pistachios, with 144 milligrams, 104 milligrams, and 83 milligrams respectively in ¼ cup.

One nut that's gotten a particularly bad rap, coconut, may actually be especially helpful for battling high cholesterol. It's true that coconut contains more saturated fat (one of the unhealthiest kinds of fat) than butter does, ounce for ounce. However, more than half of coconut's saturated fat is lauric acid. When researchers analyzed 60 studies, they discovered that even though lauric acid raises LDL (bad) cholesterol, it boosts HDL (good) cholesterol even more. So in the end, this is good for your overall cholesterol profile.

A nut that has gotten more favorable press than the coconut is the almond. And here's one reason why. Researchers at Tufts University in Boston found that almonds' skins are particularly rich in antioxidants that help to remove LDL cholesterol. The scientists found that an extract of almond-skin flavonoids reduced LDL oxidation by 18 percent in hamsters.

Help from Fiber

You know that eating whole grains, beans, and fresh fruits will help keep your digestive system in top shape, but you may want to eat these foods to reduce cholesterol, too. They're filled with soluble fiber, a substance that forms a gummy gel in the digestive tract, which helps lower cholesterol.

A study of people in China, conducted by researchers from Johns Hopkins University in Baltimore, found that cholesterol levels in men who ate about 3 ounces of oats a day were 11 percent lower than those of men who rarely ate oats. In addition, the blood pressures of the men who ate oats were 8 percent lower.

"This study suggests that eating a high-fiber diet can have a beneficial effect on blood cholesterol and blood pressure," says Jiang He, MD, PhD, professor and chairman of the department of epidemiology at the Tulane University School of Public Health and Tropical Medicine in New Orleans. "It further suggests that adopting a high-fiber diet could reduce the death rate from cardiovascular disease in the United States."

In another study, researchers from the USDA put 25 people on heart-healthy diets for 5 weeks. They gave some of the people 3 grams of soluble fiber each day from barley—about the amount in a half-cup. When compared with the other people, who didn't get the barley, their total cholesterol levels dropped by 9 percent.

The Daily Value (DV) for fiber is 25 grams. In practical terms, this means eating 2 to 4 servings of fruit, 3 to 5 servings of vegetables, and 6 to 11 servings of breads, cereals, and grains a day, says Joanne Curran-Celentano, PhD, RD, associate professor of nutritional sciences at the University of New Hampshire in Durham. "Eating oatmeal or oat bran cereal several times a week will add even more soluble fiber to your diet," she adds. Other good sources of soluble fiber include pinto beans, red kidney beans, Brussels sprouts, and sweet potatoes.

Drink Up

Two very different beverages—milk and wine—may help improve cholesterol levels, though obviously we don't recommend drinking them together, and fat-free or low-fat milk is best. One study found that after 4 weeks of consuming 1,060 milligrams of calcium and 490 milligrams of phosphorus (a combination found in dairy products such as milk) in supplement form, the cholesterol levels of healthy people were reduced by 6 percent, compared with people who didn't get the supplements. One 8-ounce glass of milk provides about a third of the amounts taken in the study.

Another study, conducted in Boston, found that averaging five wine drinks a week cut the risk of having dangerously low HDL levels by a whopping 78 percent. It's important to keep in mind that while this amount of wine may improve your HDL cholesterol, drinking more heavily can raise blood pressure (another risk factor for heart disease) and have other damaging effects on your health. So be judicious.

The Asian Superfood

We feed soybeans to chickens. But in Asian countries, people eat soybeans as well as soy foods such as tofu nearly every day. These foods contain compounds that help lower cholesterol, and this may explain, at least in part, why cholesterol levels in Japan are so much lower than they are in the United States.

Studies have shown that replacing protein from animal sources with about 1½ ounces of soy protein a day can lower total cholesterol by 9 percent. It lowers dangerous LDL cholesterol even more, by 13 percent.

Tofu and other soy foods contain compounds called phytoestrogens, says James W. Anderson, MD, professor of internal medicine in the department of endocrinology and molecular medicine at the University of Kentucky in Lexington. Researchers believe that these compounds help transport LDL cholesterol from the bloodstream to the liver, where it's broken down and excreted. They also may prevent the LDL from oxidizing, making it less likely to clog the coronary arteries.

To get the cholesterol-lowering benefits of soy, you need to eat two or three servings of soy foods a day, says Dr. Anderson.

Cloves of Protection

Garlic lovers say that you can't eat too much of the "stinking rose," and it certainly can't hurt. When it comes to cholesterol, some research suggests that this pungent bulb can significantly lower cholesterol; other research says it does nothing.

Garlic contains a compound called allicin that may change the way in which the body uses cholesterol. When researchers analyzed data from five of the most reliable scientific studies on garlic and cholesterol, they found that eating one-half to one clove of garlic a day lowered blood cholesterol an average of 9 percent. Recent research at Stanford University in California, however, found that eating raw garlic didn't affect cholesterol levels at all.

When using garlic, it's a good idea to mince or crush it, since this releases more of the allicin. Even if you eat a lot of garlic, however, don't count on it to be a magic

THE MONOUNSATURATED EDGE

"The component in food that has the biggest effect on blood cholesterol levels is saturated fat," says Mark Kantor, PhD, of the University of Maryland in College Park. Saturated fats, which are found mostly in animal foods such as red meats, whole and 2% milk, egg yolks, butter, and cheese, can increase the amount of harmful low-density lipoprotein (LDL) cholesterol in the bloodstream as well as the total amount of cholesterol.

Every day, the average American eats the fat equivalent of a full stick of butter. Experts strongly recommend decreasing the amount of fat in your diet.

But while it's a good idea to reduce the total amount of fat in your diet, there's one type of fat that you can feel good about eating. Research suggests that having moderate amounts of monounsaturated fat, the kind found in avocados, olive oil, and canola oil, can lower levels of bad LDL cholesterol, while leaving the beneficial high-density lipoprotein (HDL) untouched.

Researchers have known for a long time that people in Greece, Spain, and other Mediterranean countries where olive oil is used every day have some of the lowest rates of heart disease in the world. Indeed, even when their cholesterol levels are fairly high, they're about half as likely to die of heart disease as an American with the same cholesterol reading. Research suggests that olive oil may somehow improve the liver's ability to remove LDL cholesterol from the bloodstream.

Even so, olive oil can't take credit for all the benefits. People in the Mediterranean region also eat a lot of fresh fruits and vegetables, plus they walk more than Americans and are less likely to be overweight.

If you do decide to add more olive oil to your diet, use it in moderation, adds Dr. Kantor. It may be better than other oils, but it's still 100 percent fat. "Cut back on all fats," he says, "and consume olive oil in moderation. Don't increase the total amount of oil in your diet."

bullet. "Eating garlic on top of a diet high in saturated fat and cholesterol is unlikely to do you any good," says Mark Kantor, PhD, associate professor of nutrition and food science at the University of Maryland in College Park.

Help from the Deep

In addition to knowing your cholesterol levels, there's another number to watch: your level of blood fats called triglycerides. People with high levels of triglycerides are more likely to have low levels of protective HDL. Conversely, lowering your level of triglycerides can help decrease your risk of heart disease.

Salmon, tuna, and other oily fish contain fats called omega-3 fatty acids, which have been shown to lower triglycerides. In a study at the University of Western Australia in Perth, two groups of men followed a low-fat diet. Those in one group ate a variety of protein foods, while those in the second group ate 3 to 5 ounces of fish a day. After 3 months, men in both groups had drops in cholesterol. But the men who ate fish also experienced a 23 percent reduction in triglycerides.

Omega-3s may do more than lower triglycerides. Research suggests that they may raise levels of beneficial HDL cholesterol as well. Men in the Australian study who ate fish had a 15 percent increase in HDL. It appears that as fish is added to a low-fat diet, triglycerides go down, and HDL levels go up.

In another study, researchers at the University of Guelph in Ontario, Canada, found that women who took 2.8 grams of omega-3 fats for a month had 8 percent higher HDL levels than the women who took a placebo (dummy pill).

Finally, fish is also low in calories and saturated fat, making it a perfect addition to a cholesterol-reducing diet. To get the maximum benefits from omega-3s, plan on eating 3 to 4 ounces of fish two times a week, recommends Dr. Curran-Celentano.

Incidentally, if you're a fan of canned tuna, you're in luck since it also contains omega-3s. However, be sure to buy chunk light tuna packed in water (canned albacore tuna has been linked to high levels of mercury). Three ounces contains approximately 90 calories and less than 1 gram of fat, while the same amount of tuna canned in oil contains 168 calories and nearly 7 grams of fat.

> ## Doctor's Top Tip
>
> "Eat one to two small fistfuls of almonds a day," says Cyril Kendall, PhD, a research scientist in the department of nutritional sciences at the University of Toronto. This amount—1 to 2 ounces—of raw, unblanched almonds each day caused a significant reduction in cholesterol in a University of Toronto study. Even better news? The addition of this amount of almonds to the diet didn't result in any weight gain.

Coffee

THIS BREW'S GOOD FOR YOU

Pop quiz: What's the number one source of antioxidants in Americans' diets? Blueberries? Strawberries? Oranges? No, no, and no. It's coffee.

Researchers at the University of Scranton in Pennsylvania found that no other food or beverage comes close to providing as many antioxidants in our diets as coffee. Truth be told, of all the fruits and beverages studied, dates have more antioxidants per serving than coffee, but because people drink a whole lot more coffee than they eat dates, coffee wins out as the number one source of antioxidants.

And perhaps that's not a bad thing at all.

"A lot of new research suggests that coffee—in moderation—is fine," says Molly Kimball, RD, a sports and lifestyle nutritionist at the Ochner Health System's Elmwood Fitness Center in New Orleans. "One or two cups a day can be helpful, but more than that is counterproductive. Coffee has been linked to a decrease in the risk of Parkinson's disease, for example. It also reduces the risk of gallstones, so it may be helpful if you have a family history of them or are prone to them. And the polyphenols—a type of antioxidant—in coffee are the same as those in fruit and wine."

Brew Up Some Antioxidants

Antioxidants are substances that help ward off disease by mopping up harmful oxygen molecules called free radicals, which naturally accumulate in the body. Free radicals damage healthy tissues throughout the body, causing changes that can lead to heart disease, cancer, and other serious conditions. The antioxidants in coffee may protect against colon cancer, diabetes, and Parkinson's disease, studies show. Both regular and decaf coffee offer the same amount of antioxidants.

One study, for example, found that coffee (decaf in particular in this study) offers protection against lung cancer. Researchers at Roswell Park Cancer Institute in Buffalo, New York, studied 993 former smokers. They found that the people who drank at least 2 cups of decaf each day were 36 percent less likely to develop lung cancer than those who drank caffeinated black tea or coffee.

Another study, in Japan, found that people who drank coffee on a daily or almost daily basis had about half the risk of developing a type of liver cancer compared with people who never drank coffee. Most interesting, the risk of cancer decreased with an increase in the amount of coffee consumed each day.

More Cancer Protection

The antioxidants in coffee offer protection against cancer. But there might be another reason why researchers found that drinking two or more cups of coffee (decaf in this study) may lower the incidence of rectal cancer by a whopping 52 percent. Researchers think that by increasing bowel movements, coffee speeds things through the body, decreasing the risk. (They have no idea why decaf offered more protection than regular coffee, however.)

Get a Java Jolt

It's not likely to come as a surprise to anyone that coffee makes you more alert. But researchers couldn't say for sure if it was the coffee that truly had the effect, or if it was merely a reversal of the negative effects of caffeine withdrawal.

A British study found that it's more likely a positive effect of the coffee. Researchers in Wales gave 60 people, all regular caffeine consumers, a long battery of tests in one evening to tucker them out. They were told to drink their regular amounts of beverages with caffeine. Another evening, they were given two beverages without caffeine and given the tests again. A third evening, they were given two beverages with caffeine and given the tests a third time. The researchers found that after drinking the caffeinated beverages, the people had better moods and did better on the tests as well. So, the researchers concluded, a daily cup or two of coffee boosts mood and alertness. (But of course it does! Any Starbucks devotee could have told them that.)

Know When to Say When

But before you chug that 32-ouncer, know that you can have too much of a good thing. Too much regular coffee can give you that feeling that you've had so much caffeine your molecules are vibrating. But also a study found that people who drank two or more cups of java a day had higher levels of inflammatory markers linked to heart disease.

> ### Doctor's Top Tip
>
> "The best way to enjoy your coffee is caffeinated with milk, for extra calcium," says Jennifer Ramos Galluzzi, PhD, of Housatonic Community College in Bridgeport, Connecticut.
>
> Why caffeinated? Most of the studies that found benefits to drinking coffee were done on caffeinated coffee, so it's likely that some of those benefits may have come from the caffeine. "Limit your caffeinated coffee drinking to one or two cups a day, though," Dr. Galluzzi adds.

"Caffeinated coffee can, of course, interfere with sleep," says Kimball. "And you should talk with your doctor before drinking coffee if you have blood pressure issues, because coffee can increase heart rate."

GETTING THE MOST

Don't be cool. For some reason, conventional wisdom says to store coffee beans in the refrigerator or freezer. Ignore it! Coffee stored in the fridge or deep freeze is exposed to fluctuating temperatures, and therefore condensation. Each time the coffee is exposed to water, it's brewed a tiny bit, which waters down the flavor. Instead, keep coffee in an airtight canister in a cabinet.

Filter it out. "Studies have shown that boiled, unfiltered coffee consumption is related to elevated cholesterol levels because of the cafestol, a compound in the coffee," says Jennifer Ramos Galluzzi, PhD, assistant professor in the science department at Housatonic Community College in Bridgeport, Connecticut.

Detox, fast. If you've had too much coffee, you'll know it by a flush on your face or a twitch in your muscles. (Or by noticing the empty Styrofoam cups littering your desk.) Headaches usually start after drinking 200 to 500 milligrams of caffeine, the amount in 2 to 5 cups of coffee. To flush the caffeine out of your system, drink plenty of water.

Colds and Flu

FOODS THAT FIGHT INFECTION

Since the beginning of time, people have been catching colds, and trying—without success—to come up with a cure for them.

The common cold is one of the most prevalent causes of illness in the world, says Rallie McAllister, MD, MPH, a board-certified family physician at Nathaniel Mission Clinic in Lexington, Kentucky, and author of *Healthy Lunchbox: The Working Mom's Guide to Keeping You and Your Kids Trim*. If you're like most adults, you'll succumb to an average of two to four colds each year. With each infection, you can expect to spend somewhere in the neighborhood of 8 to 10 days coughing, sniffling, sneezing, and feeling miserable in general.

The common cold is caused when one of more than 200 cold-causing viruses invades the cells of your nose and throat. These viruses are tiny, but they're practically indestructible. Antibiotic drugs that stop bacteria in their tracks can't even put a dent in viruses. Medicines strong enough to kill most cold-causing microbes would probably kill you in the process, says Dr. McAllister.

The flu, which is also caused by a virus, affects 5 to 20 percent of the people in the United States each year. About 36,000 people die from flu each year.

Fortunately, there is a flu shot. The Centers for Disease Control and Prevention (CDC) in Atlanta recommends that anyone who doesn't want to get the flu should get a flu shot. Studies show that the vaccine is effective in 70 to 90 percent of healthy people under age 65, as long as the match between the vaccine and circulating virus is close.

According to the CDC, among people over age 65 living outside of nursing homes, the flu shot is 30 to 70 percent effective in preventing hospitalization for the flu, and also for pneumonia. Among people over age 65 living in nursing homes, the flu shot is 50 to 60 percent effective in preventing hospitalization for the flu or pneumonia and 80 percent effective in preventing death from the flu.

The only way to avoid colds and flu entirely would be to become a hermit, living far from the sneezes of co-workers, the runny noses of children, and the coughs of strangers on city streets.

Since secluding yourself on a desert island won't pay the bills, however, one of the best strategies is to eat all the immunity-boosting foods you can find. As it turns out, there are plenty to choose from. Research has found that some of the foods we eat every day contain powerful compounds that can help stop viruses from taking hold. Even when you're already sick, choosing the right foods will ease the discomfort and possibly help you get better more quickly.

Eat for Immunity

Colds and flu get their starts when just a few viruses slip into your system. Once they're inside, they immediately set to work making more viruses. If your immune system doesn't stop them early on, they multiply to enormous numbers, and that's when you start feeling sick.

One way to stop this microbial invasion is by eating a food that might surprise you—yogurt. Researchers in Sweden gave 262 people either a supplement containing a healthy bacteria that's added to some yogurts, called *Lactobacillus reuteri*, or a placebo (dummy pill). After taking either the supplement or the placebo once a day for 80 days, the researchers found that the people who took the supplement were 2½ times less likely to have caught a cold than the placebo-popping people.

The researchers think that the bacteria in yogurt stop viruses from binding to tissue. The catch is, not just any brand will do. In the United States, the only yogurt brand currently with *Lactobacillus reuteri* is Stonyfield Farm.

The other, less surprising, way to stop the microbial invasion is to eat more fruits and vegetables. These foods contain a variety of substances that strengthen the immune system, making it better able to destroy viruses before they make you sick. Research has shown, for example, that many fruits and vegetables contain a compound called glutathione, which stimulates the immune system to release large numbers of macrophages, specialized cells that seize viruses and mark them for destruction. Avocados, watermelons, asparagus, winter squash, and grapefruit are all rich in glutathione. Okra, oranges, tomatoes, potatoes, cauliflower, broccoli, cantaloupe, strawberries, and peaches are also good sources.

Another powerful compound in many fruits and vegetables is vitamin C. Doctors have been debating for years whether vitamin C can help prevent colds—and they're still debating. When you're already sick, however, getting extra vitamin C in your diet has been proven to relieve cold symptoms and help you get better more quickly.

Vitamin C lowers levels of histamine, a defensive chemical released by the immune system that is responsible for causing stuffiness and other cold and flu symptoms. At the same time, vitamin C appears to strengthen white blood cells, which are essential for fighting infection.

After reviewing 21 scientific studies published since 1971, researchers at the University of Helsinki in Finland concluded that getting 1,000 milligrams of vitamin C a day can reduce cold symptoms and shorten the duration of the illness by 23 percent.

Of course, you'd have to eat a lot of oranges, broccoli, and other foods rich in vitamin C to get that much of this important nutrient. So drink your C instead. Orange juice, which has 61 milligrams of vitamin C in a 6-ounce serving, is probably your best choice, although cranberry and grapefruit juices also contain a lot of vitamin C.

Raise a Glass

To mount an even stronger defense against the flu, consider filling your glass with red wine instead of juice. One study conducted in Rome found that resveratrol, the polyphenol found in red wine, actually stopped influenza cells from replicating. Wondering which wine is best? Pick up a Pinot Noir from California. When researchers at the University of Mississippi tested 11 red wines, they found that Pinot Noirs from California have the most resveratrol. It's important to keep in mind, however, that alcohol can come with some unwanted effects. For example, drinking heavily can raise blood pressure and have other damaging effects on your health. So, if you do drink, do so in moderation.

Bulbs of Health

Garlic has been used throughout history for treating virtually every type of infection. Now there's increasing evidence that it can help protect against colds and flu as well.

Garlic contains dozens of chemically active compounds. Two of them, allicin and alliin, have been shown to kill germs directly. Plus, garlic appears to stimulate the immune system to release natural killer cells, which destroy even more germs.

To get the benefits of garlic, however, you have to eat a lot of it—as much as an entire bulb a day to combat colds and flu, says Elson Haas, MD, director of the Preventive Medical Center of Marin in San Rafael, California, and author of *Staying Healthy with Nutrition.*

Unless you have developed a taste for it, you probably can't eat that much raw garlic. Microwaving or baking garlic until it's tender, however, will take away some of the burn and sweeten the taste, says Irwin Ziment, MD, professor emeritus at the

University of California, Los Angeles. "The softened garlic still seems to be quite potent," he adds.

Hot and Helpful

Research has shown that two traditional treatments for colds and flu—a cup of hot tea and a steaming bowl of chicken soup—are among the most-potent home remedies there are. Both of these, along with chile peppers and other spicy foods, contain compounds that can relieve congestion and keep the immune system strong.

Tea, for example, contains a compound called theophylline, which helps break up congestion. Tea also contains quercetin, a compound that may help prevent viruses from multiplying.

Instead of black tea, though, you might want to sip chamomile. Researchers in London (where else?!) found that people who drank 5 cups of chamomile tea a day for 2 weeks had increased blood levels of polyphenols. These plant-based chemicals have been associated with antibacterial activity.

Chicken soup is another folk remedy that has been proven to be effective. In fact, having a bowl of chicken soup is one of the best ways to relieve stuffiness and other cold and flu symptoms. In laboratory studies, for example, researchers at the University of Nebraska Medical Center in Omaha found that chicken soup was able to prevent white blood cells from causing inflammation and congestion in the airways.

When a cold has your nose so stuffy that you feel like you're breathing through a thick blanket, you may want to take a bite of hot pepper. Jalapeños, ground red pepper (cayenne), and their fiery kin contain a compound called capsaicin. This compound, which is similar to a drug in cold and flu medications, will help you breathe easy again, says Dr. Ziment.

In addition, several studies have shown that capsaicin can help stop sickness before it starts. In one study, researchers in Korea found that mice given capsaicin had nearly three times more antibody-producing cells after 3 weeks than mice that weren't given any capsaicin.

You can get plenty of capsaicin from fresh hot peppers, of course, but the peppers don't need to be fresh for you to get the benefits, adds Dr. Haas. Mixing ¼ teaspoon of ground red pepper in a glass of water and drinking it can be very effective. "It's heating, but not irritating," he says.

Constipation
THE FIBER EXPRESS

There's not much that people don't talk about these days. Spend a few minutes around the water cooler, and you'll hear about sex, divorce, and the details of a colleague's prostate surgery.

The one thing people don't talk about, even with their doctors, is constipation. If they did, constipation probably would no longer be the most common digestive complaint—affecting more than 4 million Americans chronically—because they'd find out that it's easy to treat. For most people, simply getting more fiber and fluids in their diet can put an end to constipation for good.

Just Passing Through

Unlike vitamins and minerals, fiber isn't absorbed by the digestive tract. Instead, it spends a long time in the intestine, absorbing large amounts of fluid. And that's precisely its constipation-fighting secret.

When fiber absorbs water, stools gradually swell, getting bigger and wetter. Unlike small stools, which can accumulate for days before moving on, large stools are moved out of the intestine much more quickly, says Marie Borum, MD, MPH, professor of medicine at George Washington University Medical Center in Washington, D.C. And because large stools are much softer than small ones, there's less straining when they do move, she adds.

All fruits, vegetables, legumes, and whole-grain foods contain healthful amounts of fiber. Doctors once believed that insoluble fiber, the kind found mainly in whole wheat, was the only choice for beating constipation. As it turns out, however, both insoluble and soluble fiber (the kind found primarily in legumes, oats, and many fruits) can help keep the intestine working smoothly. "Both types of fiber add bulk, soften the stool, and speed transit time," says Dr. Borum. The reason that constipation is so common is that most Americans simply don't get enough fiber. On average, we only get about 11 grams a day, a lot less than the Daily Value (DV) of 25 grams, says Pat Harper, RD, a dietitian based in Pittsburgh. Since virtually all plant foods contain healthy quantities of fiber, you don't have to work very hard to get the necessary amounts. A 1-cup serving of Wheaties has 3 grams of fiber, or 12 percent of the DV, and Kellogg's Raisin Bran has 8 grams in the same size serving, or 32 percent

GOOD MORNING, JOE

Coffee drinkers have always known that a morning cup of their favorite jolt does more than pop their eyes open. It appears to wake up the digestive tract as well.

It's not your imagination. The caffeine in coffee stimulates the large intestine, causing it to contract, says Pat Harper, RD, a dietitian based in Pittsburgh. "A cup or two of coffee in the morning can help you stay regular," she says. In fact, some doctors recommend that anyone who is constipated try drinking a cup of coffee rather than taking an over-the-counter laxative.

The problem with coffee, of course, is that when you drink a lot of it each day, it removes more fluids from your body than it puts in. It's fine to use coffee as a morning wake-up call, Harper says. It's a good idea, however, to limit yourself to fewer than five cups a day.

of the DV. A half-cup of cooked kidney beans has 3 grams of fiber, or 12 percent of the DV, and an apple also has about 3 grams.

There is one problem with adding more fiber to your diet. When your body isn't used to it, it can cause cramping and gas, Dr. Borum warns. To get the benefits without the grief, she recommends that you gradually add fiber to your diet over a period of several months. "A lifetime of not getting enough fiber can't be fixed in a week," she says. But if you gradually increase the amount of fiber you get each day, you probably won't have any discomfort at all, she adds.

Want to add fiber to relieve constipation without the adverse effects? Research suggests that a combination of rye bread, which is high in fiber (one slice of rye bread has 2 grams of fiber, or 8 percent of the DV for this nutrient) and yogurt containing the bacteria *Lactobacillus GG* might just be the ticket. Researchers think that the rye bread treats the constipation, and the yogurt relieves the adverse gastrointestinal effects of the extra fiber. While *Lactobacillus GG* is not presently sold in the United States, you can buy it in supplement form in this country.

Water Works

We often think of water as being sort of an add-on to a healthful diet, not an essential ingredient in its own right. But not getting enough water is a very common cause of constipation, Dr. Borum says. After all, stools can absorb large amounts of water. When they don't get enough, they get hard, sluggish, and more difficult to pass. This is particularly true when you're eating more fiber, which must be accompanied by fluids in order to keep things moving smoothly.

You can't depend on thirst to tell you when it's time to drink, Dr. Borum adds. The thirst mechanism isn't all that sensitive to begin with, and often it stays silent even when your body needs more fluids. What's more, the urge to drink naturally gets weaker with age, which is one reason that constipation is more common in older folks.

To avoid walking on the dry side, Dr. Borum recommends drinking at least six to eight full glasses of water a day. Or, if you don't want to drink that much water, make up the difference by having soups or juices.

Beverages containing alcohol or caffeine, however, really shouldn't count toward your daily fluid total because they're diuretics, meaning that they actually remove more fluids from your body than they put in, says Dr. Borum.

Several studies have proven the link between not drinking enough water and constipation. Scientists in Germany gave eight men 2,500 milliliters (85 ounces) of water each day for 1 week and then 500 milliliters of water (16 ounces) each day for another week. The researchers found that even this relative short period of fluid deprivation decreased stool frequency and weight.

So, fiber is good, and water is good, but both is better! Researchers in Italy divided 117 people with chronic constipation into two groups. For 2 months, both groups ate a standard diet with about 25 grams of fiber a day. The first group was allowed to drink as much water as they wanted (which turned out to be not too much), but the second group drank 2 liters (about 2 quarts) of mineral water each day. The researchers found that the 25 grams of fiber each day relieved the people's constipation, but their constipation was relieved even more when they drank 1.5 to 2 liters of water a day.

Pruning the Problem

Prunes are probably the oldest home remedy for constipation—and, researchers have discovered, one of the most effective.

Prunes contain three ingredients that help keep digestion on track. For starters, they're very high in fiber, with 3 grams of the rough stuff, or about 12 percent of the DV, in just three prunes. They also contain a compound called dihydroxyphenyl isatin, which stimulates the intestinal contractions that are necessary for regular bowel movements. Finally, prunes contain a natural sugar called sorbitol, which soaks up enormous amounts of water in the digestive tract and helps keep the system active.

If you don't happen to care for prunes, you can get some of the same benefits by eating raisins. In one study, for example, people were given 4½ ounces of raisins a day. At the end of the study, the average time it took for stools to move through the digestive tract was cut in half, from two days to one.

Like prunes, raisins are very high in fiber, with a snack-size box providing about 2 grams, or 8 percent of the DV. In addition, they contain a compound called tartaric acid, which acts as a natural laxative, Dr. Borum explains.

Hold the Cheese

For people prone to constipation, limiting foods that have little or no fiber, such as cheese, ice cream, meat, and processed foods, is also important, according to researchers at the National Digestive Diseases Information Clearinghouse.

As a double whammy, cheese and other dairy products contain an insoluble protein called casein, which slows digestion and worsens constipation.

Corn

KERNELS AGAINST CHOLESTEROL

In Mitchell, South Dakota, right in the middle of the corn belt, residents pay homage to the harvest. Their shrine is the Corn Palace, a mansion built in 1892 that's decorated—murals, minarets, towers, and all—with 3,000 bushels of corn.

It isn't necessary to take corn that seriously, but it does deserve a place of honor at your dinner table. Because corn is high in fiber, it can help lower cholesterol. And because it's very high in carbohydrates, it provides quick energy while delivering virtually no fat.

"Corn is really an excellent basic food source," says Mark McLellan, PhD, dean of research for the University of Florida's Institute of Food and Agricultural Sciences and director of the Florida Agricultural Experiment Station, both in Gainesville. "When combined with other vegetables in the diet, it is a good source of protein, carbohydrates, and vitamins."

'Ears to Preventing Cancer

Corn, which is native to America, has been a staple food here since primitive times, with meal made from corn dating back about 7,000 years. Today, the United States is still one of the largest commercial growers of corn. But this humble food's health benefits often get overlooked. It turns out that corn might be a powerful ally in the fight against cancer.

One study, conducted at the University of Southern California Keck School of Medicine in Los Angeles, found that an orange-red carotenoid found in corn, beta-cryptoxanthin, was protective against lung cancer. The scientist found that men who ate the most food containing beta-cryptoxanthin had a 15 to 40 percent reduction in lung cancer risk, compared with the men who ate the least.

Another study, this one conducted at the University of Maryland School of Medicine in Baltimore, found that a component of fiber that's found in abundance in corn, inositol hexaphosphate, prevents the growth of colon cancer cells in test tubes. Researchers say it stops the cancer cells from dividing.

Corn Can Be a Problem

When you think of food allergies, the foods that probably come to mind are shellfish, peanuts, or other common offenders. But many people are sensitive to processed corn as well. In fact, cereals made from corn are among the top five allergy-causing foods.

What's more, corn cereals are known for triggering flare-ups in people with irritable bowel syndrome, a condition that causes abdominal pain and cramping. Several studies have found that corn may cause problems in over 20 percent of people with this problem.

Corn is included in many products, so if you're sensitive to it (or think you might be), be sure to read labels carefully before buying. For example, people who are allergic to corn might have to avoid foods containing corn syrup as well.

Kernels against Cholesterol

Corn contains a type of dietary fiber called soluble fiber. When you eat corn, this fiber binds with bile, a cholesterol-laden digestive fluid produced by the liver. Since soluble fiber isn't readily absorbed by the body, it passes out in the stool, taking the cholesterol with it.

You've heard a lot about how oat and wheat bran can lower cholesterol. Corn bran is in the same league. In a study at Illinois State University in Normal, researchers put 29 men with high cholesterol on a low-fat diet. After 2 weeks on the diet, some of the men were each given 20 grams (almost ½ tablespoon) of corn bran a day, while others received a similar amount of wheat bran. During the 6-week study, those on the corn bran plan had a drop in cholesterol of more than 5 percent and about a 13 percent drop in triglycerides, blood fats that in large amounts can contribute to heart disease. Those who were given wheat bran showed no change beyond the initial drop caused by being on a low-fat diet.

A Bushel of Nutrients

The beauty of corn is that it provides a lot of energy while delivering a small number of calories—about 83 per ear.

Corn is an excellent source of thiamin, a B vitamin that's essential for converting food to energy. An ear of corn provides 0.2 milligram of thiamin, 13 percent of the

Daily Value (DV) for this nutrient. That's more than you'll get in three slices of bacon or 3 ounces of roast beef.

And since fresh sweet corn consists primarily of simple and complex carbohydrates, it's a superb energy source, says Donald V. Schlimme, PhD, professor emeritus of nutrition and food science at the University of Maryland in College Park. "It fulfills our energy needs without providing us with a substantial amount of fat," he says. What little fats there are in corn are the polyunsaturated and monounsaturated kinds, which are far healthier than the saturated fats found in meats and high-fat dairy foods.

GETTING THE MOST

Make sure it's mature. When you buy fresh corn at the supermarket, look for ears that have full, plump kernels. "Purchase corn at the optimum stage of maturity," Dr. Schlimme advises. "Under those conditions, the level of nutrients is higher."

To see if corn is ripe, puncture one of the kernels with your fingernail. If the liquid that comes out isn't milky-colored, the corn is either immature or overripe, and you should pass it by.

Get the whole kernel. No matter how diligent you are when eating corn on the cob, you invariably leave a lot behind. To get the most out of each kernel, you're

In the Kitchen

Corn on the cob is so easy to prepare, it's essentially nature's fast food. Just strip off the husk and corn silk, drop the ears in a steamer, and wait until it's done a few minutes later. To maximize the taste, here are a few tips you may want to try.

Gotta wear shades. Heat rapidly converts the sugar in corn to starch, so buy corn that's refrigerated or at least been kept in the shade.

Cook it right away. When corn sits around, its natural sugar turns into starch, giving up the natural sweet taste. So it's best to cook corn soon after it is picked.

Hold the salt. When cooking corn in boiling water, don't add salt. This will draw moisture from the kernels, making them tough and hard to chew.

Strip the kernels. When you have a craving for fresh corn but don't want to wrestle with the cob, just strip the kernels off. Hold the cob upright in a bowl. Using a sharp knife, slice downward, cutting away a few rows at a time. When all the kernels are removed, scrape the dull side of the blade down the sides of the cob to extract the sweet, milky juice.

better off buying frozen or canned corn. Or you can cut the kernels from the cob with a knife. Unlike eating it right off the cob, "you get more of the corn's benefit by having a mechanical cut that takes the entire kernel off," Dr. McLellan says.

Buy it vacuum-packed. While canned corn can be almost as nutritious as fresh, it loses some of its value when it's packed in brine, a salty liquid that leaches nutrients from food during processing, says Dr. Schlimme. To get the most vitamins, look for vacuum-packed corn, which doesn't contain brine. Corn that's vacuum-packed (it will say so on the label) usually comes in short, squat cans, he says. Or choose frozen corn instead. Studies at the FDA showed that frozen corn is just as nutritious as fresh.

Spicy Black Bean and Corn Salad

1 **can (15 ounces) black beans, rinsed and drained**

2 **cups frozen corn kernels, thawed and drained**

4 **jalapeño peppers, seeded and chopped**

2 **tomatoes, chopped**

1 **small red onion, chopped**

2 **cloves garlic, minced**

2 **tablespoons fresh lime juice**

1 **tablespoon extra-virgin olive oil**

2 **teaspoons chili powder**

In a large bowl, combine the beans, corn, peppers, tomatoes, onion, and garlic.

In a cup, stir together the lime juice, oil, and chili powder, and pour over the salad; toss well.

Makes 4 servings

PER SERVING

Calories: 193	Cholesterol: 0 mg
Total fat: 4.5 g	Sodium: 283 mg
Saturated fat: 1 g	Dietary fiber: 8 g

Diabetes

THE NEW APPROACH

Most people with diabetes should eat a diet that's higher in carbohydrates, particularly the complex kind, than was formerly believed. While your doctor, dietitian, or nutritionist will determine your personal need for carbohydrates, most people should be getting approximately 50 percent of their total calories from carbohydrates, says Stanley Mirsky, MD, associate clinical professor of metabolic diseases at Mount Sinai School of Medicine in New York City and the author of *Controlling Diabetes the Easy Way.*

It may sound strange, but there's never been a better time to have diabetes. Gone are the days when a doctor handed you a list of what you could and couldn't eat—the same list he gave to everyone else who came in the door. New evidence has significantly altered the one-size-fits-all dietary approach to this condition.

For example, even though it's best to eat sugar in moderation, for most people with diabetes, it's no longer forbidden. Some may be advised to cut back on fat and eat more carbohydrates; others will be told just the opposite. In fact, it's not unusual these days for two people with diabetes, even if they are the same age, same weight, and in the same overall condition, to have totally different diets for controlling it.

Yet one aspect of diabetes has stayed the same. Diet—what you eat, and in some cases, what you don't—is at the heart of any treatment plan. Along with maintaining a healthy weight and getting regular exercise, eating right helps keep blood sugar and fats at steady levels, which is the key to keeping problems under control.

Hunger Amidst Plenty

Before seeing how you can use food to treat or prevent diabetes, here's a quick look at what this condition is. The fuel that keeps our bodies running is sugar. Doctors call it glucose. Soon after we eat, glucose pours into the bloodstream and is carried to individual cells throughout the body. Before it can enter these cells, however, it requires the presence of a hormone called insulin. And therein lies the problem.

People with diabetes either don't produce enough insulin, or the insulin they do produce doesn't work efficiently. In either case, all that glucose in the bloodstream isn't able to get inside the cells. Rather, it hovers in the bloodstream, getting more and more concentrated as time goes by. Not only do individual cells go hungry, which can cause fatigue, dizziness, and many other symptoms, but all that concentrated sugar becomes toxic, eventually damaging the eyes, kidneys, nerves, immune system, heart, and blood vessels.

The most serious form of diabetes—and the least common—is type 1, or insulin-dependent, diabetes. It occurs when the body makes little or no insulin of its own. People with type 1 diabetes must take insulin to replace their own missing supplies.

Far more common is type 2, or non-insulin-dependent, diabetes. People with this condition, which occurs mainly in those over age 40, produce some insulin, but generally not enough. They may take oral medications, but usually don't require insulin injections, at least not in the early stages of the disease.

The Healing Power of Food

Experts have long recognized that what you eat can play a critical role both in preventing and controlling type 2 diabetes. Perhaps the best way to understand the effects of diet on diabetes is to look at two similar groups of people who differ primarily in what they eat.

Consider the Pima Indians. Researchers discovered that Pimas who live in Mexico and eat a lot of corn, beans, and fruits are seldom overweight and rarely develop diabetes. By contrast, the Pima Indians in Arizona eat an Americanized diet that is high in sugar and fat. They commonly develop diabetes by age 50.

Fuel Up with Carbs

Carbohydrates, which are found in most foods except meat, fish, and poultry, are the body's main source of energy. There are two types. Complex carbohydrates, called starches, include foods like rice, beans, potatoes, and pasta. Simple carbohydrates, called sugars, include the natural sugars found in milk, fruits, and vegetables as well as white table sugar and honey. The body turns both complex and simple carbohydrates into glucose, which is either immediately converted into energy or stored until needed.

If you have diabetes, a helpful way to plan your meals is to use a system called the glycemic index (GI). Scientists at the University of Sydney in Australia developed the glycemic index, which ranks carbohydrates according to their effects on your insulin-regulating system. All carbs are not created equal, however. Some carbohydrates are broken down into sugars slowly, and they slowly release those sugars into your bloodstream. Other carbohydrates are broken down lightning fast, and their sugars zip right into your bloodstream.

The index is based on the standard of table sugar, which enters your bloodstream almost instantly, causing a fast spike in your blood sugar levels, which requires a big jolt of insulin to stabilize. The index compares how fast other carbs are broken down into sugars with this table sugar standard. High-GI foods, such as cookies and cakes, affect your body like table sugar does—quickly spiking blood sugar levels. Low-GI foods, such as vegetables and some fruits, release their sugars into the bloodstream more slowly, easing out insulin more slowly.

Look for the glycemic index values of foods on product labels soon. But if you do decide to eat the low-GI way, bear in mind that it's not a perfect system. Because the glycemic index only considers carbs, it can make some healthy foods (like carrots) look bad and other not-so-healthy foods (like peanut M&Ms) look good. That's why researchers have developed an improved system called the glycemic load. The glycemic load (GL) also takes into consideration fiber and fat, both of which affect the digestion of carbohydrates. Like the glycemic index, you can find the GL of foods in books and online.

Toss One Back

Beer is probably the last thing you'd expect to be on a diabetes-friendly diet. But researchers at Boston Medical Center found that mild to moderate alcohol consumption—of beer and wine specifically—was associated with a lower risk of hyperinsulinemia (having too much insulin in the blood, which is often associated with diabetes). The people in the study who drank 20 drinks per month were 66 percent less likely to be diagnosed with an obesity-related condition, such as diabetes, than those who abstained.

Don't look at this as a license to binge, however, and talk with your doctor before adding alcohol to your diabetes diet! Safe upper limits are one drink per day for women and two for men. A drink is defined as 12 ounces of beer, 5 ounces of wine, or 1½ ounces of liquor.

Healing Fiber

A high-fiber diet has been shown to relieve everything from constipation to heart disease. Research suggests that it can also play a powerful role in controlling blood sugar, says James W. Anderson, MD, professor of internal medicine in the department of endocrinology and molecular medicine at the University of Kentucky in Lexington.

There are two types of fiber, soluble and insoluble. Both play a role in stabilizing blood sugar.

Here's how soluble fiber helps: Because it forms a gummy gel in the intestine, soluble fiber helps prevent glucose from being absorbed into the blood too quickly. This in turn helps keep blood sugar levels from rising or dipping too drastically.

In addition, soluble fiber seems to increase cells' sensitivity to insulin, so more sugar can move from the blood into the cells. In studies conducted by Dr. Anderson, people with type 2 diabetes who ate a high-fiber (and high-carbohydrate) diet were able to improve their blood sugar control by an average of 95 percent. People with type 1 diabetes on the same diet showed a 30 percent improvement.

Research now shows that insoluble fiber may play a role in diabetes prevention as well. Insoluble fiber is found in whole-grain products, vegetables such as green beans and dark green leafy vegetables, fruit skins and root vegetable skins, seeds, and nuts. In a study conducted at Harvard University, averaging 10 grams of cereal fiber each day (from foods such as whole-grain breads, rice, and pasta) lowered the risk of type 2 diabetes by 36 percent.

It's really very easy to increase your fiber intake. Try eating at least five servings of fruits and vegetables each day. Eat more whole-grain bread. (The first ingredient should be 100 percent whole-wheat flour or stone ground whole-wheat flour. Another clue is that the bread should provide 1½ to 2 grams of fiber per slice. Don't be fooled by just a brown color, which can simply be molasses!) Use whole-grain cereals and whole-wheat pasta instead of white pasta. And swap out beans for meat in some meals. You don't have to be fanatical about counting fiber grams. You can easily get enough by eating 3 to 5 servings of vegetables, 2 to 4 servings of fruits, and 6 to 11 servings of breads, cereals, pasta, and rice a day.

Two great sources of fiber are Brussels sprouts and beans. A half-cup serving of Brussels sprouts contains 4 grams of fiber, with 2 grams of soluble fiber. (That's more fiber than you'll get in a cup of pasta.) A half-cup of kidney beans contains nearly 7 grams of fiber, almost 3 grams of it soluble.

Increase your fiber intake slowly to avoid some uncomfortable digestive issues, and drink more water to help keep the fiber moving through your system.

Help from Vitamins

Perhaps it's appropriate that vitamin D—also known as the "sunshine vitamin" because your body makes vitamin D from time spent out in the sun—is helpful for diabetes.

While going outside on a sunny day is a good way to get vitamin D, possibly the easiest way to get this vitamin in your diet is by drinking fortified milk. Having one glass of fortified milk will provide about 100 IU, or 25 percent of the Daily Value (DV) for this vitamin. And another great reason to do that is because you'll also get milk's calcium. One cup of fat-free milk contains more than 300 milligrams of calcium, which is almost a third of the DV for this mineral.

Why is calcium important for people with type 2 diabetes? It turns out that calcium is key in the fight against this disease. When Harvard University scientists studied the diets of more than 41,000 men for 12 years, they found that for every daily serving of low-fat dairy foods the men ate each day, their risk of developing type 2 diabetes dropped by 9 percent. The researchers think that the calcium in low-fat dairy plays a role. But probably the best strategy is to get both vitamin D and calcium together, and of course you can get that combo in one convenient package—a carton of milk.

Two other important vitamins for diabetes care are C and E. In fact, if you have diabetes, fruits and vegetables rich in vitamins C and E may be your ticket to healthier eyes, nerves, and blood vessels. These vitamins are known as antioxidants. They help protect your body's cells from free radicals, naturally occurring, cell-damaging molecules that may pose particular risks to people with diabetes.

What's more, vitamin C may provide even more direct benefits. In one study, Italian researchers gave 40 people with diabetes 1 gram of vitamin C every day. After 4 months, the patients' abilities to use insulin had significantly improved, perhaps because vitamin C helps insulin penetrate cells.

The DV for vitamin C is 60 milligrams. Oranges and grapefruit are excellent sources of vitamin C, but they're not the only ones. One cup of chopped, steamed broccoli, for example, contains more than 116 milligrams, or almost twice the DV for vitamin C. Half a cantaloupe has about 113 milligrams of vitamin C, and one red bell pepper has 140 milligrams.

Even though vitamin C is essential for people with diabetes, this nutrient is readily destroyed during cooking. For example, boiled broccoli may retain only 45 percent of its vitamin C. Steaming, which can preserve 70 percent of the C, is better. Best of all is microwaving, which preserves as much as 85 percent.

Another way to increase your intake of vitamin C is to pick the ripest fruits. Scarlet tomatoes, garnet strawberries, and deep chartreuse kiwifruit are much more nutrient-dense than fruits that haven't yet hit their prime.

Vitamin E, which is good for the heart, may be particularly important for people with diabetes, who are two to three times more likely to develop heart disease than people who do not have the disease. And research suggests that, like vitamin C, it may help insulin work better. Finnish scientists studied 944 men and found that those with the lowest levels of vitamin E in their blood were four times more likely to have diabetes than those with the highest levels. Vitamin E may somehow help insulin carry sugar from the blood into cells in muscles and tissues, the researchers speculate.

Vitamin E also helps keep blood platelets, which are elements in blood that help it clot, from becoming too sticky. This is particularly important in people with diabetes, whose platelets tend to clump more readily and lead to heart disease.

To get the most vitamin E, you need to occasionally use oils rich in polyunsaturated fats, like soybean oil, corn oil, and sunflower oil. Of course, these oils don't provide the benefits of the monounsaturated fats found in olive oil and canola oil. Used in moderation, however, they will help boost your vitamin E to healthy levels.

Wheat germ is another excellent source of vitamin E, with ¼ cup containing 6 IU, or 20 percent of the DV. Other good sources of this vitamin include kale, sweet potatoes, almonds, avocados, and blueberries.

Chrome-Plated Protection

It's not just vitamins that can help control diabetes. The trace mineral chromium, found in broccoli, grapefruit, and fortified breakfast cereals, has been shown to help regulate blood sugar, says Richard A. Anderson, PhD, a research chemist with the USDA Human Nutrition Research Center in Beltsville, Maryland.

Tests show that people with diabetes have lower levels of chromium circulating in their blood than people without the disease. In one study, eight people who had difficulty regulating blood sugar were given 20 micrograms of chromium a day. After 5 weeks, their blood sugar levels fell by as much as 50 percent. People without blood sugar problems who were given chromium showed no such changes.

In two more recent studies, scientists found that chromium may help control the health risks of diabetes. In one study, researchers studied 27 people with diabetes for 10 months and found that insulin sensitivity was twice as good in those who took chromium as in people who took a fake supplement. Another study, this one in Slovenia, found that in people with diabetes, taking chromium supplements for 3 months shortened QTc intervals, which is a heart rhythm that may become fatal if the interval lengthens.

It's true that the people in these studies took chromium supplements. But because experts aren't sure that taking chromium supplements is safe, it's best to boost your chromium supplies by eating foods that provide it. One cup of broccoli, for example, contains 22 micrograms, or 18 percent of the DV. A 2½-ounce waffle has almost 7 micrograms, or 6 percent of the DV. And 1 cup of grape juice contains 8 micrograms, or 6 percent of the DV.

When you're trying to get more chromium, barley is a good choice. One animal study done in England found that barley can help keep blood sugar levels under control. This grain makes great soups and breads and is a nice addition to casseroles.

To help your body retain the most chromium, it's helpful to eat lots of complex carbohydrates, like pasta and bagels, says Dr. Richard Anderson. Eating lots of sugary foods, on the other hand, will cause your body to excrete chromium. So even though it's fine to enjoy an occasional sugary snack, the emphasis should really be on the healthier whole foods, he says.

The USDA recommends eating whole grains—such as whole-wheat flour, whole-wheat bread, and brown rice—instead of refined grains—such as white flour, white bread, and white rice—whenever possible. Whole grains provide many health benefits, in addition to helping your body retain chromium.

Magnesium for Glucose Control

Experts estimate that 25 percent of people with diabetes are low in the mineral magnesium. The problem is even worse in those who have diabetes-related heart disease or a type of eye damage known as retinopathy. Since low levels of magnesium have been linked to damage to the retinas, it's likely that upping your intake of this mineral may help protect your eyes.

Good sources of magnesium include baked halibut, which contains 91 milligrams of magnesium per 3-ounce serving, or 23 percent of the DV. Cooked spinach is also good: 1 cup contains 157 milligrams, or almost 40 percent of the DV. And a half-cup serving of long-grain brown rice has 42 milligrams, or 11 percent of the DV.

Putting It All Together

Treating and preventing diabetes with foods involves more than just eating a few good foods. It's really a whole diet in which all the separate elements—fiber, vitamins, minerals, and so forth—come together in one good plan. Consider working with a dietitian to develop a meal plan that promotes blood sugar control, coordinates with your medications, and is tailored to your preferences and lifestyle.

> ## Doctor's Top Tip
>
> Most people with diabetes should eat a diet that's higher in carbohydrates, particularly the complex kind, than was formerly believed. While your doctor, dietitian, or nutritionist will determine your personal need for carbohydrates, most people should be getting approximately 50 percent of total calories from carbohydrates, says Stanley Mirsky, MD, of Mount Sinai School of Medicine.

Fatigue

WHAT TO EAT WHEN YOU'RE FEELING BEAT

Every day is the same. You slap the snooze button five or six times, then crawl out of bed—no time for breakfast. Struggle through the morning, fueled by generous mugs of strong coffee. Drag yourself to lunch. Drag yourself back to your office, and muscle through the afternoon. Then drag yourself back home, where all you want is takeout, TV, your quilt, and the couch.

You're exhausted just thinking about it.

Fatigue in this country is at near-epidemic proportions. Fully half of all adults who seek medical treatment complain of fatigue. But it doesn't have to be this way. Making even small changes in your diet, experts say, can have a substantial effect on your energy levels.

Brain Fuel

There are some foods that make us sleepy and droopy, while others give us energy to burn. It's only in recent years, however, that scientists have begun understanding why. The answer, as it so often does, begins in the brain.

To a large extent our feelings, moods, and energy levels are controlled by neurons—nerve cells in the brain that communicate with the help of chemical messengers called neurotransmitters. Studies have shown that changes in the levels of neurotransmitters such as dopamine and norepinephrine can dramatically affect energy levels, which is why they're sometimes called wake-up chemicals. Studies show that people tend to think more quickly and feel more motivated and energetic when their brains are producing large amounts of these chemicals.

Our diets provide the raw materials needed for the production of these neurotransmitters. What we eat—or don't—can play a large role in how we feel. "We're talking about a whole symphony of brain chemicals that ebb and flow throughout the day," says Elizabeth Somer, RD, author of *Food and Mood* and *Nutrition for Women*.

The building block for dopamine and norepinephrine, for example, is the amino acid tyrosine. Tyrosine levels are elevated when you eat high-protein foods such as fish, chicken, or low-fat yogurt.

"Make sure to eat some protein along with carbohydrates at each meal or snack," says Molly Kimball, RD, a sports and lifestyle nutritionist at the Ochner Health System's Elmwood Fitness Center in New Orleans. "For instance, instead of having whole-wheat toast with jelly or fruit with juice for breakfast, have whole-wheat toast with peanut butter or fruit with cottage cheese. The carbohydrates alone cause a rapid release of blood sugar and a rapid drop in energy, but the protein helps even that out."

You don't have to down huge amounts of protein to get the energizing effects. Eating just 3 to 4 ounces of a protein-rich food, like a broiled chicken breast or a hard-boiled egg, "feeds" your brain enough tyrosine to get the dopamine and nor-epinephrine flowing.

Even though protein-rich foods can help boost energy, the fats that often come with them can drag you down. Digesting fats diverts blood from the brain, which can make you feel sluggish. So don't overload a turkey sandwich with high-fat cheese and mayonnaise; dress it with mustard, lettuce, and tomatoes instead, recommends Somer.

Back to Basics

While much research has focused on the intricacies of brain chemistry, eating for energy can also be as simple as getting more fruits and vegetables and essential minerals like iron.

A study of 411 dentists and their wives found that those who consumed at least 400 milligrams of vitamin C a day reported feeling less fatigue than those consuming less than 100 milligrams. In both cases, of course, the amount of vitamin C was considerably higher than the Daily Value (DV) of 60 milligrams.

It's easy to boost the amounts of vitamin C in your diet. An 8-ounce glass of orange juice, for example, contains 82 milligrams of vitamin C, or about 132 percent of the DV. A half-cup of strawberries has 42 milligrams, or 70 percent of the DV, and a half-cup of cooked chopped broccoli has 58 milligrams, or 97 percent of the DV.

Iron is also essential for energy. Even small iron-deficiencies can leave you weary. Fortunately, iron is very easy to get in the diet. Eating a half-cup of quick-cooking Cream of Wheat, for example, provides 5 milligrams of iron, or 50 percent of the Recommended Dietary Allowance (RDA) for men. Red meats are another good source of iron. You don't need much. A 3-ounce serving of broiled flank steak, for example, contains 2 milligrams of iron, or 20 percent of the RDA for men.

The Ups and Downs of Carbohydrates

Whereas eating high-protein foods often leaves us feeling energized, eating starchy foods like pasta and potatoes, especially for lunch, often leaves us nodding. The explanation, once again, is found in brain chemistry.

FOOD FOR THOUGHT

It has been hammered into us since grade school: Start the day with a good breakfast. But while eating breakfast does seem to boost performance in children, it's not so clear whether it's equally important for adults.

While a number of studies have suggested that skipping breakfast can cause fuzzy thinking and fatigue, some experts say that the evidence isn't convincing. "In terms of human evolution, the notion of organized meals is very new," says Arthur Frank, MD, medical director of the Obesity Management Program at George Washington University Hospital in Washington, D.C. Indeed, studies on human performance indicate that people who regularly skip breakfast may actually experience an energy slump on occasions when they do eat it.

While Dr. Frank certainly isn't opposed to the idea of having breakfast, "you shouldn't feel obligated to eat it," he says. "Follow your body's lead."

Of course, if you frequently find yourself feeling tired as the day wears on, skipping breakfast could be making the problem worse, says Wahida Karmally, DrPH, RD, CDE, director of nutrition at the Irving Center for Clinical Research at Columbia University Medical Center. She recommends starting the day with a breakfast that is high in complex carbohydrates and blended with protein—whole-grain cereal with low-fat or fat-free milk and fresh fruit, for example, or whole-wheat toast topped with low-fat cheese.

Eating high-carbohydrate foods like potatoes or rice causes an amino acid called tryptophan to be delivered to the brain. This, in turn, jump-starts the production of serotonin, a "calm-down" chemical that regulates mood. And it doesn't take a lot of carbohydrates. Eating as little as 1 ounce of rice, for example, can get the serotonin flowing.

In one study, researchers in England gave people a variety of lunches to see how their energy levels fared. One lunch was low-fat, high-carbohydrate; another was medium-fat, medium-carbohydrate; and the third was high-fat, low-carbohydrate. As you might expect, the people eating the high-carbohydrate (and also the high-fat) lunches reported feeling more drowsy and muddled than those getting the lower-carbohydrate fare.

"What you want to do is balance your carbohydrate-protein mix so that the bulk of your diet comes from complex carbohydrates, laced with a bit of protein," Somer says. "That's how most people will improve their energy levels."

Paradoxically, the opposite is true in people known as carbohydrate cravers.

Experts aren't sure why, but these people tend to get an energy boost after eating high-carbohydrate meals or snacks. Researchers at the Massachusetts Institute of Technology in Cambridge speculate that carbohydrate cravings are the body's attempt to boost low serotonin levels.

If you're one of those people who seem to get energy after eating starchy foods, don't fight it, advises Somer. Enjoy a baked potato, bread, pasta, or other starchy food at lunch. While you're at it, feel free to eat a starchy snack—like whole-wheat crackers or a banana—to stave off fatigue at midday.

Incidentally, it's generally better to eat several small meals a day instead of two or three large meals. Smaller meals will help keep blood sugar levels stable, which will help stave off fatigue, says Wahida Karmally, DrPH, RD, CDE, a registered dietitian on the Nutrition Advisory Committee at New York–Presbyterian Hospital/Columbia University Medical Center and director of nutrition at the Irving Center for Clinical Research at Columbia University Medical Center.

> ## Doctor's Top Tip
>
> "Drink more water," says DicQie Fuller, PhD, DSc, scientific advisor for Z-Health Corporation in Chicago. "It allows the enzymes to work throughout your body, assisting in the proper digestion of food for energy. I personally recommend hydrating with pure water rather than soda, coffee, and juice."

Snooze Foods

It's 3 p.m. Do you know where your energy is?

Not at the coffee cart. While a cup or two of coffee early in the day has been shown to boost alertness and mental functioning, drinking large amounts day after day tends to lower energy levels. The same thing is true of sweet pick-me-ups like doughnuts. The quick surge of energy, for some people, is often followed by an equally quick—and longer-lasting—crash.

"Sugar can contribute to feelings of fatigue, particularly if you're sensitive to it," says Larry Christensen, PhD, chairman of the department of psychology at the University of South Alabama in Mobile and an expert on the effects of sugar and caffeine on mood.

Unlike starches, which gradually release their energy into the bloodstream, sugars (called glucose) careen in all at once, causing blood sugar to spike. To cope with the sugar surge, the body releases insulin, which quickly removes sugars from the blood and carries them into individual cells. The result, of course, is lower levels of blood sugar. And the lower the level of sugar in your blood, the more fatigued you become.

Sugar can also cause fatigue by indirectly stimulating production of serotonin, which, as we've seen, is the brain chemical that plays a calming role. That's exactly what you don't need when you're fighting off fatigue.

Experts aren't sure why caffeine tends to sap your energy instead of revving you up, says Dr. Christensen. They do know that the caffeine buzz caused by cup after cup of coffee—or cola, tea, or other caffeine-containing drinks—is often followed by the caffeine crash.

To get reenergized, many people simply drink more coffee. This creates a cycle that can leave you alternately jittery and heavy-lidded.

In one study, people with a history of fatigue, depression, and moodiness were put on a sugar- and caffeine-free diet for 2 weeks. Not surprisingly, many of them quickly improved on this diet. More interesting is what happened later. When they resumed getting caffeine and sugar in their diets, 44 percent got fatigued all over again.

Fish

HEALTH FROM THE DEEP

For years, Americans have wisely been reducing the amount of fat in their diets. But there's one fat you may want to get more of instead of less: the fat in fish. When it comes to healthy eating, fish swims to first place.

Cold-water fish contain a number of polyunsaturated fats, which are known collectively as omega-3 fatty acids. Omega-3s benefit the fish by helping them stay warm in chilly waters. In people, the same fats go a long way toward promoting better health.

Consider Greenland's Eskimos. They eat fish to their hearts' content, which may be why they have very low levels of heart disease. Similar benefits have been observed in fish eaters around the world. People are simply a lot less likely to die from heart disease when fish plays a role in their diets. There is compelling research that the oils in fish may do far more than protect the heart, however.

Perhaps most significant, a team of scientists at the Harvard School of Public Health reported that overall mortality was 17 percent lower among people who ate fish twice a week compared with people who ate little or no seafood.

A big reason for these protective effects is omega-3s' ability to reduce inflammation. "As we eat more processed foods, such as cookies, crackers, and fast food, we get a lot of omega-6 fatty acids," says Gretchen Vannice, MS, RD, research coordinator at Nordic Naturals, who has studied omega-3 fatty acids extensively. "Omega-6 fatty acids increase inflammation. And omega-3 fatty acids decrease inflammation, so if we don't get enough omega-3s to counteract the omega-6s, we're in a constant state of inflammation. And inflammation puts us at risk for a whole host of conditions, including heart disease, overweight, and even depression," she says. "We should get a ratio of 4:1 omega-6s to omega-3 fatty acids, but most people get an estimated 15 to 20:1, so we're way undernourished with omega-3s."

Swim Away from Heart Disease

In the 1980s a round of studies reported that a diet high in fish could help protect against heart disease, prompting many Americans to trade some of their red meat and poultry for a couple of fish meals each week. They made the right choice.

Research has shown that people who eat fish are less likely to die from heart disease than their non-fish-eating counterparts. A recent study done at the Harvard School of Public Health reported that the death rate from heart disease was 36 percent lower among people who ate fish twice a week compared with people who ate little or no seafood.

In a study done at King's College in London, participants ages 45 to 70 increased their omega-3 intake by eating fish until their ratio of omega-6s to omega-3s was 3:1. As a result, their triglycerides went down, lowering their risk of heart disease.

The omega-3s in fish appear to work by putting the brakes on the body's production of inflammatory prostaglandins, leukotrienes, and thromboxane, naturally occurring compounds that, in large amounts, may cause blood vessels to constrict, elevating blood pressure. These compounds also may promote unwanted clotting in the bloodstream, which can lead to heart disease.

The ability of omega-3s to prevent clotting is particularly important, says James Kenney, PhD, RD, director of nutrition research and educator at the Pritikin Longevity Center and Spa in Aventura, Florida. Clots that form in the bloodstream can block the flow of blood to the heart or brain, possibly causing heart attacks or strokes. Further, the oil found in fish appears to raise levels of high-density lipoprotein cholesterol, the good cholesterol that helps keep fatty sludge from depositing in the arteries.

Research shows that fish can offer particular benefits to people who have already had one heart attack. Having two fish meals (up to a total of 12 ounces of fish) a week may reduce the chances of suffering a second, fatal heart attack.

In addition to its favorable effects on clotting and cholesterol, the oil in fish appears to help keep the heart beating in a healthy rhythm. This is important because potentially serious heartbeat irregularities, called arrhythmias, may lead to cardiac arrest, in which the heart stops beating entirely. There is increasing evidence that the omega-3s in fish somehow fortify the heart muscle and keep it beating regularly. In one study, people getting nearly 6 grams of omega-3s a month—the equivalent of having a 3-ounce serving of salmon weekly—had half the risk of cardiac arrest as those who ate no omega-3s.

As a result of the heart-protective benefits of fish, the American Heart Association recommends that all adults eat fish at least two times a week. However, the AHA also notes that some types of fish may contain high levels of mercury, PCBs (polychlorinated biphenyls), dioxins, and other environmental contaminants. Levels of these substances are generally highest in older, larger, predatory fish and marine mammals. Fish with potential for the highest mercury contamination are shark, swordfish, king mackerel, and tilefish. Eating a variety of fish will help minimize any potentially adverse effects due to environmental pollutants.

Fighting Cancer

Nutritionists have long advised us to eat less fat, especially the fats in meats and dairy products, to reduce the risk of certain types of cancer. But the fat in fish is a healthy exception. "There's excellent evidence that eating fish provides protection against colorectal cancer," says Bandaru S. Reddy, PhD, professor of research in the department of chemical biology at Rutgers University in New Brunswick, New Jersey.

In the Kitchen

While fresh fish delivers some of the most delicate flavors imaginable, it goes bad in a hurry. One day may be all it takes to turn a beautiful, flavorful fish into a dish you'd rather forget. To get the best taste from fish every time, here's what you can do:

Follow your nose. Fresh fish should smell just slightly briny. Off odors develop in the gut cavity first. When buying fish, always take a sniff in the belly area to make sure the fish is clean and fresh.

Incidentally, beware of fish that has been prewrapped in plastic. Unless the fish has been frozen, it can go bad very quickly.

Look at the eyes. When buying whole fish, look at the eyes; if the fish is fresh, they will be clear, bright, and bulging. Eyes that are slightly milky or sunken are an indication of the condition of the fish—that freshness is waning.

Check the gills. The gills should be moist and bright red, almost burgundy. If they are gray or brown, the fish is old, and you should pass it by.

Press the flesh. The flesh on fresh fish should be firm and springy. If you press it with your finger, and the indentation remains, the fish is old and won't deliver the best flavor.

Fish protects against cancer in much the same way that it helps prevent heart disease—by reducing the body's production of prostaglandins. In large amounts, prostaglandins act as tumor promoters—that is, they encourage cancer tumors to grow, says Dr. Reddy.

In a study of people in 24 European countries, British researchers found that people who regularly included fish in their diets were much less likely to get cancer. Indeed, they estimated that having small servings of fish three times a week, in addition to decreasing intake of animal fats, would reduce the death rate from colon cancer in men by nearly one-third.

Better Breathing

You wouldn't think that eating fish could improve breathing difficulties caused by smoking, but that's exactly what researchers have found. Consumption of fish has been linked with better lung function in adults.

There's only so much that the occasional tuna steak can do to protect you from developing lung disease if you smoke. But if you're trying to quit or if you live with someone who smokes, eating fish is one way to reduce the damage. "If you smoke, you are under big-time oxidative stress, which will increase inflammation," says Vannice. "Omega-3 fatty acids in fish help protect cell walls, which will reduce the oxidative stress. Plus, omega-3s will help your nerves and therefore lower your anxiety level—a big thing for people who are trying to quit," she says.

Multiple Protection

The omega-3 fatty acids in fish also help protect against autoimmune diseases, such as rheumatoid arthritis, and help prevent dementia and Alzheimer's disease, says Vannice. In addition, two studies have shown that taking fish oil in addition to exercising for 45 minutes, three times a week, leads to a lower percentage body fat, suggesting that fish oil may also aid in weight loss.

GETTING THE MOST

Shop for salmon. All fish provide some omega-3s, but salmon is perhaps the best choice, with a 3-ounce serving of Chinook (king) salmon providing 3 grams.

Don't fish for farm-raised varieties. "Farm-raised fish are often fed grains instead of their natural diets, which affects the fat in their bodies—when they are fed omega-6 fats in the grains, they become sources of omega-6 fats," says Jana Klauer,

MD, a New York City–based physician, who specializes in the biology of fat reduction and is the author of *How the Rich Stay Thin*.

Look for deep colors. The more deeply colored the salmon, the more omega-3s it provides. As a rule of thumb, the more expensive varieties of salmon generally have the most omega-3s.

Shop for variety. It's not only salmon that has omega-3s. Other good sources include Spanish mackerel, tuna, sardines, anchovies, whitefish (fresh, not smoked), and herring.

Enjoy it canned. One of the easiest ways to get more omega-3s into your diet is to pick up a can of water-packed chunk light tuna (avoid albacore, which has been linked to mercury). If you're making tuna salad, choose a low-fat or fat-free mayonnaise, or skip the mayo altogether and use a mustard instead. The unhealthy fats in regular full-fat mayonnaise will more than offset the benefits of the healthy fats in the fish.

Use your microwave. The high cooking temperatures used in conventional cooking methods such as broiling can destroy nearly half the omega-3s in fish. Microwaving has little effect on these beneficial oils, however, so it's a good cooking choice for getting the most benefits from your fish.

Microwave-Steamed Salmon with Leeks

4 Chinook (king) salmon fillets (4 ounces each)

1 large leek

1 tablespoon grated fresh ginger

1 tablespoon dry sherry

2 teaspoons reduced-sodium soy sauce

Rinse the salmon with cold water. Pat dry with paper towels.

Trim both the tough green part and the root end from the leek and discard them. Cut the leek in half lengthwise. Rinse thoroughly with cold water, pulling apart the layers to remove all the grit.

Cut the leek into very thin slices. Spread two-thirds of the slices evenly over a large microwaveable plate. Cover loosely with waxed paper, and microwave on high for 30 seconds.

In a small bowl, combine the ginger, sherry, soy sauce, and the remaining leek slices.

Place the salmon on the plate over the microwaved leek slices, skin side down and with the pieces arranged in spoke-fashion so the thickest parts face outward. Pour the ginger mixture evenly over the top. Cover loosely with waxed paper.

Microwave on high for 4 to 6 minutes, or until the salmon is opaque in the center. Test for doneness by inserting the tip of a sharp knife in the center of 1 fillet.

Let stand for 5 minutes before serving.

Makes 4 servings

PER SERVING

Calories: 229
Total fat: 11.9 g
Saturated fat: 2.9 g

Cholesterol: 75 mg
Sodium: 232 mg
Dietary fiber: 0.9 g

Mediterranean Tuna Wrap

2 pieces Armenian flatbread (lavash)

1 can (6 ounces) water-packed chunk light tuna, drained

4 tablespoons fat-free dill vegetable dip

1 can (2.25 ounces) black olives, drained and sliced

10 baby carrots, sliced lengthwise

1 cup mixed salad greens

Place the lavash on a cutting board.

In a small bowl, combine the tuna, vegetable dip, and olives. Spoon the tuna mixture down the middle of each lavash.

Cover the tuna mixture with the sliced carrots, then cover the carrots with the salad greens.

Tuck in one or both ends of each lavash, and roll up tightly. Slice each crosswise in half.

Makes 2 servings

Cook's Notes: *You can easily double or triple this recipe for a crowd. Use leftover dip with leftover baby carrots for healthy snacks.*

PER SERVING

Calories: 277
Total fat: 5.5 g
Saturated fat: 0.5 g

Cholesterol: 53 mg
Sodium: 794 mg
Dietary fiber: 4 g

Gallstones
CLEANING UP THE CLUTTER

Even though your body needs some cholesterol, this thick, gummy substance has earned a reputation for being nothing but trouble—and with good reason. In large amounts, cholesterol not only contributes to heart disease, high blood pressure, and stroke; it also plays a role in the formation of gallstones. And although gallstones may be small nuggets, they can cause large amounts of excruciating pain. So needless to say, the more you can do to avoid these little buggers, the better.

As the name suggests, gallstones form in the gallbladder, which is simply a storage area for bile (also known as gall), which the body uses to digest fats in the small intestine. This bile is normally in a liquid state and contains small particles of cholesterol, protein, and fat.

But when you get too much fat and cholesterol in your diet, there's a tendency for these particles to come together and form gallstones, says Henry A. Pitt, MD, professor of surgery and director of the Hepatopancreatobiliary Surgery Fellowship at Johns Hopkins Hospital in Baltimore.

So it makes sense that the best advice for people who are prone to stones is to eat fewer red meats and whole-fat dairy foods and less of anything else that contains large amounts of fat and cholesterol, says Dr. Pitt.

Another way to help prevent gallstones is to eat smaller, more frequent meals. Since gallstones are caused by buildups of debris, making the gallbladder contract more often will help remove debris before it compacts into stones. The gallbladder contracts every time you eat, so having several small meals a day rather than two or three large ones will help keep it active and debris free. A group of researchers at the University of Rome watched gallbladder motion with

---

Doctor's Top Tip

Foods that come in packages, such as processed foods and fast foods, contain the bad fats and oils that contribute to gallstones, says Kaayla Daniel, PhD, a board-certified clinical nutritionist in Santa Fe, New Mexico. "The average American diet contains a lot of partially hydrogenated oils and vegetable oils (aka trans fats), and these fats cause bile to become thick and congested, which leads to gallstones," she says. "Plus, you will be doing your whole body a disservice because these fats aren't just bad for the gallbladder—they have been linked to diseases such as heart disease, cancer, obesity, and multiple sclerosis, just to name a few," she says.

ultrasound and found that frequent meals kept the bile turnover high, which made people less likely to form stones. Drinking a lot of water will also help keep stones from forming.

People who are overweight are much more likely to form gallstones than those who are lean, adds Michael D. Myers, MD, a physician in private practice in Los Alamitos, California. "For every pound of fat you have in your body, you produce 10 milligrams of cholesterol," Dr. Myers explains. So in addition to cutting down on high-fat foods, it's a good idea to add more fruits, vegetables, legumes, and whole grains to your diet, since these foods are the cornerstone of any weight-loss plan.

Even though losing weight can help prevent gallstones, losing too much, too fast can have the opposite effect, because it causes cholesterol in the gallbladder to rise, Dr. Myers says. And a similar reaction occurs in people on an extremely low-fat diet. What's more, if you seriously cut back on the amount of food you eat, your gallbladder will naturally be less active, permitting stone-forming sludge to accumulate.

If you're counting calories, staying in the range of 1,000 to 1,200 calories a day will help you lose weight without making you more prone to stones, says Dominic Nompleggi, MD, PhD, professor of medicine and surgery and director of the nutrition support service at the University of Massachusetts Medical Center in Worcester.

Ginger

THE PUNGENT HEALER

HEALING POWER

Can Help:

Prevent motion sickness

Soothe stomach upset

Relieve migraines

Reduce clotting in blood

Provide arthritis relief

Roman doctors kept it handy during military marches. Pythagoras, Greek philosopher and geometry whiz, touted it for digestive health. And King Henry VIII of England was convinced that it would protect against the plague, although there's no evidence that ginger is that good. But there's plenty of evidence that this gnarled, piquant root can help relieve dozens of conditions, from high blood pressure, motion sickness, and other digestive complaints to migraines, headaches, arthritis, high cholesterol, and even dangerous blood clots. This is why millions of people worldwide swear by ginger as a healing food.

Help for the Heaves

As anyone who has suffered from motion sickness knows, even a mild bout can derail the best-laid vacation plans. That's why nearly every thorough travel checklist, along with reminders to buy sunscreen and feed the cat, includes the notation, "Bring Dramamine."

The next time you travel, you may want to stop at the supermarket instead of the pharmacy, however. As it turns out, ginger is one of the best motion sickness remedies you can buy.

In a classic study conducted by Daniel B. Mowrey, PhD, director of the American Phytotherapy Research Laboratory in Salt Lake City, 36 motion-sickness-prone students were strapped into tilted rotating chairs and spun until they felt ill. Half were given 200 milligrams of dimenhydrinate (Dramamine) before the ride, and half were given ginger. Those who were given the Dramamine could only take the stomach-churning ride for about 4½ minutes—and most gave up even sooner. The half given ginger, however, had less nausea and dizziness than the drug-tested group and were therefore able to withstand the ride for the full 6 minutes.

In another study, Dutch researchers tested the effects of ginger on seasick naval cadets and found that ginger pills reduced the cadets' nausea and vomiting, providing relief for as long as 4 hours.

Experts aren't sure exactly why ginger suppresses a queasy stomach. But researchers in Japan have suggested that gingerols, one of the compounds in ginger, may be somehow responsible for blocking the body's vomiting reflex.

To use ginger for combating motion sickness, try taking about ¼ teaspoon of fresh or powdered ginger 20 minutes before getting in a car or on a boat. Repeat every few hours as needed.

You can also use ginger to help relieve a run-of-the-mill upset stomach, says Janet Maccaro, PhD, ND, a holistic nutritionist in Ormond Beach, Florida, who is president of Dr. Janet's Balance By Nature Products. Prepare a cup of ginger tea by adding three or four thin slices of fresh ginger to a cup of boiling water, and sip as needed. Or drink a cup after dinner to aid in digestion, she says.

Relief for Migraines

If you're one of the millions of Americans who suffer from migraine headaches, ginger may help prevent both the pain and the resulting nausea. In a small study, researchers at Odense University in Denmark found that ginger may short-circuit impending migraines without the unpleasant side effects of some migraine-relieving drugs. It appears that ginger blocks the action of prostaglandins, substances that cause pain and inflammation in blood vessels in the brain.

And in a study done at the Headache Care Center in Springfield, Missouri, 30 people with a history of migraines were given an over-the-counter combination of feverfew and ginger (called GelStat) at the early, mild pain phase of a migraine headache. Two hours after treatment, 48 percent of the participants were pain free, and 34 percent reported a migraine of only mild severity. Overall, 59 percent of the participants said they were happy with the effectiveness of the ginger-containing GelStat, indicating that its ingredients may be a good first-line treatment for migraines.

Research on the role of ginger in migraines is still preliminary, so experts are reluctant to recommend specific treatment plans for using ginger to fight migraines. If you feel a headache coming on, you may want to try taking ⅓ teaspoon of fresh or powdered ginger, which is the amount suggested by the Danish researchers.

Aid for Arthritis

Are the joints in your fingers so stiff and sore that you can't even fumble the childproof cap off the aspirin bottle in an attempt to get some relief? You may want to add ginger to your medicine chest.

In a review of various therapies for osteoarthritis, researchers at the Musculoskeletal Research Center in New York City found that ginger extract was among the experimental therapies that showed promise in being able to slow or even reverse osteoarthritis.

Doctor's Top Tip

Whenever possible, buy ginger that is grown in Africa or India, says Stephen Fulder, PhD, a private research consultant and author of *The Ginger Book*. Studies show that varieties of ginger from these continents are more potent than the common Jamaican kind.

You can't tell the difference in gingers just by looking, though. Ask the produce manager at the supermarket or health food store. He should be able to tell you where the ginger was grown.

And in a Danish study, researchers studied 56 people who had rheumatoid arthritis or osteoarthritis and who treated themselves with fresh or powdered ginger. They found that ginger produced relief in 55 percent of people with osteoarthritis and 74 percent of those with rheumatoid arthritis.

Some experts speculate that ginger may ease arthritis pain the same way it helps block migraines, by blocking the formation of inflammation-causing prostaglandins that cause pain and swelling.

To soothe arthritis pain, brew a mild tea by putting three or four slices of fresh ginger in a cup of boiling water, suggests Charles Lo, MD, a doctor of Chinese medicine in private practice in Chicago. You can also try downing ½ teaspoon of powdered ginger or up to an ounce (about 6 teaspoons) of fresh ginger once a day.

Help for the Blood

Blood clotting can be a good thing. When you cut your finger, for example, platelets—components in blood that help it clot—help "stick" the wound together to stop the bleeding and start the healing process.

But these sticky platelets can also cling to artery walls as well as to each other. When that happens, clots stop being beneficial and start becoming something to worry about. Many people routinely take aspirin to help keep their blood clear of clots that could lead to strokes or heart attacks.

The gingerol in ginger has a chemical structure somewhat similar to that of aspirin. Research suggests that getting ginger in the diet—although at this point experts aren't sure how much—may inhibit the production of a chemical called thromboxane, which plays a key role in the clotting process.

GETTING THE MOST

Use it fresh. Ginger comes in a variety of forms, including fresh, dried, crystallized, and powdered. It's best to use it fresh, advises Dr. Lo. "Fresh ginger is more active than dried," he says. Crystallized ginger is the next best thing, he adds. To find the freshest ginger and get the most healing compounds, shop for ginger that looks healthy. "Avoid ginger with soft spots, mold, or dry, wrinkled skin," Dr. Lo advises.

Enjoy it often. To extract the most health benefits from ginger, consume it as often as possible, says Dr. Lo. But you don't need to go ginger-crazy to get the healing benefits. Less than an ounce a day will do. "Drinking a few cups of ginger tea or adding a small amount of fresh ginger to a stir-fry should be enough."

Make a ginger marinade for meats. Mix fresh ginger, minced garlic, olive oil, and light soy sauce for a marinade for chicken, beef, or fish, says Dr. Maccaro. "They use ginger for a marinade in Japan, and it's a wonderful way to get the health benefits," she says.

Double-Ginger Gingerbread

¾ **cup unsweetened applesauce**

½ **cup molasses**

¼ **cup fat-free egg substitute**

3 **tablespoons canola oil**

1½ **cups all-purpose flour**

1 **teaspoon baking soda**

1 **teaspoon ground ginger**

1 **teaspoon ground cinnamon**

⅛ **teaspoon salt**

⅓ **cup finely chopped candied ginger**

Preheat the oven to 350°F.

In a large bowl, combine the applesauce, molasses, egg substitute, and oil. Stir to mix well.

In a medium bowl, combine the flour, baking soda, ground ginger, cinnamon, and salt. Stir to mix. Add to the applesauce mixture, and

stir until just mixed. Mix in all but 1 tablespoon of the candied ginger.

Pour the batter into an 8- × 8-inch nonstick baking dish. Bake until a knife inserted in the center comes out clean, 25 to 30 minutes.

Cool on a wire rack. Cut into squares. Sprinkle each piece with the remaining candied ginger just before serving

Makes 9 servings

Cook's Note: *A dollop of fat-free sour cream makes a delicious topping for the ginger-bread.*

PER SERVING

Calories: 211
Total fat: 4.8 g
Saturated fat: 0.4 g

Cholesterol: 0 mg
Sodium: 192 mg
Dietary fiber: 1 g

Grapefruit
THE POWER OF PECTIN

Grapefruit may be the biggest citrus fruit around, but in terms of popularity, it sometimes gets rolled aside. Its sour taste just isn't as appealing to some people as its sweeter kin, like oranges, tangerines, or clementines.

But in the health game, grapefruit, particularly the darker red variety, is a shining star. Grapefruit contains a number of antioxidant compounds—not just vitamin C, but also such things as lycopene, limonoids, and naringin. Together, these compounds can help reduce cold symptoms and also help decrease the risks of heart disease and cancer.

What these substances have in common is their ability to fight excess dangerous oxygen molecules in the body called free radicals. While free radicals are a natural part of metabolism, they can have dangerous effects as well. Grapefruit essentially acts as a chemical "mop" that helps clean up problems before they occur.

In addition, grapefruit contains large amounts of pectin, a type of fiber that can significantly lower cholesterol, thus reducing your risk for the health conditions high cholesterol brings on, such as heart disease, high blood pressure, and stroke.

Red with Health

One of the compounds in red (and pink) grapefruit that gives the fruit its distinctive hue is lycopene. Also found in tomatoes and red bell peppers, lycopene "is a very important, very potent antioxidant and free-radical scavenger," says Paul Lachance, PhD, executive director of the Nutraceuticals Institute at Rutgers University in New Brunswick, New Jersey. "Our cancer and heart disease situations would be a lot worse if not for the lycopene in our foods."

Grapefruit is also an excellent source of limonoids, which, like vitamin C, have been shown to have anticancer properties. A 6-ounce glass of grapefruit juice, for example, contains more than 100 milligrams of various limonoid compounds. In a study conducted at the Department of Nutrition and Food Science at Texas A & M University, researchers gave rats five different diets, including one diet containing grapefruit pulp powder and one containing limonin, and then measured their rates of colon cancer. The two diets that were protective against colon cancer were the grapefruit powder and limonin diets, indicating that both grapefruit and the limonoids they contain are protective against colon cancer.

Finally, grapefruit is an excellent source of vitamin C. It's one of the few foods that can provide more than the entire Daily Value (DV) for this vitamin in one serving. A cup of grapefruit sections contains 88 milligrams of vitamin C, a whopping 146 percent of the DV.

While vitamin C is a powerful antioxidant, it also helps bind skin cells together. "Vitamin C is especially important for holding collagen bundles together, which helps wounds heal," says Jana Klauer, MD, a New York City–based physician. If you don't get enough of this vitamin, your cuts will be slower to heal, and your gums may bleed. Vitamin C has also been shown to relieve cold symptoms by reducing levels of histamine, a naturally occurring chemical that makes your nose run.

Pectin Power

Grapefruit has received a lot of attention in recent years due to its generous supply of pectin, a type of soluble fiber that can help lower cholesterol to healthy levels. It does this by forming a gel in the intestine that helps block the absorption of fats into the bloodstream.

Research has shown that pectin can help lower cholesterol levels, as well as prevent risk of heart disease and stroke. One such study was done by the late James Cerda, MD, a former professor of medicine at the University of Florida College of Medicine in Gainesville. Dr. Cerda found that animals given a diet containing 3 percent grapefruit pectin for 9 months had more than 5 percent of their artery walls covered with plaque. In animals not given pectin, plaque covered 14 percent of the artery walls.

A 4-ounce serving (about ½ cup) of grapefruit provides 1 gram of pectin. The fibrous compound is found not only in the grapefruit flesh but also in the peel and the thin white layer just beneath the peel.

GETTING THE MOST

Eat the sections. When you eat a grapefruit by scooping out the flesh, you leave about half the pectin behind. To get the most fiber, experts say, peel the grapefruit and eat the entire section.

Sip your juice. Grapefruit juice is a concentrated source of the antioxidant naringin. You can make your own juice, but this may be one juice variety where commercial is better; during commercial processing, parts of the healthful grapefruit peel go into the juice.

Buy it red. Both red (and pink) grapefruits contain more lycopene than the white varieties. Experts say good choices include Ruby Red, Flame, and Star Ruby.

Honey-Marinated Grapefruit

4 ruby grapefruit

2 tablespoons honey

1 tablespoon finely chopped fresh mint

Grate about 1 teaspoon of the zest from 1 grapefruit. Cut that grapefruit in half through the middle, and squeeze the juice into a small bowl; set aside.

Place the honey in a small microwaveable bowl. Microwave on medium for 20 to 30 seconds, or until warm. Add the grapefruit juice and zest. Mix well.

Peel the remaining 3 grapefruit with a sharp paring knife, cutting away most but not all of the white pith below the peel. Carefully separate the grapefruit into sections. Remove any seeds, and pierce each section in 1 or 2 places with the tip of the knife so the marinade can permeate the grapefruit.

Arrange the grapefruit sections on dessert plates. Pour the honey mixture over the sections. Let stand for at least 15 minutes to let the flavors blend. Chill, if desired. Sprinkle with the mint before serving.

Makes 4 servings

PER SERVING

Calories: 110	Cholesterol: 0 mg
Total fat: 0.3 g	Sodium: 5 mg
Saturated fat: 0 g	Dietary fiber: 3.8 g

Grape Juice
A DRINK FOR THE HEART

Grape juice made its debut in this country toward the end of the 19th century, when certain teetotaling churches decided that they needed to serve a nonalcoholic substitute for wine for Communion.

Modern-day teetotalers are still toasting the grape juice innovation. Purple grape juice provides similar benefits to red wine (both red wine and purple grape juice contain powerful compounds that can help lower cholesterol, prevent hardening of the arteries, and fight heart disease) without the unwanted health effects of alcohol.

Giving Your Heart Some Juice

Researchers might never have stumbled across the health benefits of purple grape juice and its spirited sibling, red wine, had it not been for the heart-healthy folks from the country that also brought us croissants, berets, and Brigitte Bardot.

A few years back, scientists discovered a phenomenon that they dubbed the French paradox. What they found was that while the French ate almost four times as much butter and three times as much lard, smoked just as many (or more) cigarettes, and had higher cholesterol and blood pressure than Americans, they fell victim to heart attacks 2½ times less often.

At least part of the French secret to heart health, researchers believe, is red wine. Red wine contains compounds called flavonoids, which have been linked to lower rates of heart disease.

If red wine confers protection, the researchers thought, why not the purple grape juice from where the wine comes?

As it turns out, the researchers were right. "Purple grape juice gives you most of the benefits of red wine without the alcohol," says Janet Maccaro, PhD, ND, a holistic nutritionist in Ormond Beach, Florida, who is president of Dr. Janet's Balance By Nature Products and the author of *Natural Health Remedies A-Z*. Among the most powerful ingredients in purple grape juice are flavonoids—some of the same flavonoids found in red wine. Studies suggest that flavonoids may help lower cholesterol, prevent cholesterol from sticking to artery walls, and keep blood platelets from sticking together and forming dangerous clots in the bloodstream, thus helping to prevent stroke.

Great Grapes

Scientists are still unraveling the mysteries of exactly how purple grape juice helps protect against heart disease. What they do know is that it appears to help in more than one way.

The flavonoids in purple grape juice are among the most powerful antioxidants around—maybe even better than vitamins C or E, says John D. Folts, PhD, professor of medicine and director of the coronary thrombosis laboratory at the University of Wisconsin Medical School in Madison. In your body, they help prevent bad low-density lipoprotein (LDL) cholesterol from oxidizing—the process that enables cholesterol to stick to your artery walls and create blockages.

A study published in the *American Journal of Clinical Nutrition* showed that purple grape juice has the power to reduce LDL cholesterol and triglycerides—both of which help to lower risk for heart disease.

Keeping LDL cholesterol in check is a good start against heart disease. But you also need to keep the platelets, components in blood that cause it to clot, from sticking together unnecessarily. The flavonoids in purple grape juice do that, too, Dr. Folts says. A study at the University of Wisconsin found that when purple grape juice was given to laboratory animals, abnormal clotting was significantly reduced. So drinking purple grape juice gives you two benefits for the price of one.

Actually, it's more than two.

Purple grape juice is also a fair source of potassium, with 8 ounces providing 334 milligrams, or 10 percent of the Daily Value. This is important because potassium

---

Doctor's Top Tip

Research shows that purple grape juice acts as a natural antioxidant. In fact, in a recent study that measured the antioxidant power of more than 1,000 foods and beverages, Welch's 100 percent grape juice made from Concord grapes had the second highest antioxidant capacity overall, and the number one antioxidant capacity for a beverage.

The study, which was published in the *American Journal of Nutrition*, named blackberries as the top antioxidant food and grape juice as a close second. "Many high-antioxidant fruits and vegetables can be identified by their deep, dark coloring," says Carla McGill, PhD, RD, a nutrition scientist at Tropicana in Chicago.

To get an antioxidant boost, drink an 8-ounce serving of 100 percent grape juice each day. Throw a small bottle in your lunch box or briefcase, and keep a larger bottle in the fridge at home. No washing, chopping, or peeling required—just pour and serve.

helps control high blood pressure and protect against stroke, furthering grape juice's power to combat cardiovascular disease.

The Missing Link

While purple grape juice does contain powerful compounds, it doesn't contain a lot of them. In fact, you need about three times as much grape juice as wine to get the same protective effects, says Dr. Folts.

All of a grape's protective flavonoids are in the "must," a chunky mixture of grape skins, pulp, seeds, and stems that is used to make wine and grape juice, says Dr. Folts. When this must is fermented to make wine, a lot of the flavonoids are drawn into the liquid, he explains. Since grape juice is never fermented, you get only the flavonoids that are drawn into the juice during the heating and processing stages.

The compounds that end up in the drink are still plenty strong, though, he adds. You just need more juice to get them.

GETTING THE MOST

Pour a big glass. Since you need to drink more grape juice than wine to get the same health benefits, you'll want to down up to 12 ounces a day, Dr. Folts says.

Chill out with a nonalcoholic wine spritzer. "In the summer, I make a drink called a grape juice chiller, which is a mixture of club soda and grape juice," says Dr. Maccaro. "It's a great nonalcoholic and refreshing way to get your flavonoids," she says.

Drink it dark. "Since flavonoids are what give juice its rich purple hue, if you're looking for the grape juice with the most flavonoids, pick the darkest of the bunch," advises Dr. Folts.

Drink juice, not drink. So-called grape drink is nothing but a watered-down, sugared imitation of the original article. Nutritionally, it doesn't compare. So when you want the benefits of grape juice, be sure to buy the real thing.

Greens

NATURE'S BEST PROTECTION

Double coupons, good gas mileage, supersizing for only a dollar more—if there's one thing that Americans appreciate, it's getting more for less. That is why we really ought to love leafy green vegetables. They deliver more nutrients in fewer calories than virtually any food out there.

"You get so many important nutrients from leafy green vegetables—magnesium, iron, calcium, folate, vitamin C, and vitamin B_6—plus all the cancer- and heart disease–fighting phytochemicals," says Michael Liebman, PhD, professor of human nutrition at the University of Wyoming in Laramie. "These are the most nutrient-dense foods available."

Experts are quick to note, however, that America's favorite "salad starter"—the bland-tasting iceberg lettuce—doesn't count as a "leafy green" vegetable. Of all the foods in this powerhouse family, iceberg is the runt. Far better are such things as kale, Swiss chard, dandelion greens, beet greens, turnip greens, spinach, and chicory.

Leaves for the Heart

To some extent, the difference between people who have heart attacks and those who don't may be how many trips they make to the salad bar, provided that bar isn't stocked with iceberg lettuce only.

A review done at Harokopio University in Athens, Greece, revealed that the high consumption of wild greens and the healthful omega-3 fatty acids they provide was previously underestimated as a crucial protective part of the Mediterranean diet, which is high in olive oil, fruits, and vegetables, and low in meats and full-fat dairy products, and has been linked with a lower risk of heart disease.

And researchers from the Jean Mayer USDA Human Nutrition Research Center on Aging at Tufts University in Boston and the Framingham Heart Study in Massachusetts studied more than 1,000 people between the ages of 67 and 95 to learn what dietary factors affect heart health. In this, as in so many issues touching on food, the answer boiled down to chemistry—specifically, to an amino acid called homocysteine.

HEALING POWER
Can Help:

Control blood pressure

Reduce the risk of heart disease

Reduce the risk of cancer

Protect against vision loss

Homocysteine is a natural compound that is harmless as long as the body keeps it in check. When it reaches high levels, however, it becomes toxic and may contribute to clogged arteries and heart disease. The researchers found that among people with the most clogged arteries, 43 percent of men had high levels of homocysteine in their blood.

What's the connection with greens? The body uses folate and vitamins B_{12} and B_6 to keep homocysteine under control. Many of the people in the study were falling short of these vital nutrients—especially the B vitamin folate and vitamin B_6.

In a more recent review from Serbia, researchers looked at the relationship between homocysteine and cardiovascular disease. This research supported the findings in the Framingham Heart Study, showing that a low intake of folate, vitamin B_6, and vitamin B_{12} increases levels of homocysteine and thus increases overall risk of cardiovascular disease.

Luckily, greens can help. As it turns out, leafy greens are outstanding sources of folate, and they also provide vitamin B_6. That's why experts advise adding plenty of leafy green vegetables to your diet to counteract homocysteine levels.

In the Kitchen

With the exception of residents of the Southern states, Americans as a rule aren't all that familiar with cooking greens. Those of us who live in other areas of the country throw them in salads and maybe put them on sandwiches. But why limit yourself to raw leaves? Greens are very easy to cook once you know a few tricks.

Trim the stems. While the leaves are often surprisingly tender, the stems on leafy greens can be unpleasantly tough and should probably be discarded or used in vegetable stock. Before cooking greens, separate the leaf from the stem by running a sharp knife alongside the stem and center rib.

Make sure your greens are clean. Since the leafy greens grow close to the ground, and the frilly leaves readily capture dirt and grit, it's important to wash all parts of greens thoroughly. The easiest way is to fill the sink or a large bowl with cold water and swish the greens around, allowing any dirt or sand to sink to the bottom. When the greens are clean, transfer them to a colander to drain.

Cut thick greens into ribbons. When cooking thick greens like kale or Swiss chard, it's helpful to cut them into ribbons, or small pieces. This will help them cook more quickly and become tender.

Boil them quickly. The easiest way to prepare greens is to submerge them briefly in boiling water. Drop the greens in a cup of boiling water, cover, and cook for about 4 minutes, or until tender. You can then sauté them more quickly, if desired, for certain stir-fries and other recipes.

Cooked spinach is probably your best bet for managing homocysteine. A half-cup of Popeye's favorite snack delivers 131 micrograms of folate, or 33 percent of the Daily Value (DV) for this vitamin. It also contains 0.2 milligram of vitamin B_6, or 10 percent of the DV.

In addition to these important B vitamins, certain greens—particularly beet greens, chicory, and spinach—provide the heart-healthy minerals magnesium, potassium, and calcium. These minerals, along with sodium, help regulate the amount of fluid that your body retains. All too often, researchers say, people have too much sodium and too little of the other three, leading to high blood pressure.

Even though eating leafy greens is an excellent way to help regulate blood pressure, the calcium from spinach and beet greens isn't well-absorbed by the body. Be sure to eat a wide variety of greens to meet all your mineral needs.

Meat of the Diet

Large studies overwhelmingly show that many cancers occur least often in countries where people regard leafy greens, along with a wide variety of fruits and vegetables, as the "meats" of their meals.

In one study, researchers compared 61 men with lung cancer in Chile with 61 men of similar age and smoking habits who were cancer free. The one difference they found was that men with cancer consumed significantly fewer carotenoid-rich foods, especially Swiss chard, chicory, and spinach as well as beets and cabbage, than those without the disease.

Another study done at Banaras Hindu University in India looked at the role of

---

FOOD ALERT

When Spinach Means Stones

Popeye probably never had kidney stones, because if he had, he wouldn't have kept downing all those cans of spinach.

Spinach, along with Swiss chard and beet greens, contains high amounts of oxalates, acids that the body cannot process and that are passed through the urine. For people who are sensitive to oxalates, eating too many of these greens could contribute to the formation of kidney stones. So if you're prone to stones, says Michael Liebman, PhD, professor of human nutrition at the University of Wyoming in Laramie, choose low-oxalate vegetables such as Brussels sprouts and green peas rather than spinach, chard, and beet greens.

vegetables in protecting against gallbladder cancer. The study looked at the vegetable consumption of 153 people with gallbladder cancer and 153 people without gallbladder cancer and put them into three categories: no or rare consumption of vegetables, consumption 1 to 2 days a week, or consumption at least 3 days a week. The researchers found that the people with the highest reported intake of vegetables—particularly, leafy green vegetables—had the lowest rate of gallbladder cancer.

A similar protective benefit was found between leafy green vegetable intake and stomach cancer in a study done at the University of Occupational and Environmental Health in Kitakyushu, Japan.

And leafy green vegetables seem to be protective against prostate cancer as well. An Australian study looked at the diets of 130 men with prostate cancer and 274 men without the disease, and found that the risk of prostate cancer decreased as certain foods—one of them being spinach—increased.

The carotenoids, which are found in large amounts in most leafy greens, are like bodyguards against cancer-causing agents, explains Frederick Khachik, PhD, adjunct professor in the department of chemistry and biology at the University of Maryland in College Park. He and fellow researchers believe that certain cancers are brought on by the constant onslaught of free radicals—harmful oxygen molecules made by our bodies and also found in air pollution and tobacco smoke—which attack our bodies' healthy cells. Carotenoids counteract free radicals by acting as antioxidants, meaning that they step between the free radicals and our bodies' cells, neutralizing the free radicals before they can do damage, he explains.

"There is also plenty of evidence that carotenoids may fight cancer by activating the body's detoxification enzymes—called phase II enzymes—which are responsible for ridding the body of harmful, often cancer-causing, chemicals," says Dr. Khachik.

"Dark green leafy vegetables are among the best sources of some very important carotenoids, like lutein, alpha-carotene, and the one that everyone's familiar with, beta-carotene," he says. While all leafy greens are rich in carotenoids, the granddaddy is spinach, with a half-cup providing 1 milligram of beta-carotene.

Seeing Green

Carrots must be good for your eyes, the old joke has it, since you never see a rabbit wearing glasses. According to research, it's probably not only carrots that are good for the eyes but also all the leafy greens rabbits munch.

In one study, scientists from the Massachusetts Eye and Ear Infirmary in Boston compared the diets of more than 350 people with advanced age-related macular degeneration (AMD)—the leading cause of irreversible vision loss among older adults—with the diets of more than 500 people without the disease. They found that people who ate the most leafy green vegetables—particularly spinach and collard greens—were 43 percent less likely to get macular degeneration than those who ate them less frequently.

And a Dutch study published in the *Journal of the American Medical Association* looked at the relationship between dietary intake of vitamins E and C, zinc, and beta-carotene and age-related macular degeneration in more than 4,000 older adults at risk for the condition. A high intake of all four nutrients was associated with a 35 percent decrease in AMD risk, indicating that all four antioxidants are protective.

Experts believe that carotenoids protect the eyes in much the same way as they work against cancer, by acting as antioxidants and neutralizing the tissue-damaging free radicals before they harm the body—in this case, the macular region of the eye.

Smile and Say "Greens"

In some parts of the world, like rural China, where vegetarianism is a way of life, people meet their daily calcium needs not by drinking milk but by eating greens.

In fact, 1 cup of turnip or dandelion greens can deliver about 172 milligrams of calcium, or 17 percent of the DV for this mineral. That's more than you'd get from a half-cup of fat-free milk.

There is a catch, though. One problem with getting calcium from leafy green vegetables is that some of them contain high amounts of oxalates—compounds that block calcium absorption, says Dr. Liebman. "Spinach, Swiss chard, collards, and beet greens have the most oxalates, so don't eat these as a source of calcium," he says. "The others are fine. Research has shown that the calcium in kale is particularly well-absorbed."

Pumping Up at the Salad Bar

If you're among the many folks who are cutting back on meats these days, you may be cutting down on a very important mineral as well—iron. Here again, the leafy greens can help. Many green vegetables, especially spinach and Swiss chard, are

> ## Doctor's Top Tip
>
> They may all fall under the umbrella term of "greens," but they actually come in many rich colors and textures, and you should eat the full range. One way to guarantee a nice greens buffet is with a greens mixture called mesclun. This mix may include arugula, frisée, mache, radicchio, dandelion greens, mizuna, oakleaf lettuce, and sorrel—all these greens serve up healthful vitamins and minerals, says Jana Klauer, MD, a New York City–based physician who specializes in the biology of fat reduction. "You can also make up your own batch by mixing and matching greens. Choose leaves that add interesting flavors, colors, and textures, such as endive, kale, escarole, Swiss chard, or baby spinach," she says. "Salads don't have to be boring. Get creative with your greens," she suggests.

good sources of iron, a mineral your body needs to produce red blood cells and transport oxygen.

A half-cup of cooked spinach has 3 milligrams of iron, or 30 percent of the Recommended Dietary Allowance (RDA) for men. The same amount of Swiss chard provides 2 milligrams, which is 20 percent of the RDA for men.

Unfortunately, the iron found in plants isn't as readily absorbed by the body as the iron found in meats—unless it's accompanied in the same meal by vitamin C. Good news again. Along with their high doses of iron, leafy green vegetables also contain ample amounts of vitamin C, which substantially improves iron absorption.

But while all the leafy greens provide good amounts of vitamin C, the greens for this important vitamin are chicory (a half-cup serving has 22 milligrams, or 37 percent of the DV) and beet and mustard greens, which both provide almost 18 milligrams, or 30 percent of the DV.

In addition, beet greens and spinach are rich sources of riboflavin—a B vitamin that is essential for tissue growth and repair as well as helping your body convert other nutrients into usable forms. A half-cup of cooked spinach or beet greens provides 0.2 milligram of riboflavin, or 12 percent of the DV.

Go Deep

To get the maximum health benefits from greens, eat the darkest ones you can find. "The deeper the color of greens, the more benefits they provide," says Janet Maccaro, PhD, ND, a holistic nutritionist in Ormond Beach, Florida, who is president of Dr. Janet's Balance By Nature Products and the author of *Natural Health Remedies A-Z*. "The darker, the better. So go for spinach, kale, and other greens with a deep tone for good health," she says.

GETTING THE MOST

Cook them quickly. To cook or not to cook? That's often the question asked by people who want to maintain high levels of nutrients in vegetables. The answer with leafy greens, experts say, is yes, no, and maybe a little.

"It's always a trade-off between increasing the digestibility of nutrients when you cook foods and losing some nutrients in the cooking process," says Dr. Liebman. "But while it's great to eat them raw, you're more likely to eat more of certain vegetables if they're cooked. Just watch your cooking method. You don't want to boil them to death. Any quick-cooking method, such as blanching, is fine. One of the best cooking methods for retaining nutrients is microwaving," he says.

Steak and Spinach Salad with Pomegranate Dressing

- 6 **tablespoons 100% pomegranate juice**
- 2 **tablepoons white wine vinegar**
- 4 **teaspoons Dijon mustard**
- 4 **teaspoons extra-virgin olive oil**
- 1 **teaspoon honey**
- 12 **cups loosely packed baby spinach leaves**
- 1 **cup juice-packed mandarin oranges, drained**
- ½ **cup pomegranate seeds**
- ¼ **cup roasted, unsalted almonds**
  Salt and freshly ground black pepper
- 12 **ounces lean steak, such as top round or London broil**

In a small bowl, whisk together the juice, vinegar, mustard, oil, and honey.

In a large bowl, combine the spinach, oranges, pomegranate seeds, and almonds. Add all but 3 tablepoons of the dressing and salt and pepper to taste. Toss well.

Lightly coat a large skillet with cooking spray, and heat over medium-high heat. Add the steak and cook for 5 minutes per side for medium-rare. Remove from the heat and set aside for 3 minutes.

Slice the steak thinly, and top the salad with the slices. Drizzle with the remaining dressing. Serve immediately.

Makes 4 servings

PER SERVING

Calories: 356
Total fat: 15 g
Saturated fat: 3 g

Cholesterol: 41 mg
Sodium: 238 mg
Dietary fiber: 5 g

Romaine and Watercress Salad with Anchovy Vinaigrette

½ teaspoon anchovy paste
½ teaspoon Dijon mustard
Salt (optional)
1 tablespoon balsamic vinegar
1 tablespoon red wine vinegar
6 tablespoons extra-virgin olive oil
Freshly ground black pepper
1 small head romaine lettuce
2 bunches watercress, large stems discarded

In a salad bowl, combine the anchovy paste, mustard, and salt (if using). Add the balsamic and red wine vinegars, and mix with a fork. Add the olive oil slowly while whisking constantly. Taste for seasoning, adding the pepper and more salt, vinegar, and oil to taste.

When ready to serve, add the romaine and watercress, and toss to coat.

Makes 6 servings

PER SERVING

Calories: 136	Cholesterol: 0 mg
Total fat: 14 g	Sodium: 96 mg
Saturated fat: 2 g	Dietary fiber: 1 g

Mustard Greens with Smoked Turkey

2 pounds mustard greens
1 cup finely chopped onions
¾ cup chopped smoked turkey breast
2 cloves garlic, minced
1 tablespoon white wine vinegar
Hot pepper sauce

Tear the leaves of the greens away from the stems and discard the stems. Tear the greens into bite-size pieces.

Coat a large nonstick skillet with cooking spray. Scatter the onions, turkey, and garlic evenly in the skillet, and warm over medium heat. As soon as the skillet starts to heat up, add as much of the greens as the skillet will hold. (If necessary, add the remainder after the first batch cooks down enough to make room for them.) Cover tightly and cook until the greens wilt and soften, 7 to 8 minutes. Stir to combine. Sprinkle with the vinegar and add hot pepper sauce to taste.

Makes 4 servings

PER SERVING

Calories: 62	Cholesterol: 14 mg
Total fat: 1.2 g	Sodium: 304 mg
Saturated fat: 0.3 g	Dietary fiber: 2.6 g

Headaches

FEED YOUR HEAD RIGHT

In some ways, headaches are an unavoidable consequence of the horn-honking traffic jams, daily office politics, family squabbles, and late nights that go hand-in-hand with modern life.

Yet stress and noise aren't the only things causing heads to throb. Many of the foods we eat, from hot dogs and cheese to chocolate brownies, can cause headaches. Not eating certain foods can also cause problems. This may explain, in part, why Americans spend billions of dollars per year on over-the-counter and prescription pain relief. That's a lot of extra-strength aspirin, acetaminophen, and ibuprofen. And given the recent warnings about the link between these over-the-counter pain remedies and liver damage and stomach bleeding, you may want to think twice before you down these pills to stop your head from pounding.

While changing your diet won't eliminate headaches entirely, it can reduce their frequency and keep the pain under control. Best of all, relief won't come from a safety-sealed bottle that delivers health risks along with pain relief, but rather from the foods you eat.

Two Types of Pain

Before considering specific foods, it's helpful to understand the main types of headaches. The most common type, called muscle-contraction or tension headache, is usually caused by kinked-up neck and scalp muscles.

The second type, which includes migraines, is called vascular headache. This type of headache is caused by the expansion and contraction of blood vessels in the face, head, and neck. Vascular headaches can be extremely painful and in some cases, even disabling, as anyone who gets migraines can attest.

Both vascular and tension headaches can be caused by almost anything—stress, fluctuating hormone levels, or even changes in the weather. But substances found in foods—natural compounds as well as chemicals added during processing—are frequently to blame, says Melvyn Werbach, MD, assistant clinical professor of psychiatry at the University of California, Los Angeles, and author of *Healing through Nutrition* and *Nutritional Influences on Illness*.

Common Triggers

Although experts aren't sure exactly what causes migraines, they have identified a number of foods and additives that may set the headache process in motion.

A huge culprit is tyramine (see "Doctor's Top Tip" at left). Nitrites are another common cause of headache pain. Used to preserve cured meats such as bologna, hot dogs, and meats packaged in a can, nitrites can cause blood vessels in the head and body to dilate painfully.

And monosodium glutamate (MSG), a preservative and flavor enhancer used in a variety of foods, including lunch meats, canned and dry soups, and frozen dinners, can be a problem. It's also a common additive in Chinese cooking. The term *Chinese restaurant syndrome* was coined to describe MSG-related headaches. Luckily, a lot of Chinese restaurants have caught on to the headache side effect that sometimes goes along with their fare and have removed all MSG from their cooking processes.

There's no easy way to avoid all of these substances or to be sure which one—or which combination of them—is causing the problem. To keep track of which foods cause your head to throb, keep a headache diary, says Alan M. Rapoport, MD, cofounder and director of the New England Center for Headache in Stamford, Connecticut, and assistant clinical professor of neurology at Yale University School of Medicine. The minute you feel the first twinge of a headache coming on, make a list of everything you've eaten in the past 24 hours. Eventually, you'll gain a better understanding of which foods may be to blame so you can avoid them in the future.

The Carbohydrate Connection

Central to the headache-food equation is a feel-good brain chemical called serotonin, which transmits messages from one nerve cell to another. Low levels of serotonin in the brain are often associated with headaches, says Dr. Rapoport. Therefore, raising the levels of serotonin can ease headaches or even prevent them entirely.

One way to boost serotonin in the brain is to increase the amount of complex carbohydrates in your diet. "There's no doubt that following a diet high in complex

---

Doctor's Top Tip

The best way to deal with a headache is not to get one in the first place. And the foods that cause headaches most often are those that contain tyramine, an amino acid that triggers the body to release hormones that cause blood vessels to constrict, says John Neustadt, ND, medical director of Montana Integrative Medicine in Bozeman. At some point, the blood vessels fight back and dilate, setting off the familiarly unpleasant throb. To avoid this head-pounding compound, stay away from chocolate, beer, aged dairy products, bananas, nuts, beans, and other tyramine foods if you're headache prone, he says.

---

carbohydrates and low in fat can be very helpful for some people with migraine, although we don't know exactly why," says Dr. Rapoport.

If you're prone to headaches, it might be a good idea to eat more foods that are high in fiber and complex carbohydrates, such as fresh vegetables, whole grains, and dried beans and other legumes, Dr. Rapoport advises.

But even though a high-carbohydrate diet can often ease pain, there are some people for whom it can actually make headaches worse. If you have low blood sugar, or hypoglycemia, for example, you may find that you do better if you consume fewer carbohydrates. "Having low levels of sugar in the brain can set off a headache," says Dr. Werbach. "These people may do well on a so-called hypoglycemic diet, which is usually a low-carbohydrate diet." And beyond headaches, a high-carbohydrate diet can be detrimental for people with certain health conditions, such as metabolic syndrome or diabetes.

If you've noticed that your headaches often occur after you've eaten a lot of carbohydrates, says Dr. Werbach, try eating slightly more protein in the form of lean meats, eggs, or low-fat cheese.

The Benefits of B_6

Vitamin B_6 has been shown to keep the nervous system healthy and bolster the immune system, and as if that weren't enough, studies also suggest that it may help relieve migraines. The brain uses vitamin B_6 to increase serotonin levels, explains Dr. Rapoport, "so a good intake of B_6 might help relieve migraines, even if you're not deficient in it."

The Daily Value (DV) for vitamin B_6 is 2 milligrams. One medium potato or one banana contains 0.7 milligram of B_6, or 35 percent of the DV. A 3-ounce serving of baked or broiled swordfish has 0.3 milligram, or 15 percent of the DV.

Your doctor may also advise getting larger amounts (up to 150 milligrams) of vitamin B_6 through a multiple vitamin. You shouldn't take B_6 supplements unless prescribed by a doctor, however, because getting too much B_6 can cause damage to the nervous system.

Minerals for Relief

While the exact underlying reasons aren't yet clear, certain minerals, particularly magnesium, calcium, and iron, seem to help prevent and treat both migraine and tension headaches.

People who suffer from chronic migraines often have low levels of magnesium in their brain cells. Studies suggest that correcting a magnesium deficiency may help relieve migraine, says Dr. Rapoport.

Ready-to-eat breakfast cereals are good sources of magnesium; some brands contain more than 100 milligrams of magnesium, or 25 percent of the DV, in a 1-ounce serving. Nuts, seeds, and dark green leafy vegetables are also rich in magnesium. Nuts are also loaded with fat, however, so you'll want to eat them in moderation (no more than a handful a day), and get most of your magnesium elsewhere.

Calcium is another mineral that has been linked to headache relief. One study found that people who consumed 200 milligrams of calcium a day (20 percent of the DV) had fewer headaches than those who consumed less.

Dairy foods are the best sources of calcium. Topping the list is milk, with 1 cup of fat-free milk containing 302 milligrams, or 30 percent of the DV. Other good sources of calcium include ice milk, with 176 milligrams per cup, or 18 percent of the DV, and low-fat fruit yogurt, with 312 milligrams per cup, or 31 percent of the DV. There are many nondairy sources of calcium as well, among them broccoli, with 72 milligrams in 1 cup, and Swiss chard, with 101 milligrams in 1 cup.

Last on the list of minerals that may help prevent headaches is iron. Not getting sufficient iron in the diet can lead to anemia, a condition in which the body doesn't get enough oxygen. To compensate, blood vessels dilate to admit more blood, says Dr. Rapoport. "This dilation compresses the nerves in the walls of the vessels, causing head pain," he explains. "Consuming more dietary iron may indirectly relieve headaches by treating the anemia."

It's generally easy to meet the DV of 18 milligrams for iron. A large baked potato, for example, has 7 milligrams, while 1 cup of Swiss chard has nearly 4 milligrams. Meats are even better sources; they contain heme iron, a type of iron that is more readily absorbed by the body than the nonheme iron in vegetables. A 3-ounce serving of broiled top round steak has 3 milligrams of iron, and the same amount of roasted white turkey meat has 1 milligram.

Spicy Relief

When you're searching for a drug-free form of migraine relief, you might want to try a spoonful of the popular spice ginger. "Ginger is good for headaches because it stimulates circulation," says Janet Maccaro, PhD, ND, a holistic nutritionist in Ormond Beach, Florida, who is president of Dr. Janet's Balance By Nature Products and the author of *Natural Health Remedies A-Z*.

A study done at the Headache Care Center in Springfield, Missouri, showed ginger's power at preventing headaches. Thirty people with a history of migraine were given an over-the-counter combination of feverfew and ginger (called GelStat) at the early, mild pain phase of a migraine headache. Two hours after treatment, 48 percent of the participants were pain free, and 34 percent reported a mild headache. Overall, 59 percent of the participants said they were happy with the effectiveness of the ginger-containing GelStat, indicating that its ingredients may be a good first-line treatment for migraines.

And researchers at Odense University in Denmark believe that ginger blocks the action of prostaglandins, substances that cause pain and inflammation in blood vessels. Therefore, it might help prevent impending migraines without the side effects of some migraine-relieving drugs.

If you feel a migraine coming on, you might try taking ⅓ teaspoon of powdered ginger, the amount suggested by the Danish researchers.

When taking ginger, it's even better to use the fresh rather than the powdered form because it's more active, says Charles Lo, MD, a doctor of Chinese medicine in private practice in Chicago. He advises grating the ginger or pushing it through a garlic press; these methods release more of the potent juices than does slicing or chopping it. Or you can make a spicy ginger tea by steeping a teaspoon of the grated root in a cup of boiling water for at least 5 minutes, says Dr. Lo.

The Coffee Cure

There's a reason some over-the-counter headache relievers can make you feel jumpy. "Caffeine is often an ingredient in pain relievers," says Fred Sheftell, MD, cofounder and codirector of the New England Headache Center in Stamford, Connecticut. For some people, sipping a cup of their favorite aromatic brew may work as well as popping an over-the-counter painkiller. The caffeine in coffee can counter a headache by temporarily constricting dilated blood vessels, which may be causing the pain, says Dr. Sheftell.

But don't overdo it with the coffee. Too much java will eventually cause the blood vessels to dilate painfully again. Dr. Sheftell recommends that people who are headache-prone drink no more than 2 cups (5 ounces each) a day, which together contain about 200 milligrams of caffeine, depending on the strength of the brew.

Heartburn

PUTTING OUT THE FIRE

If you've ever had heartburn, you know the name is appropriate. It feels as though a fire is raging in your chest. The pain can be so intense, in fact, that some people rush to the emergency room in the fear they're having a heart attack.

But contrary to its name and its sensation, heartburn has nothing to do with the heart. It occurs when acid-laden digestive juices in the stomach head in the wrong direction and surge upward into the esophagus, the tube that connects the mouth with the stomach. Normally, a tight little muscle at the base of the esophagus, called the lower esophageal sphincter (LES), prevents juices from escaping. But if that sphincter relaxes, juices splash upward and cause the "burn" that is heartburn.

There are some foods that make heartburn more likely. Likewise, there are foods that will quickly put the fire out. So before you rush to the pharmacy for an antacid, make a pit stop in your kitchen.

"Modifying the diet remains one of the first lines of treatment for people with heartburn," says Suzanne Rose, MD, professor of medical education and medicine and gastroenterology at Mount Sinai Hospital in New York City.

Inside Healing

One food that can help control heartburn is ginger, says John Hibbs, ND, a naturopathic doctor and clinical faculty member at Bastyr Center for Natural Health in Seattle. Ginger helps strengthen the holding power of the LES, which can help keep acid where it belongs. If you don't like the spiciness of fresh ginger, make a ginger tea by adding ½ to 1 teaspoon of freshly grated ginger (or ¼ to ½ teaspoon of powdered ginger) to a cup of hot water. Let it steep for 10 minutes, strain, and enjoy.

It's a good idea not to lie down soon after eating, says Dr. Rose. When your stomach is full, it's much easier for acid to rise up into the esophagus, especially when you lie down and gravity is working against you. Remain upright, whether on your feet or sitting in a chair, to help keep the acid down, she says.

Common Offenders

An estimated 60 million Americans experience heartburn at least once a month, and up to 15 million are thought to experience it daily. What's more, Americans get more calories from fat than people from any other country on the planet. A coincidence? Researchers don't think so. Studies have shown that foods high in fat, like butter and red meat, can temporarily reduce the holding power of the LES. In one study, researchers at Bowman Gray School of Medicine of Wake Forest University in Winston-Salem, North Carolina, found that people who ate high-fat meals were exposed to acid about four times as long as those eating leaner fare.

Chocolate is another offender for some people, Dr. Rose adds. Not only is it high in fat, it may contain other compounds that can relax the LES even more. In another study at Bowman Gray, researchers found that when people ate chocolate, stomach acid splashed into the esophagus for up to an hour afterward.

It's not only high-fat foods that can be a problem for heartburn sufferers, however. Onions, for example, can bring on heartburn in some people. Researchers aren't exactly sure what it is about onions that can light the fire, but for some, heartburn can flare up after only one slice of onion.

Peppermint, which is often added to candy, ice cream, and baked goods, frequently causes heartburn as well, Dr. Rose adds. In one study, researchers at the State University of New York at Buffalo found that when people ate peppermint, their esophageal muscles lost some holding power within just a few minutes.

And coffee, tomatoes, citrus fruits, and fried foods can also trigger heartburn, says John Neustadt, ND, medical director of Montana Integrative Medicine in Bozeman. So if you notice your heartburn worsens after eating one or more of these foods, try to avoid them, he says.

Finally, if you're suffering from a bout of heartburn, be careful about eating spicy foods until your esophagus has a chance to heal, says Dr. Rose. Many people don't think twice about dousing tender esophageal tissues with hot peppers or a swig of orange juice. You don't have to give up your favorite foods entirely, she says. Just avoid them for a few days until your heartburn is feeling better.

Doctor's Top Tip

The most recent development in heartburn research was a study that compared how quickly a meal was ingested rather than a type of food per se, says Donald Castell, MD, professor of medicine and the director of the esophageal disorders program at the Medical University of South Carolina in Charleston. "The study was hospital-based and probably developed originally because the interns and residents ate their meals so quickly and then ran off to see another patient," he says. "What they found was that if you took the same meal—a turkey burger, fries, and a Coke—and looked at people who ate that meal in 5 minutes versus people who ate it in 30 minutes, there was a significantly greater amount of acid reflux in the quick-eating group than in the leisurely eating group," he says. So if you have a problem with heartburn, take some time to relax and enjoy your food—no matter what you're eating—rather than scarfing it down.

Heart Disease

PRIMING YOUR PUMP

Doctors haven't always known what was best for our hearts. Only a few decades ago, little attention was paid to diet, and even smoking was thought to be acceptable by some.

Everything Has Changed

After almost 50 years of investigating what makes heart disease our worst public-health enemy, scientists have come up with some pretty simple and straightforward answers. Regular exercise is important, of course, as is staying away from cigarettes or quitting smoking if you picked up the habit. But perhaps the most important of all is having a healthy diet. Reaching for the right foods is the most effective way to lower cholesterol and high blood pressure, two of the biggest risk factors for the heart.

All too often, however, we reach for the wrong foods. So, to put confusion to rest, here are some of the best—and worst—foods for preventing heart disease, starting with fats. While there are some fats that we'd be better off avoiding, others aren't so bad, it turns out, and some might even be healthful.

The Bad Fats

We all know that saturated fat, the kind found primarily in animal foods, such as red meat, butter, and others, is incredibly dangerous for the heart. Study after study has shown that the more saturated fat people get in their diets, the higher their risks for heart disease.

Foods high in saturated fat raise levels of artery-clogging low-density lipoprotein (LDL) cholesterol, says Michael Gaziano, MD, associate professor of medicine at Harvard Medical School, both in Boston. What's more, foods high in saturated fat are often high in cholesterol as well.

The danger is so great that the American Heart Association recommends that we limit our intake of saturated fat to less than 7 percent of our calories each day. Suppose, for example, that you normally get 2,000 calories in a day. This means your upper daily limit for saturated fat is 14 grams. This means that in addition to eating fruits, vegetables, and other low-fat foods, you could have 3 ounces of extra-lean ground beef (which contains 5 grams of saturated fat), a serving of macaroni and cheese (6 grams), and a half-cup of low-fat frozen yogurt (3 grams).

Another type of problem fat, called trans fatty acids, has been shown to dramatically increase the amount of cholesterol in the bloodstream, says Dr. Gaziano.

Ironically, trans fatty acids (which are made when manufacturers add hydrogen to vegetable oils to turn the liquid oils into solid fats like margarine and shortening) were meant to be a healthful alternative to the saturated fat in butter. But it appears that trans fatty acids may be even more harmful than saturated fats. Trans fats raise the bad LDL cholesterol *and* lower the good HDL (high-density lipoprotein) cholesterol, increasing the risk of cardiovascular disease, heart attack, and stroke.

Trans fats appear to be so dangerous, in fact, that some US cities, including New York City, have begun banning them from being used as ingredients in french fries, doughnuts, and other foods fried in frying shortenings. And it's not only margarine and fried foods that may be a problem. Many cookies, cakes, and other snack foods contain "partially hydrogenated oil," which is also high in trans fatty acids. Because of the health risk posed by trans fatty acids, the American Heart Association recommends you limit your daily intake to less than 1 percent of your total calories.

Some Better Fats

Unlike saturated fat and trans fatty acids, some fats are relatively healthful. Here's an easy way to recognize them. Look for the "un," as in polyunsaturated and monounsaturated fats. While these "un-fats" are still high in calories, in small amounts, they play several beneficial roles.

Polyunsaturated fats (found in soy, corn, safflower, sesame, and sunflower oils, as well as nuts and seeds) help your body get rid of newly formed cholesterol; therefore, they keep cholesterol levels down and reduce cholesterol deposits on artery walls. Monounsaturated fats also appear to help lower cholesterol levels as long as the rest of the diet is very low in saturated fats. Although they are a good substitute for saturated fat, both polyunsaturated fats and monounsaturated fats should be used in moderation because their high calorie counts can lead to weight gain. No more than 30 percent of your calories should come from fat.

"Picking either polyunsaturated or monounsaturated fats over saturated fat or trans fats is a winning choice," says Christopher Gardner, PhD, assistant professor of medicine at the Stanford Prevention Research Center in Stanford, California.

Nuts are particularly good sources of these healthful fats. In a study of Seventh-Day Adventists, researchers found that those who consumed nuts at least four times a week had almost half the risk of fatal heart attacks of those who rarely ate them.

Although the American Heart Association recommends less than 30 percent of calories from fat, many health-care professionals, including Dr. Gaziano, recommend even less. "I tell people to aim for getting about 20 to 25 percent of total calories from fat, most of which should be in the form of monounsaturated and polyunsaturated fat," says Dr. Gaziano.

There's yet another kind of healthful fat, perhaps the king of healthful fats, called omega-3 fatty acids. Found in most fish (but particularly in oily, cold-water fish) and also in flaxseed and certain dark greens, omega-3s can help prevent clots from forming in the bloodstream. In addition, they help lower triglycerides, a type of blood fat that, in large amounts, may raise the risk for heart disease.

Studies show that eating fish twice a week (salmon is a good choice, because it contains high levels of omega-3s) can help keep your arteries clear and your heart working well. In a study done at the Harvard School of Public Health, scientists found that the death rate from heart disease was 36 percent lower among people who ate fish twice a week compared with people who ate little or no seafood. The study, which was published in the *Journal of the American Medical Association,* also showed that overall mortality was 17 percent lower among the regular seafood eaters.

Feast on Folate

Almost 30 years ago, a Harvard pathologist suggested that a vitamin deficiency could be a major cause of heart disease. The theory sounded so wacky that nobody listened. Now, instead of laughing, scientists are busy researching, because evidence suggests that folate, a B vitamin abundant in beans and dark green leafy vegetables, may play a major role in preventing heart attacks.

An Italian study published in the *European Journal of Clinical Nutrition* looked at the relationship between folate intake and heart attack risk in nearly 1,000 individuals, half who had a history of one nonfatal heart attack and half who had not. Researchers found that the individuals with a higher intake of folate were less likely to have suffered a heart attack than those with a low intake of the B vitamin.

Folate is responsible for lowering levels of an amino acid called homocysteine. While the body needs homocysteine to produce muscle and bone tissue, in large amounts, it can injure blood vessels, causing hardening of the arteries.

"High homocysteine levels are an important contributor to heart disease," says Dr. Gardner. "And it appears that homocysteine can be brought down easily with modest amounts of folate in the diet."

You don't need a lot of folate to get the benefits. The Daily Value (DV) of 400 micrograms may be plenty, says Dr. Gardner. Spinach is a good source of folate, with 1 cup of cooked spinach containing 263 micrograms, or nearly 66 percent of the DV. Lentils are even better, with a half-cup containing 179 micrograms, or 45 percent of the DV. Even a 6-ounce glass of orange juice contains 36 micrograms of folate, or 9 percent of the DV.

Aiming for Antioxidants

Doctors have known for years that the body's LDL cholesterol is bad news, and now they also understand why.

Every day, your body produces harmful oxygen molecules called free radicals, which damage cholesterol. This harmful process, called oxidation, is what causes cholesterol to stick to the lining of artery walls.

Fruits, vegetables, and other foods containing antioxidants, such as beta-carotene and vitamins C and E, are the best protection against oxidation and heart disease. In fact, one group of antioxidants, called flavonoids, is thought to be the reason that the Dutch and French have such healthy hearts, despite some unhealthy eating habits.

A study in the Netherlands, for example, found that men who ate the most flavonoid-rich foods, particularly apples, tea, and onions, were half as likely to have heart disease as those who ate the least. Flavonoids may also explain why the French, who eat more fat and cholesterol than we do, have heart disease death rates 2½ times lower than ours.

"Foods containing flavonoids, including green tea, dark chocolate, and red wine, seem to protect against heart disease by improving endothelial function, which means that arteries are more flexible and able to deal with stresses of dietary fat, exercise, and increases in blood pressure," says Joe A. Vinson, PhD, professor of analytical chemistry at the University of Scranton in Pennsylvania, who specializes in the study of flavonoids.

Doctors still aren't sure which foods—or which compounds found in foods—are the most effective. An Italian study looked at the intake of certain flavonoids and the risk of heart attack in 760 patients under age 79 with a history of nonfatal heart attack and 682 patients with no history of heart attack. Researchers found that the patients with the highest intake of flavonoids called anthocyanidins—found in cherries, blueberries, and other brightly colored fruits—had the lowest risk of heart attack.

The American Heart Association recommends eating at least five servings a day of a large variety of fruits and vegetables. One serving is equal to ½ to 1 cup of cooked or raw vegetables, ½ cup of fruit juice, or 1 medium piece of fruit.

"You just can't lose by eating plenty of fruits and vegetables," says Dr. Gardner. "Study after study shows that people who eat the most of these healthful foods have the lowest rates of heart disease."

Fortify Your Heart with Fiber

Your grandmother called it roughage. Today, we call it fiber. But whatever it's called, it's an important part of any heart protection plan.

Fiber, especially the soluble kind found in beans, fruits, and whole grains, binds with cholesterol in the body and helps remove it along with the waste, says Diane Grabowski-Nepa, RD, a dietitian and nutritional counselor at the Pritikin Longevity Center in Santa Monica, California.

The DV for fiber is 25 grams, but most Americans don't get nearly enough. "The average consumption of fiber per person is 15 grams a day, but we need 25 to 30 grams for optimum health," says Jana Klauer, MD, a New York City–based physician who specializes in the biology of fat reduction and is the author of *How the Rich Stay Thin*. Super sources of fiber include whole grains and flaxseed, beans such as chickpeas, kidney beans, and lima beans, berries such as blueberries, strawberries, and raspberries, and dried fruits like figs, apples, and peaches. Overall, Dr. Klauer recommends fruits and vegetables as the best sources of fiber. "Per 100 calories, nonstarchy fruits and vegetables typically contain about eight times more fiber than whole grains, plus they supply added vitamins and minerals," she says.

Sip a Little Health

It's a tradition in many countries to raise a glass of wine and give a toast to good health. As it turns out, what's in that glass can make the toasts come true.

Studies have shown that drinking moderate amounts of alcohol raises levels of beneficial HDL cholesterol. Plus, alcohol acts like motor oil in the blood. It makes platelets, the tiny disks that aid in clotting, a little more slippery, so they're less likely to stick together and cause heart-damaging clots in the bloodstream.

A study done at the Institut Municipal d'Investigacio Medica in Barcelona, Spain, looked at the association of nonfatal heart attack and amount and types of alcoholic beverages consumed in 244 men with a history of nonfatal heart attack and 1,270 healthy male controls. The researchers found that total alcohol consumption (beer, wine, or liquor) of up to 30 grams per day (adjusted for lifestyle and cardiovascular disease risk factors) was associated with a decreased incidence of nonfatal heart attack. Alcohol consumption of 20 grams or less per day decreased the risk even more. And alcohol consumption higher than 30 grams did not decrease risk of nonfatal heart attack. These results suggest that moderate alcohol consumption is protective against heart attack, regardless of the type of alcohol consumed, but higher amounts of alcohol are not.

That said, red wine does happen to be particularly good because it also contains heart-healthy flavonoids. A Norwegian study looked at the relationship between drinking red wine and plasma viscosity (blood plasma that is more viscous is more likely to clot and lead to heart attack or stroke). Healthy, nonsmoking volunteers were instructed to drink a glass of wine every day for 3 weeks and then to abstain from alcohol for 3 weeks. Researchers measured their plasma viscosity at the start of the study, after the first 3 weeks of wine drinking, and after the second 3 weeks of abstaining from wine. They found that viscosity levels dropped after the 3 weeks of wine drinking and remained lower through the second 3 weeks, suggesting that a daily glass of red wine helps lower plasma viscosity and, therefore, risk of heart attack and stroke.

To get the benefits of alcohol without the health problems, doctors advise drinking in moderation. For men, this means having no more than two drinks a day. (A drink is defined as 12 ounces of beer, 5 ounces of wine, 1½ ounces of 80-proof liquor, or 1 ounce of 100-proof liquor.) Drinking more than two drinks is counterproductive healthwise and poses dangers such as high blood pressure, obesity, stroke, suicide, and accidents. Therefore, the American Heart Association cautions people not to start drinking if they do not already drink alcohol.

Herbs

HEALING THE NATURAL WAY

Imagine marinara sauce without oregano. Baked potatoes without chives. No one who enjoys food would want to live in a world without herbs.

But herbs do more than add rich flavor to sauces or a tangy zip to potatoes and tofu. For millions of people worldwide, herbs also act as the medicines they depend on to stay healthy.

"Before the discovery of modern pharmaceuticals, both Europeans and Americans relied on herbs," says William J. Keller, PhD, vice president of health sciences and educational services at Nature's Sunshine Products in Provo, Utah. Even today, people in European nations use herbal medicines nearly every day. In this country, however, we'd pretty much cast them aside—until about a decade or so ago, says Dr. Keller.

Doctors are discovering that many herbs work as well as prescription and over-the-counter drugs for relieving common conditions, and for a very simple reason. The active ingredients in herbs are often virtually identical to the chemicals found in drugs. When you take an aspirin, for example, you get the benefit of a compound called acetylsalicylic acid, which works to ease pain, lower fever, and reduce inflammation. But before there was aspirin, people made tea from willow bark. Willow contains a compound called salicin, which has many of the same effects as aspirin.

And it's not just "simple" over-the-counter drugs that have herbal counterparts. Many prescription drugs also resemble—or are actually made from—herbs. The cancer drug etoposide, for example, is extracted from the root of the mayapple plant, and the heart drug digitalis contains compounds similar to those found in purple foxglove (do not eat the foxglove plant, however, as it is poisonous in its raw form). Researchers estimate, in fact, that up to 30 percent of the drugs we use today contain ingredients that are very similar to compounds found in plants.

From Plants to Penicillin

Today researchers use sophisticated equipment and expensive tests to discover which herbs are the most effective. For the original herbalists, however, "research" often meant watching animals in the wild to see which leaves, bark, or berries they turned

In the Kitchen

To preserve the healing powers of herbs, you have to dry and store them properly. Here's how:

- When drying leaves or flowers, tie small bunches of herbs together, and hang them upside down in a dry, well-ventilated area such as an attic or large pantry. To prevent herbs from getting dusty, hang them inside paper bags with holes punched in the sides to allow air to circulate. Be careful not to crush the herbs, which will cause the precious oils to dissipate.

- When drying roots, cut them into thin pieces, thread them on a length of string, and hang them to dry.
- To dry seeds, hang the entire plant upside down in a paper bag with holes punched in it, and allow it to dry; as the plant dries, the seeds will fall to the bottom of the bag.
- To keep dried herbs fresh, store them in tightly sealed jars in a cool, dark place. When they are properly stored, dried herbs will retain their potency for a year or more.

---

to whenever they were ill. Over the years, herbalists (and many doctors) became pretty knowledgeable about which herbs were best for which conditions.

By the middle of the 20th century, however, scientists were less interested in the herbs themselves than in the medicinal compounds they contained. "With the advancement of laboratory chemistry, it became possible to isolate and purify the chemical compounds from plants to make pharmaceutical drugs," says Mark Blumenthal, executive director of the American Botanical Council in Austin, Texas, and editor of the journal *HerbalGram*.

The new drugs offered a lot of advantages over their leafy predecessors. With laboratory precision, it was possible to make millions of pills, each with exactly the same strength. Drugs were also convenient. It was no longer necessary to spend hours searching for and preparing herbs—hanging them to dry, extracting their oils, or brewing them into tea—since it was possible to pop a pill that did the same thing.

"It wasn't because herbs were ineffective that people quit using them, but because there were reliable, cheaper, sexier drugs, like the sulfa drugs and later, penicillin," says Blumenthal. "So herbs fell into a kind of twilight zone."

Back to Basics

Today, of course, it's much easier to find over-the-counter drugs than herbal remedies. But more and more Americans are choosing herbs over drugs in favor of a more natural way of healing.

One advantage of herbs is that they tend to cause fewer side effects than modern drugs. Most drugs are highly concentrated, which is why taking one tiny pill or capsule can have such dramatic results. Herbs, on the other hand, are much less concentrated; you don't get as much of the active ingredients in your body at one time, so you're less likely to have uncomfortable reactions.

But the main reason that people use herbs such as garlic, echinacea, and feverfew is that they really work—which is why, in just 1 year, German physicians wrote 5.4 million prescriptions for ginkgo, an herb that has been shown to improve bloodflow to the brain. They also wrote more than 2 million prescriptions for echinacea, an immunity-boosting herb that's often used for treating colds and flu.

Some evidence has shown that taking echinacea as soon as you start feeling ill shortens the duration of the infection.

Of all the healing herbs, garlic is perhaps the best-studied, and with good reason. It contains compounds that have been shown to lower cholesterol and high blood pressure, two of the leading risk factors for heart disease. In a landmark study, people in two groups were given 2½ ounces of butter for several weeks. Half of these people were also given an extract containing the equivalent of seven cloves of garlic every day. Not surprisingly, people in both groups had increases in cholesterol. The garlic eaters, however, showed less of an increase than those who did not eat garlic. What's more, they actually had a 16 percent decrease in triglycerides, another type of blood fat that has been linked to heart disease.

Feverfew is an herb that has received scientific attention because it appears to help prevent migraines. In one study, for example, researchers at University Hospital in Nottingham, England, gave migraine-prone people capsules of feverfew every day for 4 months. At the end of the study, the number of migraines in the group had dropped 24 percent.

And, in a study done at the Headache Care Center in Springfield, Missouri, 30 people with a history of migraine were given an over-the-counter combination of feverfew and ginger (called GelStat) at the early, mild pain phase of a migraine headache. Overall, 59 percent of the participants said they were happy with the effectiveness of the feverfew-containing GelStat, indicating that its ingredients may be a good first-line treatment for migraines.

Adding Flavor to Food

In addition to their medicinal properties, some herbs add fabulous flavors to recipes and can therefore act as a healthful substitute for salt, says Jana Klauer, MD, a New York City–based physician who specializes in the biology of fat reduction and is the author of *How the Rich Stay Thin*. Instead of salt, throw fresh thyme, dill weed, peppermint, basil, rosemary, garlic, parsley, tarragon, and other herbs into your foods to make them flavorful.

Putting Them to Work

When you're used to opening a bottle and popping a neat little pill into your mouth, getting used to the various herbal remedies can take a little time. Apothecaries and natural food stores often stock hundreds of healing herbs—packed into capsules, dissolved in oils, or lying loose in covered glass jars. It's not always easy to know which form to choose or how to prepare the herbs once you get them home. Here are a few tips for getting started.

Choose the right form. Many herbal remedies come in three forms: as pills or capsules, as liquids (called extracts and tinctures), and in their natural form as leaves, bark, roots, and flowers. Each form provides healing benefits, but they act in slightly different ways, says Debra Brammer, ND, a naturopathic doctor and clinical faculty member and associate clinical dean for the naturopathic medicine department at Bastyr University Natural Health Clinic in Seattle.

When you're sick and want fast relief, herbal extracts are usually best because they're absorbed very quickly by the body, says Dr. Brammer. While they're not as convenient as taking a pill—you have to measure them, using a dropper or a teaspoon, into a glass of water or juice—they go to work almost instantly, she says.

When you're using herbs for long-term protection—to strengthen the immune system, for example—it doesn't matter how quickly they work. What does count is convenience in buying and taking them, since you're going to be using the herbs almost every day. Nothing's easier than taking herbs in pill or capsule form. Just be sure to check the label before buying them, Dr. Keller adds. Herbal pills should be standardized, which means that they contain a precise amount of the healing herb. Products that aren't standardized may contain little or none of the herb's active compounds.

You can also buy herbs in their natural form or ground into a powder. These are used for making teas, says Dr. Brammer. While herbal teas work somewhat more slowly than extracts, they're absorbed by the body faster than pills or capsules. Plus, many people enjoy the taste of freshly brewed herbal teas. "The ritual of brewing the tea and sipping it slowly is so relaxing that it often makes people feel better," Dr. Brammer adds.

Shop for freshness. The one problem with using fresh herbs is that they give up their benefits over time. "It's a bad sign if the herbs are lying in bins in the store's front window, with the sun pouring in, since herbs lose their potency when exposed to light and air," says Dr. Keller.

Before buying herbs, put your nose to work, Dr. Keller advises. Fresh herbs

(continued on page 142)

THE HEALING HERBS

There are literally thousands of herbs that are used for healing around the world. Most herbs can be taken in capsule, tablet, tea, or liquid forms. Here are some of

Herb	Benefits	How to Use
Anise	Helps relieve gas.	Crush 1 tsp seeds, and steep in boiling water to make a tea.
Chamomile	Good for indigestion and gas, insomnia, and for easing sore throat.	Pour boiling water over 1–2 Tbsp herb, and steep to make a tea.
Echinacea	Strengthens the immune system.	Take ½ tsp tincture three times a day at the first sign of a cold. Or pour boiling water over ½ tsp coarsely powdered dried herb, and steep to make a tea.
Fennel	Helps settle the stomach.	Crush 1–2 tsp seeds, and steep in boiling water to make a tea.
Feverfew	Helps prevent and relieve migraines.	Eat 2–3 fresh leaves a day.
Garlic	Helps lower cholesterol and high blood pressure and reduces the risk for heart disease.	Eat 1–6 cloves a day.
Gentian	Stimulates appetite and improves digestion.	Pour boiling water over ½ tsp finely cut or coarsely powdered herb, and steep to make a tea.
Ginkgo	Helps prevent blood clots and increases bloodflow to the brain. Eases anxiety.	Take a 40-milligram capsule three times a day for 1–2 months.
Horehound	A mild expectorant that's good for coughs.	Pour boiling water over 1½ tsp finely cut leaves, and steep to make a tea.
Lemon balm	A calming herb that also helps ease cold sores.	Pour boiling water over 1–2 tsp finely chopped leaves, and steep to make a tea.
Licorice root	Helps heal sore throat and ulcers.	Pour boiling water over ½ tsp finely chopped root, and steep to make a tea. Do not use for more than 4–6 weeks at a time. Avoid if you have high blood pressure.
Lovage	Relieves gas and fluid retention.	Pour boiling water over ½–1 tsp finely cut root, and steep to make a tea. Repeat three times a day when using as a diuretic.

the most popular healing herbs and instructions for using them. Of course, if you are pregnant or breastfeeding or have serious health problems, be sure to talk to your doctor before using medicinal herbs.

Herb	Benefits	How to Use
Milk thistle	Good for liver problems such as hepatitis and cirrhosis.	Take a 200-milligram capsule once a day.
Nettle	Helps relieve fluid retention.	Pour boiling water over 2 tsp finely cut leaves, and steep to make a tea.
Oregano	Good for parasitic infections and for blocking the effects of carcinogens in cooked meats.	Add generous amounts of whole leaves or powdered herb during cooking.
Parsley	A digestive aid and mild diuretic.	Add generous amounts of leaves and stems during cooking.
Peppermint	Eases upset stomach and reduces gas.	Pour boiling water over 1 Tbsp dried leaves, and steep to make a tea.
Rosemary	Eases digestion and helps stimulate appetite.	Pour boiling water over 1 tsp finely chopped leaves, and steep to make a tea.
St.-John's-wort	Eases nervousness and anxiety, improves memory and concentration, and has antiviral and anti-inflammatory effects.	Take a 250-milligram capsule once a day.
Savory	Relieves gas and diarrhea and stimulates appetite.	Add generous amounts of crushed leaves during cooking.
Thyme	Eases cough and upper respiratory infections.	Pour boiling water over 1 tsp dried herb, and steep to make a tea.
Uva ursi	Helps relieve fluid retention.	Pour cold water over 1 tsp coarsely powdered leaves (bearberry), and let stand for 12–24 hours to make a tea.
Valerian	Good for insomnia.	Pour boiling water over 2 tsp finely cut root, and steep to make a tea.
Willow bark	Helps ease pain, fever, and headaches.	Pour boiling water over 1–2 tsp finely chopped bark, and steep to make a tea.
Yarrow	Good for indigestion and for stimulating the appetite.	Pour boiling water over 1 heaping tsp finely chopped herb, and steep to make a tea.

should smell fresh. "Don't buy herbs that smell musty or look moldy, dry, or discolored," he says. And once you get them home, be sure to store them in an airtight container in a cool, dark place, such as a kitchen cupboard away from the stove.

Shop often. Even though it's convenient to buy in bulk, dried herbs won't keep indefinitely, says Dr. Brammer. To get the most healing power, she says, it's best to buy herbs in small amounts and replenish the supply a bit more frequently.

Treat them with respect. Even though herbs are often gentler than modern medicines, they can cause side effects, such as upset stomach, says Dr. Keller. It's a good idea to take healing herbs with meals rather than on an empty stomach. And because herbs are medicine, be sure to check with your doctor before taking them, especially if you're taking other medications for serious conditions such as diabetes or heart disease, says Dr. Keller. Also, because some herbs can act as blood thinners, be sure you tell your doctor about all herbs you are taking before you have surgery.

Insomnia

RESTFUL FOODS

When life gets hectic, we've all found ourselves wishing that there were more hours in the day. Sometimes, unfortunately, we get our wish—at the expense of our sleep.

Few things are more miserable than lying awake, frustrated and tired, when everyone else is sleeping soundly. Insomnia is usually temporary, of course, caused by too much coffee, perhaps, or anxiety about tomorrow's work. But sometimes insomnia really sticks around—not just for days but for weeks, months, or even years. After a few nights spent staring at the ceiling, you may feel as if you'll never be rested again.

You're not alone. A 2003 poll by the National Sleep Foundation found that half of adults in America ages 55 and older reported at least one symptom of insomnia three or more times a week, including having trouble falling asleep, waking during the night, waking too early and not being able to go back to sleep, or not feeling refreshed in the morning.

The next time you find yourself tossing and turning, get out of bed, put on your slippers, and head for the kitchen. There's good evidence that what you eat before going to bed can help turn out the lights on insomnia.

Nosh to Nod

Remember dear old Dad sawing logs on the La-Z-Boy after dinner? He wasn't just dodging the dishes. He was responding to one of the body's most inflexible commands: "First you eat, then you sleep."

"When you put food in your stomach at night, you should be able to sleep better," says David Levitsky, PhD, professor of nutrition and psychology at Cornell University in Ithaca, New York. "Eating draws blood into the gastrointestinal tract and away from the brain. And if you draw blood away from the brain, you're going to get sleepy."

In fact, researchers are learning more about the link between your stomach and sleep. After studying the brain activity of mice, Tamas Horvath, PhD, professor of comparative medicine, obstetrics/gynecology, and neurobiology at Yale University School of Medicine, has found that blood glucose levels are the main trigger for hypocretin, cells in the brain that keep you awake. When you go to bed on an empty stomach, and your blood glucose levels are low, hypocretin cells become active, and that keeps you from going to sleep, he says.

This doesn't mean that stuffing yourself at bedtime will send you off to dreamland. In fact, eating too much too late in the evening can leave you feeling bloated and gassy, which is more likely to keep you awake than help you sleep. But having a light snack just before bedtime will help give your body the message that it's time to nod off.

Talking Turkey

Have you ever wondered why you always nod off in front of the television after a Christmas or Thanksgiving feast? It's not because of the company. Traditional holiday foods such as turkey and chicken are very high in an amino acid called tryptophan, which has been shown to affect the part of the brain that governs sleep, says Dr. Levitsky. Dairy foods are also high in tryptophan, he adds.

The body converts tryptophan into serotonin, which is then converted into melatonin. Both serotonin and melatonin make you feel relaxed and sleepy. In fact, tryptophan may be so effective that for a long time, doctors recommended tryptophan supplements to help people sleep. Even though the pills were eventually banned (due to a tainted batch imported from Japan), doctors believe that the amino acid found in foods is safe and effective as a sleep aid.

For tryptophan to be most effective, however, it's important to get it in combination with starches, according to Judith Wurtman, PhD, a researcher affiliated with the Massachusetts Institute of Technology Clinical Research Center in Cambridge and author of *The Serotonin Power Diet*. When you eat starches—a bagel, for example— the body releases insulin, which pushes all the amino acids except tryptophan into muscle cells. This leaves tryptophan alone in the bloodstream, so it's first in line to get into the brain.

Obviously, you don't want to stuff yourself with turkey before climbing into bed at night. But having a glass of milk or a piece of cheese on a cracker just before bedtime will help to boost your tryptophan levels, which will make getting to sleep a little bit easier.

A Natural Sleep Aid

Until recently, the scientific community thought that melatonin was only produced in the body. As it turns out, however, this sleep-inducing hormone is also found in a variety of foods, such as oats, sweet corn, rice, ginger, bananas, and barley, says Russell Reiter, PhD, professor of cellular and structural biology at the University of

Texas Health Science Center in San Antonio and author of *Melatonin: Your Body's Natural Wonder Drug.*

Doctors often recommend that people who have trouble sleeping take melatonin supplements. In 2004 the Agency for Healthcare Research and Quality in Rockville, Maryland, reviewed the studies showing the effects of melatonin supplements on sleep and concluded that short-term use of the supplements can help people with delayed sleep phase syndrome, or those who have trouble falling asleep before 2 a.m. However, the melatonin supplements weren't effective for treating other sleep disorders.

When the Sandman is running behind schedule, having a banana or even a bowl of oatmeal will slightly boost your melatonin levels and help prepare your body for sleep.

Sound Body, Sound Sleep

Even though scientists have identified a few key substances that help improve your chances of sleeping, there's simply no substitute for having an overall healthful diet, says James G. Penland, PhD, a research psychologist at the USDA Human Nutrition Research Center in Grand Forks, North Dakota. "A deficiency of minerals or vitamins may affect your sleep," he says. "So the better your diet, the better your sleep is likely to be."

Studies have shown, for example, that when people don't get enough iron or copper in their diets, it can take longer to fall asleep, and the sleep they do get may be less than refreshing.

The easiest way to get more of these minerals in your diet is to put shellfish on the menu. Just 20 small steamed clams, for example, will provide just over 25 milligrams of iron, or 139 percent of the Daily Value (DV), and 0.6 milligram of copper, or 31 percent of the DV. Lentils, nuts, and whole-grain foods are also good sources of iron and copper.

Magnesium is another mineral that's essential for good sleep. "It's been shown that having low magnesium levels will stimulate brain-activation neurotransmitters, which leads to overstimulation of the brain," says Dr. Penland. Not getting enough magnesium is especially common in the elderly, he adds, since they may be taking medications that block its absorption. "That's a double whammy that puts them at high risk for sleep problems," he says.

Good sources of magnesium include dried beans such as pinto and navy beans and green leafy vegetables such as spinach and Swiss chard. You can also get magnesium from soybeans, pumpkin seeds, wheat germ, and almonds.

Finally, getting plenty of B vitamins in your diet may help take the edge off insomnia. The body uses B vitamins to regulate many amino acids, including tryptophan. Niacin is particularly important because it appears to make tryptophan work even more efficiently. Lean meat is an excellent source of all the B vitamins, including niacin. Canned tuna is another good source, with 3 ounces providing 11 milligrams of niacin, or 55 percent of the DV.

In general, healthier people enjoy better sleep. Among those who reported a sleep problem to the National Sleep Foundation, 85 percent rated their health as fair or poor.

The Sleep Robbers

You know the drill. Fall into a blissfully restful sleep only to wake up once—or twice or three times—because of the urge to use the bathroom. It was the most common reason given for waking up at night by those surveyed by the National Sleep Foundation. In men, the most common reason for nightly bathroom trips is an enlarged prostate, which should be evaluated by a doctor. But if you're getting up during the night to urinate and an enlarged prostate isn't the problem, restrict your intake of liquids for 2 to 3 hours before bedtime, says William Orr, PhD, president and chief executive officer of Lynn Health Science Institute in Oklahoma City.

You already know that coffee can keep you up at night, but did you know that chocolate can also send your brain into overdrive? A serving of chocolate doesn't have as much caffeine as a cup of coffee or a cola, but it can have the same effect on your sleep, says Michael Bonnet, PhD, a sleep specialist and director of the Veterans Affairs Medical Center in Dayton, Ohio.

It's not just late-night caffeine that leaves you staring at the ceiling, Dr. Bonnet adds. Since it takes 6 to 8 hours for the body to eliminate caffeine from your system, even the coffee you had at lunch—or the chocolate bar you had in the afternoon—can keep you up at night.

Alcohol is one of the most common disturbers of sleep. A glass of wine or another alcoholic beverage at bedtime can very quickly turn off those hypocretin neurons that keep you awake, Dr. Horvath says, but unfortunately, the alcohol causes a rebound effect. Soon after falling asleep, the hypocretin cells in the brain are reactivated and wake you up.

When you're having trouble getting to sleep at night, it's a good idea to skip the nightcap and maybe have a little milk instead, Dr. Bonnet says.

When you choose to eat certain foods can also throw off your sleep schedule. If you've ever wondered why sleep eludes you at night while it threatens to overcome you in the middle of the afternoon, take a look at what you're eating for lunch and dinner. More solid foods, such as a hamburger, will make you more tired than a liquid meal, such as a bowl of soup and crackers, Dr. Orr says.

If you've just had a big meal and find yourself tired hours before your usual bedtime, resist it, Dr. Orr says. Giving in to sleep too early will only result in waking up in the middle of the night.

Irritable Bowel Syndrome
KEEPING YOUR INSIDES CALM

Doctors still aren't sure what causes irritable bowel syndrome (IBS), a miserable intestinal problem that often causes cramps, gas, diarrhea, and constipation. What they do know is that by eating a healthy diet—getting more of some foods and less of others—you can control IBS instead of having it control you.

Find Your Triggers

Perhaps the trickiest part of managing IBS is knowing which foods are most likely to trigger attacks. Since this varies from person to person, it takes time to learn which foods are safe and which aren't. "A lot of it is trial and error," says David E. Beck, MD, chairman of the department of colon and rectal surgery at the Ochsner Clinic in New Orleans.

Even though everyone with IBS reacts to foods differently, there are a few common denominators. Dairy foods, for example, are often a problem. Although children can usually enjoy milk and cheese to their hearts' content, up to 70 percent of adults worldwide produce insufficient amounts of the enzyme (lactase) needed to digest the sugar (lactose) found in dairy foods. For people with IBS, having dairy foods can be especially uncomfortable, Dr. Beck says.

You don't necessarily have to give up milk and cheese entirely, he adds. But you'll certainly want to try cutting back to see if your symptoms improve. Over time, you'll get a good idea of how much of a dairy food you can enjoy without having problems.

Eating beans often causes problems for people with IBS. Again, you don't have to rule them out entirely, Dr. Beck says. You may find that some kinds of beans bother you more than others, and some may not bother you at all.

Another food that's hard to digest is the sugar (fructose) found in soft drinks and apple and pear juices, says Samuel Meyers, MD, clinical professor of medicine at Mount Sinai School of Medicine in New York City. In addition, sweeteners like sorbitol, which are found in diet candy and chewing gum, can also be a problem. For many people with IBS, cutting back on juices and candies may be all it takes to ease the discomfort, he says.

NATURAL RELIEF

Just as the right foods can help calm an irritable bowel, there are also a number of herbs that will help keep the problem under control, says Daniel B. Mowrey, PhD, director of the American Phytotherapy Research Laboratory in Salt Lake City, and author of *Herbal Tonic Recipes*. Here's what he recommends:

Licorice root. This sweet-tasting herb, which you can use to make tea, is a natural anti-inflammatory that can help relieve irritation in the bowel, he says.

Peppermint. In one study, people with IBS who took peppermint capsules were able to eliminate all or most of their symptoms, Dr. Mowrey says. Peppermint tea is also effective, he adds.

Psyllium. The main ingredient in a number of over-the-counter laxatives, psyllium seeds, which are very high in fiber, have been shown to help relieve the pain of IBS as well as the diarrhea and constipation that may accompany it.

Forgo Fatty Foods, Fill Up on Fiber

A common cause of IBS flare-ups is fat. This is because the bowel normally contracts following a high-fat meal. For people with IBS, these normal contractions can be extremely painful, Dr. Meyers explains. Getting no more (and preferably less) than 30 percent of your total calories from fat will go a long way toward calming an irritable bowel, he says.

A sure way to eat less fat is to cook your own meals rather than eat out, says Paul Millea, MD, assistant professor of family and community medicine at the Medical College of Wisconsin in Milwaukee. Restaurants prepare food with their own benefit in mind, not yours. As a result, the food you eat at restaurants is loaded with fat and low in nutrients.

At the same time, high-fat food means low fiber, and fiber is key to avoiding IBS flare-ups for several reasons. Fiber makes stools larger, so the intestine doesn't have to squeeze as much to move them along, Dr. Beck says. In addition, the larger stools help sweep potential irritants from the bowel before they cause cramping, gas, or other symptoms. Getting more dietary fiber also will help relieve both diarrhea and constipation, which often occur in people with IBS, Dr. Beck says.

The Daily Value (DV) for fiber is 25 grams. As a starting point, Dr. Millea tells his patients to add a bowl of bran cereal to their diet every day and build up from there. "Most people will be surprised at how it affects their gastrointestinal system," he says. Although at first, the extra fiber may cause some bloating, give it time, and your body will adjust. (Avoid cereals made from corn, however, since corn tends to aggravate IBS in 20 percent of people with the problem.)

"If all Americans ate low-fat, high-fiber diets, irritable bowels would be very uncommon," Dr. Meyers says.

Stress Effects

IBS is hardly ever seen in people who are retired because its symptoms are commonly brought on by stress, says Dr. Millea. When we're under stress, we typically grab for foods that exacerbate IBS, such as coffee, soft drinks, chocolate, and fast food. That's like throwing gasoline onto the fire for most people with IBS.

"I hate to tell people to avoid stress because that essentially comes across as 'Don't live your life,'" Dr. Millea says. But it is important to be aware of the choices you make when you're under stress. Avoid stimulants such as caffeine and alcohol, add as much fiber to your diet as you can, avoid eating out, and be sure to get enough sleep and exercise.

If giving up coffee sounds impossible, try drinking less. Because both regular and decaf coffee make the bowel more sensitive, Dr. Beck recommends limiting yourself to a cup or two each day.

Swap Large Meals for Small

Finally, it's helpful to eat smaller meals. The more food you put into your body at one time, the harder the intestines have to work, and that can cause problems for people with IBS. Having several small meals is usually easier for the body to handle than having two or three big meals, says Douglas A. Drossman, MD, professor of medicine and psychiatry at the University of North Carolina at Chapel Hill School of Medicine.

Kidney Stones
RELIEF FROM THE KITCHEN

There's pain. There's agonizing pain. And then there are kidney stones.

Actually, calling them kidney barbs would be more fitting since these stones, which consist mainly of mineral salts, are sometimes studded with sharp spikes. While it's possible to pass small stones without knowing you had them, larger stones, which can range from about the size of the tip of a pen to that of a pencil eraser, cause excruciating pain as they move from the kidney through the ureter, the long tube through which urine flows. Passing a large stone has been compared to the pain of childbirth. Some women say it's worse.

Although some think kidney stones are rare, up to 10 percent of Americans will pass at least one during their lifetime, and the number is growing. Over the past 20 years, the number of people with kidney stones has been on the rise, according to the National Institutes of Health.

There are several types of kidney stones, but the most common—in fact, 80 percent of kidney stones—are those formed from calcium. Experts aren't entirely sure what causes kidney stones to form. But one thing is certain. Diet can play a key role, says Lisa Ruml, MD, an endocrinologist in Wharton, New Jersey. What you eat affects the kinds and amounts of minerals that accumulate in your urine—minerals that, in some people, lead to the formation of stones.

Perhaps the most important point is this: If you've passed one stone, the odds are good that you'll pass another. So pay attention when your doctor tells you what kind of stones you have, since this will affect the changes you make in your diet.

The stones that respond best to dietary changes are uric acid and calcium stones. The dietary changes recommended in the next few pages are given primarily with these types of stones in mind.

Stone-Crushing Potassium

Once you've experienced the pain of a kidney stone, you don't want a repeat performance. So consider making a handful of dried apricots or a baked potato a regular part of your anti-stone diet. Along with a variety of fruits and vegetables, these foods are somewhat alkaline, which helps neutralize stone-forming acids in the body.

Here's how it works. Alkaline foods increase the level of a mineral called citrate in the urine, and citrate helps block the formation of stones, Dr. Ruml explains.

To raise your levels of citrate, Dr. Ruml says, you need to get more fruits and vegetables into your diet. "Many of the foods that are high in citrates, like citrus fruits and vegetables, are also good sources of potassium."

Studies have found that choosing orange juice over other citrus is worth your while. A 2006 study found that drinking 13 ounces of orange juice three times a day, along with a diet low in calcium, had a more positive effect on reducing kidney stones than lemonade. That's because orange juice contains potassium, which increases citrate levels, while lemonade doesn't.

In a study at the University of Texas Southwestern Medical Center in Dallas, men with histories of kidney stones were given either three glasses of orange juice a day or potassium-citrate supplements. The researchers found that the juice was almost as effective as the supplements. "We recommend drinking at least a liter (a little more than 32 ounces) a day if you have stones, because of its content of potassium and citrate," says Dr. Ruml.

Help from Magnesium

Your body is full of minerals that are constantly being adjusted for balance. Eating foods that are rich in magnesium, Dr. Ruml says, can help prevent stones by lowering the amount of another mineral, called oxalate. This mineral can be a problem because it's one of the main components of kidney stones.

Fish, rice, avocados, and broccoli all are rich in magnesium. A 3-ounce fillet of baked or broiled halibut, for example, has 91 milligrams of magnesium, or 23 percent of the Daily Value (DV). A half-cup of cooked long-grain brown rice has 42 milligrams, and a floret of cooked broccoli has 43 milligrams, or 11 percent of the DV.

Here's another easy way to get more magnesium. Drink some fortified, low-fat milk. If your doctor has recommended that you restrict dairy foods, however, don't drink more than 8 ounces a day, says Dr. Ruml.

Of course, it's also helpful to get less oxalate in your diet, Dr. Ruml says. If you're prone to kidney stones, it's a good idea to limit yourself to one serving a week of oxalate-rich foods, such as black tea, chocolate, peanuts and other nuts, spinach and other leafy greens, and strawberries.

Fiber for the Stone-Prone

If you want to leave no stone unturned, getting more fiber in your diet can be a smart strategy. In a study at the Stone Clinic at Halifax Infirmary Hospital in Nova Scotia, 21 people were put on a low-stone (low-protein, low-calcium, and low-oxalate) diet. After 90 days, they followed the same diet but also were given 10 grams (a little more than ⅓ ounce) of dietary fiber in the form of high-fiber biscuits. While the original diet helped reduce the amount of calcium in the urine, the extra fiber reduced it even more.

Doctors still aren't sure how effective fiber is at treating or preventing kidney stones, Dr. Ruml adds. "It's probably safe to say that the higher your fiber intake, the more likely you are to bind calcium and oxalate in the intestine, which will lower the urinary levels of these minerals," she says.

One more point about fiber: While reducing the amount of calcium in the urine may be beneficial for people with stones, it's not so good for those trying to prevent osteoporosis, the bone-thinning disease caused by low levels of calcium. "Some people with kidney stones may be prone to osteoporosis," Dr. Ruml says. The bottom line for the stone-prone: Check with your doctor before substantially increasing your fiber intake.

> ### Doctor's Top Tip
>
> Doctors say drinking lots of water is the most important way to prevent all kinds of kidney stones. The National Institutes of Health in Bethesda, Maryland, recommends drinking enough liquids to create 2 quarts of urine every 24 hours. That's about a gallon of water a day.

The Calcium Controversy

Doctors used to commonly tell patients that they could avoid kidney stones by limiting calcium intake, but more recent studies have found that getting more calcium can actually prevent kidney stones. A Harvard study of nearly 46,000 men found that those who ate the most calcium were the least likely to form stones.

A 2002 study that followed 120 men with recurrent kidney stones for 5 years found that the men who ate a normal amount of calcium but who cut down on meat and salt were less likely to have kidney stones than men who ate the traditional low-calcium diet.

While vegetables such as broccoli and turnip greens have some calcium, the easiest way to get adequate amounts is by drinking milk and eating other dairy foods. A glass of protein-fortified fat-free milk, for example, has 351 milligrams of calcium. A cup of low-fat yogurt has 414 milligrams, and 1½ ounces of mozzarella cheese made from fat-free milk has 270 milligrams.

Because calcium supplements have been associated with an increase in kidney stones, experts recommend getting calcium from your food rather than a pill.

Meat

A MINE OF MINERALS

Americans are back in the saddle again. After a decade of searching for greener pastures, we've decided that the grass was actually pretty tasty back at the ranch. So we're stampeding back, steaks in hand, ready to hit the backyard barbecue.

Does this latest swing back to red meat mean that we're headed straight for imminent health disaster? Not at all. In moderation, lean meats—not just beef but also pork, venison, and other meats with less than 25 to 30 percent of calories from fat—can provide significant health benefits, from preventing vitamin and mineral deficiencies and boosting immunity to building stronger blood.

"People read these reports that red meat causes cancer and heart disease, so they think that they have to stop eating meat altogether," says Susan Kleiner, PhD, RD, owner of High Performance Nutrition in Mercer Island, Washington, and author of *The Good Mood Diet*. "What they don't realize is that the people in these studies are eating 10 ounces of red meat a day."

"Moderation is the key," urges Dr. Kleiner. "When it comes to red meat, you should have no more than 3 to 5 ounces a day. That's about the size of a deck of cards. For a lot of people, that looks like a garnish. But if you use just enough meat to accent a meal, you'll be able to get all the benefits without the potential detriments."

To know what a true 3-ounce serving of meat is, you may want to weigh it on a kitchen scale, says Christine Gerbstadt, MD, RD, a spokesperson for the American Dietetic Association. It's an eye-opener for people because they often don't know what a healthy serving of meat looks like.

Ironing Out Anemia

Iron deficiency is the most common nutritional deficiency in the United States. Maybe that's why fatigue, the main symptom of iron-deficiency anemia, is the number one reason that people drag themselves to see their doctors.

Meat is an important source of iron, a mineral that's essential for boosting the oxygen-carrying capability of blood. Once you've depleted your iron stores, your red

LIKE BEEF? CHOOSE LEAN CUTS

If you like eating beef, there's good news. Your favorite meat is getting leaner. In fact, many cuts of beef are 20 percent leaner than they were in 1990, according to the National Cattlemen's Beef Association, which lists 19 cuts of beef from the USDA Nutrient Database that meet government guidelines for being lean. The cuts, beginning with the leanest, include:

- Eye round roast
- Top round steak
- Mock tender steak
- Bottom round roast
- Top sirloin steak
- Round tip roast
- 95% lean ground beef

- Brisket (flat half)
- Shank crosscuts
- Chuck shoulder roast
- Arm pot roast
- Shoulder steak
- Top loin (strip or New York) steak

- Flank steak
- Ribeye steak
- Rib steak
- Tri-tip roast
- Tenderloin steak
- T-bone steak

blood cells get smaller. This makes it difficult for your lungs to send enough oxygen to the rest of your body. Without enough oxygen, you start feeling worn out. This may become even more apparent if you exercise.

In addition, those who exercise are at higher risk for anemia, says Dr. Kleiner. That's because the body uses more iron during exercise to meet the increased demand for oxygen. If you don't have enough iron to begin with, it's easy to run out while you're working up a sweat.

What's so special about meat when you can also get iron from nonmeat sources like fortified breakfast cereals, tofu, and beans? Or, for that matter, when you can take an iron supplement?

For one thing, meats are unusually rich in iron. A 3-ounce serving of top round, for example, contains 3 milligrams of iron, or 30 percent of the Recommended Dietary Allowance (RDA) for men. A 3-ounce serving of pork tenderloin has 1 milligram of iron.

Even though some plant foods are rich in iron—a baked potato, for example, contains 3 milligrams—it comes in a form that's harder for your body to absorb than the iron found in meats.

Meats contain a type of iron called heme iron, which is up to 15 percent more absorbable than nonheme iron, the kind found in plant foods. Plus, when you eat heme iron from meats, it helps your body absorb nonheme iron, so you get the maximum iron absorption from all your food, says Dr. Kleiner.

Zinc Immunity

Your immune system's duty is to keep your body from falling down on the job. Zinc's duty is to keep your immune system from doing the same. Not getting enough of this important mineral means that your immune system will have a harder time fending off infections, colds, and other health invaders.

As with iron, you can get zinc from foods besides meats, such as whole grains and wheat germ. But again, your body has a harder time retrieving zinc from plant sources, whereas the zinc in meats is readily absorbed, explains Dr. Kleiner.

By including a little meat in your diet, it's easy to meet the Daily Value (DV) of 15 milligrams of zinc. Three ounces of top round steak, for instance, provides 5 milligrams, or about a third of the DV for this essential mineral.

The Best of the Bs

For most of us, getting enough vitamin B_{12} (the DV is 6 micrograms) isn't a problem. If you eat meats, fish, eggs, poultry, or dairy products on a regular basis, you're almost certainly getting enough.

But if you don't eat these foods, and many strict vegetarians don't, you could be headed for trouble. Low levels of vitamin B_{12} can result in a rare and sometimes fatal blood disorder, called pernicious anemia, which causes fatigue, memory loss, and

In the Kitchen

Lean meats like top round steak and pork loin have all but supplanted their high-fat predecessors in healthy kitchens. To be truly good, however, they do require special handling.

To ensure that your lean meat meals are moist and flavorful, try the following cooking tips:

Start with a marinade. Marinating lean meats in the refrigerator several hours prior to preparation will infuse them with flavor and add extra liquid to help keep them moist during cooking. There are so many options for healthy marinades, says Christine Gerbstadt, MD, RD, a spokesperson for the American Dietetic Association. One easy marinade is to use ¼ cup of lemon juice, ¼ cup of vinegar, ¼ cup of a healthy oil such as canola or olive oil, and your favorite seasoning, such as fresh garlic, freshly ground black pepper, or dried herbs.

Add fat-free flavor while cooking. People tend to add fat to meat when they're cooking it to give it more flavor, Dr. Gerbstadt says, but it's just as easy and even more delicious to flavor your meat with healthier options. When grilling or broiling, add a fat-free salsa or sauce or fresh herbs to the meat near the end of cooking.

other neurological problems. And worse, you may not even know that there's a problem until it's already well advanced.

"Pernicious anemia comes on very slowly and can take up to 7 years to develop," says Dr. Kleiner. "And because one of the symptoms of the illness is deteriorating mental function, lots of people aren't even aware that there's anything wrong with them. It can take a long time to straighten this problem out, and the damage can be irreversible, especially in children."

Including small amounts of meats or other animal foods in your diet on a regular basis makes it easy to get enough vitamin B$_{12}$, says Dr. Kleiner. If you're a strict vegetarian who doesn't get vitamin B$_{12}$ from animal foods, it's essential that you take a daily supplement or eat soy foods such as tempeh and miso, which are high in this nutrient. In addition, many cereals, pastas, and other packaged foods have been fortified with vitamin B$_{12}$, she points out.

Most meats are full of other B vitamins as well. They generally provide 10 to 20 percent of the DV for B-complex vitamins: riboflavin (essential for tissue repair), vitamin B$_6$ (needed for immunity), niacin (vital for skin, nerves, and digestion), and thiamin (which helps the body convert blood sugar into energy).

GETTING THE MOST

Buy free-range. For the best healing meats, some experts advise, look for "free-range" meats or "grass-fed" beef. These are meats that come from livestock that is allowed to roam free instead of being restricted in close quarters. Because the animals aren't crammed together, the ranchers generally use fewer antibiotics and skip the growth hormones, explains Dr. Kleiner.

"Although I recommend organic, chemical-free meat, if the higher price is going to keep you from eating it, don't worry about the chemicals, and get the nutrients," recommends Dr. Kleiner. "In the long run, that's more important."

Add some variety. Although much of the research on the health benefits of meats has been done in studies with lean beef, experts are quick to note that you

(continued on page 160)

THE BEST CUTS

While meats can play a valuable role in a healthful diet, it's important to shop only for those items that are suitably low in fat—preferably with no more than 25 to 30 percent of calories coming from fat. In the following table, we've listed a few meats (and a variety of

Cut	Calories	Fat (g)	Calories from Fat	Vitamin B$_{12}$ (mcg)	Zinc (mg)
Beef—eye round	143	4	26%	2 (33% of DV)	4 (27% of DV)
Beef—top round	153	4	25%	2 (12% of DV)	5 (11% of DV)
Pork tenderloin	141	4	26%	—	3 (20% of DV)
Lamb foreshank	159	5	29%	2 (33% of DV)	7 (47% of DV)
Venison	134	3	18%	—	2 (13% of DV)
Elk	124	2	12%	—	3 (20% of DV)
Veal leg	128	3	20%	1 (17% of DV)	3 (20% of DV)
Moose	114	1	6%	—	3 (20% of DV)
Bison/ Buffalo	122	2	15%	—	2 (13% of DV)
Emu	103	3	23%	—	—

cuts) that you may want to try. Only prominent nutrients—those providing more than 10 percent of the DV—are mentioned. All nutritional information is based on 3-ounce servings.

Iron (mg)	Niacin (mg)	Vitamin B_6 (mg)	Potassium (mg)	Riboflavin (mg)	Thiamin (mg)
2 (20% of RDA for men and 13% for women)	3 (15% of DV)	0.3 (15% of DV)	—	—	—
3 (30% of RDA for men and 20% for women)	5 (25% of DV)	0.5 (25% of DV)	376 (33% of DV)	0.2 (33% of DV)	—
1 (10% of RDA for men and 7% for women)	4 (20% of DV)	0.4 (20% of DV)	457 (13% of DV)	0.3 (18% of DV)	0.8 (53% of DV)
—	14 (70% of DV)	—	—	—	—
4 (40% of RDA for men and 27% for women)	6 (30% of DV)	—	—	0.5 (29% of DV)	0.2 (13% of DV)
3 (31% of RDA for men and 21% for women)	—	—	—	—	—
—	9 (45% of DV)	0.3 (15% of DV)	—	0.3 (18% of DV)	—
4 (40% of RDA for men and 27% for women)	5 (25% of DV)	—	—	0.3 (18% of DV)	—
3 (30% of RDA for men and 20% for women)	—	—	—	—	—
4 (40% of RDA for men and 27% for women)	—	—	—	—	—

SAFER GRILLING

Grilled foods taste great, but for a long time, researchers have worried about their safety. The problem is that grilling causes certain compounds in meats to change into other compounds called heterocyclic amines, which may increase the risk for cancer. Charring or burning your meat on the grill carries the biggest risks to health.

What's a grill-chef to do? The answer, some researchers say, can be summarized in one word: marinade. In one study, researchers found that when medallions of chicken breast were marinated (or even dipped) in a mixture of olive oil, brown sugar, mustard, and other spices before being grilled, they contained 90 percent less of the dangerous compounds than nonmarinated meat that was cooked the same way. Another good rule of thumb: Don't eat the blackened or burned parts of the meat.

shouldn't limit yourself to eating beef alone. Other meats such as pork and lamb can also play a role in a healthful diet. "In the same way that you should eat a wide variety of whole grains and vegetables, you should also eat a variety of meats to ensure that you get all the nutrients they have to offer," advises Dr. Kleiner.

You might also want to take a walk on the wild side and go with game. Many people believe that game meats such as venison are tastier than more pedestrian meats such as beef. In addition, game is generally much leaner—deriving less than 18 percent of its calories from fat—while delivering the same powerhouse of B vitamins and minerals. To compare: A lean cut of beef, such as top round steak, has 34 percent calories from fat.

Horseradish-Spiked Pork and Apples

12 **ounces pork tenderloin, trimmed of fat**

2 **medium apples**

2 **tablespoons all-purpose flour**

1 **cup apple cider**

1 **tablespoon extra-hot horseradish**

Cut the pork crosswise into ¼-inch-thick slices. Core the apples and cut into thin slices.

Coat a large nonstick skillet with cooking spray, and heat over medium-high heat. Add the pork and cook until lightly golden on the bottom, about 2 minutes. Turn and cook until lightly golden on the second side and cooked through, 2 to 3 minutes longer. Test for doneness by inserting the tip of a sharp knife in a piece of the pork. Remove the pork to a clean plate, and set aside.

Reduce the heat to medium. Add the apples and cook, stirring occasionally, until they begin to turn light golden, 3 to 4 minutes. Sprinkle with the flour, and continue cooking, tossing to coat evenly with the flour.

Stir in the cider. Cook, stirring, until the sauce thickens, 3 to 4 minutes. Stir in the horseradish. Spoon the apples and sauce over the pork.

Makes 4 servings

PER SERVING ——————————

Calories: 218
Total fat: 6.3 g
Saturated fat: 2.2 g

Cholesterol: 52 mg
Sodium: 38 mg
Dietary fiber: 1.6 g

Beef and Spinach Stir-Fry

1 pound beef eye of round, trimmed of fat

1 tablespoon cornstarch

2 teaspoons canola oil

2 teaspoons grated fresh ginger

1 small onion, thinly sliced

1 bag (6 ounces) spinach, washed and trimmed

⅓ cup defatted beef broth

2 tablespoons ketchup

Freshly ground black pepper

Cut the beef across the grain into very thin slices. Place in a medium bowl. Add the cornstarch, and toss to coat.

In a wok or large skillet, heat the oil over medium-high heat until it is nearly smoking. Add the beef and ginger. Stir-fry until the beef is no longer pink on the surface, about 2 minutes. Transfer to a plate.

Add the onion to the pan, and stir-fry until softened, 1 to 2 minutes. Add the spinach, and stir-fry until just wilted, about 30 seconds.

In a small bowl, combine the broth and ketchup. Add to the pan. Add the beef. Stir-fry until the sauce is heated through and coats the beef and vegetables, 2 to 3 minutes. Season to taste with pepper.

Makes 4 servings

Cook's Note: *Serve over rice or noodles.*

PER SERVING ———————————

Calories: 207	Cholesterol: 61 mg
Total fat: 7.6 g	Sodium: 263 mg
Saturated fat: 2.1 g	Dietary fiber: 1.6 g

Muscle Cramps
EASE THEM WITH ELECTROLYTES

Whether you're on a treadmill, writing a letter, or even lying in bed at night, your muscles are constantly contracting and relaxing. As a result, they need a lot of nourishment. When they don't get it, they'll sometimes contract into tight, painful spasms known as muscle cramps. Cramps are a muscle's way of telling you it's tired, hungry, and in need of rest.

Muscle cramps are painful, but they play a protective role, says Leslie Bonci, RD, a dietitian at the University of Pittsburgh Medical Center and a spokesperson for the American Dietetic Association. Essentially, they force the muscle to remain inactive until it has time to recover, usually within a few minutes.

While you can't prevent muscle cramps entirely, choosing the right foods will make them less likely to return. Here's how it works.

Help from Minerals

Muscles don't move without orders from the brain. Before you can stand up, blink an eye, or turn the pages of this book, the brain sends electrical messages to the appropriate muscles, telling them when (and how much) to contract or relax. Minerals such as calcium, potassium, sodium, and magnesium, which are known as electrolytes, play a role in helping the messages get through, says Joel Press, MD, medical director of the Spine and Sports Rehabilitation Center at the Rehabilitation Institute of Chicago.

If you haven't been getting enough of these minerals or have sweated them out during vigorous exercise, a muscle may not get the message to relax. This can cause it to contract in a painful cramp.

Of all the electrolytes, magnesium is one of the most important, because it helps other electrolytes do their jobs, says Robert McLean, MD, associate clinical professor of internal medicine and rheumatology at Yale University School of Medicine. When you don't eat enough magnesium-rich foods, minerals such as calcium and potassium can't get into muscle-fiber cells. So even if you have an abundance of other electrolytes, without magnesium, they may be locked out and ineffective. "People who are depleted of magnesium tend to have greater irritability of the muscles and nerves," says Dr. McLean. "This irritability may cause muscle cramping."

Here are a few tips for improving your electrolyte balance:

Get magnesium from tofu, spinach, and Spanish mackerel. A serving of tofu has 128 milligrams of magnesium, or 32 percent of the Daily Value (DV). A serving of spinach has about 44 milligrams, or 11 percent of the DV, and a serving of mackerel has 82 milligrams, or 20 percent of the DV.

Include dairy in your diet. Calcium helps regulate the muscles' ability to contract. Dairy foods are the best sources. A cup of fat-free milk, for example, has nearly 302 milligrams of calcium, or 30 percent of the DV, while a serving of low-fat yogurt has 77 milligrams, or 7 percent of the DV.

Choose potassium-rich bananas and potatoes. Getting enough potassium in your diet may also be helpful for preventing cramps, says Dr. Press. Bananas are a good source of potassium, with one banana supplying 451 milligrams, or 13 percent of the DV. Potatoes are also a good source, with a half-cup containing 114 milligrams, or 3 percent of the DV.

Say no to sodium. For most people, the problem isn't getting enough sodium, it's getting too much, since this mineral is found in large amounts in many foods, particularly processed foods. And for those who are sensitive, sodium can lead to fluid retention and high blood pressure. So even if you have been getting cramps, leave the sodium alone—you're almost certainly getting enough.

Hydrate, hydrate, hydrate. Whenever you perspire, you lose fluids from the muscle cells, which can result in cramping, Bonci says. And you're more likely to get muscle cramps when you exercise in hot weather because you'll be sweating more and losing fluid, salt, and minerals that keep your muscles working optimally. Sipping water frequently throughout the day will help keep electrolyte levels in balance. When you're planning on being active, it's a good idea to drink at least 16 ounces of water or juice to prime your body with the necessary minerals.

Dodge cramps with carbs. Muscles need more than electrolytes and water to function well. They also need glycogen, a sugar that comes from carbohydrates. Getting plenty of carbohydrates in your diet will help keep muscles working well. Good sources include potatoes, rice, bananas, and bread.

Nuts

A SHELL GAME YOU CAN WIN

The ancient Persians believed that eating five almonds before drinking alcoholic beverages would prevent intoxication, or at least the hangover that might follow. They also believed that almonds would ward off witches and stimulate milk production in nursing mothers.

As nutty as this seems today, it's not surprising that ancient civilizations took their nuts seriously. Not only are nuts a compact source of energy, they also are easily stored through cold winters and hot summers, making them available throughout the year. What's more, nuts contain a number of compounds that may help prevent heart disease and cancer.

The Fat Factor

Before we talk about the health benefits of nuts, it's important to discuss one of their potential drawbacks. While nuts are high in nutrients, they're also high in fat. One-third cup of nuts typically contains anywhere from 240 to 300 calories and 20 to 25 grams of fat.

Not all types of nuts are loaded with fat, but most are. The coconut, for example, contains a lot of fat, and most of it is the dangerous saturated kind. "On the other end of the spectrum is the chestnut, which is extremely low in fat, and almost all of it is unsaturated," points out Joan Sabaté, MD, DrPH, chairman of the department of nutrition and associate professor of nutrition and epidemiology at Loma Linda University School of Public Health in California.

"It's very unfortunate that people shun nuts just because they're high in calories," Dr. Sabaté adds. "The trick to eating nuts is not overdoing it—fitting them wisely into a healthy eating plan."

If you're worried about gaining weight from eating nuts, consider this. A review of top studies by researchers at Loma Linda University found that eating nuts is not associated with obesity. For instance, people who live in the Mediterranean eat twice as many nuts as Americans, but their rates of obesity are much lower. In one study, 81 people were given raw and dry-roasted almonds to add to their diet. After

6 months, the men in the study gained less than 2 pounds (and women saw no significant weight gain). The study authors suggest that the protein and fiber in nuts may help us feel full so that we eat less of other foods.

As you add nuts to your diet, be sure to get less of other, less healthy fats, such as butter, hydrogenated margarines, and nutrient-empty snack foods such as chips and cookies, Dr. Sabaté says.

Here are some easy ways to make a healthy substitution. Choose 2 tablespoons of slivered almonds over ⅔ cup of a low-fiber cereal, or have 4 tablespoons of pistachios instead of 1 cup of cooked pasta, or add 1 tablespoon of chopped walnuts to your salad instead of ¼ cup of seasoned croutons.

Good for the Heart—and the Gallbladder

One great thing about nuts is that they contain a number of compounds that help keep the arteries open and blood flowing smoothly.

It was quite by accident that researchers at Loma Linda University discovered that eating nuts seems to protect against heart disease. They asked 26,000 members of the Seventh-Day Adventist Church, an extremely health-conscious bunch, to indicate the frequency with which they ate 65 food items.

As it turns out, the Adventists are very fond of nuts. Twenty-four percent ate nuts at least five times a week. In the population at large, by contrast, only 5 percent of people eat them that often. As the researchers discovered, this difference in nut consumption made a colossal difference in heart disease risk. Eating nuts just one to four

In the Kitchen

Blending your own peanut butter is a lot of fun. Not only does it taste good, depending on the amount of oil you add, it also has a bit less fat than the store-bought kind. Plus, it's very easy to make. Here's how:

- Buy roasted peanuts, the kind that come in a vacuum-sealed can or jar. You can also use roasted peanuts in the shell, but shelling them requires more work.
- For each cup of peanuts you use, add 1½ to 2 tablespoons of canola or another light-flavored oil. Some people will add ½ teaspoon of salt per cup of peanuts, but this is optional.
- Put the peanuts and oil in a blender, and purée until you get the texture you want—extra-chunky, chunky, or creamy.
- Transfer the peanut butter to a jar, and store in the refrigerator. It will stay fresh for 3 to 4 months. However, the oils in "natural" peanut butter will separate, so be sure to stir it well before using.

times a week reduced the risk of dying from artery-clogging heart disease by 25 percent. People who ate them five or more times per week slashed their risks in half.

Researchers aren't sure which nuts made the most difference. Among the most popular choices were peanuts, almonds, and walnuts. (Even though peanuts are technically a legume, they're nutritionally similar to nuts and, in fact, are sometimes referred to as ground-nuts.)

What is it about nuts, which are practically dripping with oil, that amazingly defats arteries? "With a few exceptions, most nuts are high in monounsaturated and polyunsaturated fats," says Dr. Sabaté. "When these types of fats replace saturated fats in the diet, they can help lower total cholesterol as well as the unhealthy low-density lipoprotein (LDL) cholesterol." At the same time, nuts don't affect levels of the heart-healthy high-density lipoprotein (HDL) cholesterol.

A study in the journal *Circulation* found that bad LDL cholesterol levels fell 4 percent and good HDL cholesterol levels rose 5 percent in people who ate 25 almonds a day.

Another thing that makes nuts healthy for the heart is an amino acid called arginine. Some arginine may be converted in the body to nitric oxide, a compound that helps expand the blood vessels. In fact, it acts much like the drug nitroglycerin, which is used to rapidly dilate arteries to permit more blood to reach the heart. Nitric oxide also appears to help keep the platelets in blood from clumping, which can further reduce heart disease risk.

"Nuts are also high in vitamin E, which may keep LDL cholesterol from oxidizing," says Dr. Sabaté. This is the process that makes cholesterol more likely to stick to artery walls and block bloodflow. Nuts have more vitamin E than any other food, with the exception of oils. Almonds and walnuts are particularly good choices. One-third cup of either nut contains about 12 IU, or 40 percent of the Daily Value (DV) for this vitamin.

Nuts also contain generous amounts of heart-healthy copper and magnesium. Magnesium appears to regulate cholesterol and blood pressure as well as heart rhythms, while copper may play a role in lowering cholesterol.

Interestingly, in the same way that nuts help keep arteries clear and free of blockages, they also help prevent gallstones, which block the release of bile from the

Doctor's Top Tip

An ounce, or one handful, a day of nuts is a healthy amount, suggests Andrew Weil, MD, clinical professor of medicine and director of the integrative medicine program at the University of Arizona in Tucson. To get the benefits of omega-3 fatty acids, choose cashews, almonds, and walnuts.

gallbladder. Researchers at Harvard Medical School followed 81,000 adults over 20 years and found that those who ate 5 or more ounces of peanuts, peanut butter, or other nuts a week were 25 percent less likely to need gallbladder surgery.

Preventing Cancer

Just as nuts contain compounds that may help prevent heart disease, they also contain compounds that may help stop cancer.

Walnuts, for example, contain a compound called ellagic acid that appears to battle cancer on several fronts. "Ellagic acid is a good antioxidant, disabling harmful oxygen molecules, called free radicals, that are known to instigate the cancer process," says Gary Stoner, PhD, professor and cancer researcher at Ohio State University in Columbus. Ellagic acid also helps detoxify potential cancer-causing substances, while at the same time helping to prevent cancer cells from dividing.

In one study, laboratory animals given ellagic acid as well as a cancer-causing substance were 33 percent less likely to develop esophageal cancer than animals given only carcinogens. In another study, laboratory animals were 70 percent less likely to develop liver tumors when they were given purified ellagic acid.

The vitamin E in nuts also appears to help in cancer prevention. In 2004, researchers at Purdue University in West Lafayette, Indiana, found that gamma-tocopherol, a form of vitamin E in walnuts and pecans, killed human prostate and lung cancer cells in the laboratory, while leaving healthy cells untouched.

A Nutritional Payload

All nuts are richly endowed with protein, and most contain a generous supply of vitamins and minerals as well as dietary fiber.

While the plain old peanut doesn't hit the charts for healing potential, it's the highest in protein of any nut, with ⅓ cup containing more than 11 grams, or 22 percent of the DV. That's more protein than you'll get from the same amount of beef or fish. Better yet, the protein in peanuts is a complete protein, meaning that it contains all the essential amino acids we can't do without. Brazil nuts, cashews, walnuts, and almonds also are good sources of protein, each containing at least 6 grams in ⅓ cup, or 12 percent of the DV.

In addition, all nuts are a good source of fiber, with ⅓ cup typically containing 1 to 2 grams—about the amount in a similar amount of Cheerios. Among the most fiber-rich nuts are pistachios (nearly 5 grams per ⅓ cup, or almost 20 percent of the DV) and almonds (just over 6 grams, or about 24 percent of the DV).

Spiced Almond Cereal Snack Mix

1 egg white

1½ teaspoons Cajun seasoning blend

1 teaspoon Worcestershire sauce

½ teaspoon garlic powder

1 teaspoon water

2 cups whole-wheat cereal squares

1½ cups whole almonds

Preheat the oven to 300°F. Coat a rimmed baking sheet with cooking spray.

In a large bowl, combine the egg white, Cajun seasoning, Worcestershire sauce, garlic powder, and water. Whisk to thoroughly mix. Add the cereal and almonds. Toss well to coat.

Spread the mixture out evenly on the prepared pan. Bake for 30 minutes, or until golden and crisp. Allow to cool. Store in an airtight tin or jar.

Makes about 3⅓ cups

PER ⅓ CUP

Calories: 139	Cholesterol: 0 mg
Total fat: 11 g	Sodium: 146 mg
Saturated fat: 1.1 g	Dietary fiber: 2.9 g

Walnut and Red Pepper Pasta Topping

⅔ cup chopped walnuts

⅔ cup chopped roasted peppers

2 cloves garlic, minced

2 tablespoons minced parsley

⅛ teaspoon salt

⅛ teaspoon crushed red pepper flakes

In a large nonstick skillet, heat the walnuts over medium heat, shaking the pan frequently, until toasted and fragrant, 1 to 2 minutes.

Stir in the roasted peppers, garlic, parsley, salt, and red pepper flakes. Cook, stirring frequently, until heated through, about 3 minutes. If the mixture starts to stick to the pan, add a little water.

Makes 1⅓ cups

PER ⅓ CUP

Calories: 149	Cholesterol: 0 mg
Total fat: 13 g	Sodium: 240 mg
Saturated fat: 1.2 g	Dietary fiber: 1.4 g

Oats

MOPPING UP CHOLESTEROL

If it weren't for horses, we probably wouldn't even know about oats, to say nothing of the great health benefits they provide. When horses were introduced in various parts of the world, oats went along as their feed. Not surprisingly, however, humans were a bit reluctant to take a taste. Samuel Johnson's 1755 *Dictionary of the English Language* defined oats as "a grain which in England is generally given to horses, but which in Scotland supports the people." It seems that the Scots were ahead of their time.

Oats are a very healthful grain. For one thing, unlike wheat, barley, and other grains, processed oats retain the bran and germ layers, which is where most of the nutrients reside. In addition, oats contain a variety of compounds that have been shown to reduce heart disease, fight cancer, lower blood sugar, improve insulin sensitivity, and help with dieting.

Help for High Cholesterol

All you have to do is watch some television before you come across a commercial that says oatmeal can help lower cholesterol, a critical move in reducing the risk of heart disease. In fact, studies show that getting more oats in the diet not only lowers total cholesterol but, more encouragingly, lowers the bad low-density lipoprotein (LDL) cholesterol while leaving the beneficial high-density lipoprotein (HDL) cholesterol alone.

A Tufts University study compared a low-calorie diet that included oats to one that didn't. Although both diets helped the study participants lose weight, those who ate oats experienced a bigger drop in blood pressure, total cholesterol, and bad LDL cholesterol.

Oats contain a type of soluble fiber called beta-glucan, which traps dietary cholesterol within a sticky gel in the intestine. Since this gel isn't absorbed by the body, it passes through the intestine, taking unwanted cholesterol with it. Americans get only about half of the recommended 25 grams of a fiber a day, and oats have more soluble fiber than any other grain.

Studies have shown that people with high cholesterol benefit from eating oats and other foods high in fiber. Weight loss helps lower cholesterol, but data from 13 studies found that the fiber from two servings of oats a day helped lower cholesterol an additional 2 to 3 percent more than modifying fat did.

Soluble fiber isn't the only thing doing the trapping. Oats also contain compounds called saponins, which in preliminary animal studies appear to bind to cholesterol and usher it out of the body. Saponins also glom onto bile acids. This is good because high levels of bile acids can cause cholesterol levels to rise.

"We used to think that saponins had only negative effects on the body," says Joanne L. Slavin, PhD, professor of nutrition at the University of Minnesota in St. Paul. "In fact, we call them anti-nutrients because they inhibit the absorption of various nutritional substances. But their positive health benefits are clearly stronger than their negative attributes."

It doesn't take a loaf of oats to lower cholesterol. Having about ¾ cup of dry oatmeal (which cooks up to about 1½ cups) or just less than ½ cup of dry oat bran (which cooks up to about 1 cup) a day can help lower total cholesterol by up to 5 percent.

A Stable of Protection

Like all plant foods, oats contain a variety of compounds that provide different kinds of protection. Three of these compounds—tocotrienols (related to vitamin E), ferulic acid, and caffeic acid—are antioxidants. That is, they help control cell-damaging particles called free radicals, which, when left unchecked, can contribute to heart disease, cancer, and certain eye diseases.

Tocotrienols, which are richly abundant in oats, pack at least two punches against heart disease. They're very effective at stopping oxidation, the process that causes LDL cholesterol to turn rancid and stick to artery walls. Indeed, tocotrienols are 50 percent more powerful than vitamin E, says David J. A. Jenkins, MD, DSc, PhD, professor of nutritional sciences at the University of Toronto. In addition, tocotrienols act on the liver, which might turn down the body's own production of cholesterol.

Battling Cancer

Some of the same compounds in oats that protect against heart disease may also help prevent cancer, says A. Venket Rao, PhD, professor of nutrition at the University of Toronto.

We've already discussed how the saponins in oats bind to bile acids. This is important because, while bile acids are necessary for the absorption and digestion of fat, they also cause problems. In the large intestine, they get converted by bacteria into a form called secondary bile acids. Secondary bile acids can damage intestinal cells, possibly setting in motion the events that lead to cancer. "By binding up bile acids and reducing the amount that can be transformed into a toxic version, saponins may help lower cancer risk," says Dr. Rao.

In addition, saponins appear to strengthen the immune system, making the body better able to detect and deactivate foreign invaders such as bacteria, viruses, and cancer cells. "In animal experiments, the addition of saponins to the diet increased the number of natural killer cells, which translates into a stronger immune surveillance system," says Dr. Rao.

Other compounds in oats protect against cancer in much the same way that they help prevent heart disease—by neutralizing cell-damaging free radicals before they cause harm.

Oats also contain generous amounts of a compound called phytic acid, says Dr. Slavin. "Although we haven't identified the exact mechanism, there's some evidence that phytic acid binds up certain reactive minerals, which may be important in preventing colon cancer."

In addition, the fiber in oats helps this food fight cancer. In 2001, 54 cancer experts wrote in a public letter that they agreed that high-fiber diets offer protection from cancer. They found more than 200 studies that said so, compared with only three studies that don't show a connection between high-fiber diets and lower risk for cancer.

In the Kitchen

Oats are among the easiest foods to cook. Just add one part oatmeal to two parts water, cover, simmer, and serve. Here are a few ways to change both the texture and the taste of oats to suit your personal preference.

Cream them with milk. Cooking oats in milk instead of water yields a much creamier porridge, which some people prefer to the firmer, water-cooked variety. Choose low-fat or fat-free milk to avoid additional fat.

Make them coarser. If you prefer your oats with a firm, slightly coarse texture, chefs advise adding the oats to water that's already boiling rather than mixing them with cold water and then raising the heat.

Change the taste. To add extra flavor to oats, you can eliminate the water or milk altogether and cook them in apple, pear, or peach juice. Since the sugars in fruit juices can readily scorch and give the cereal a slightly burnt taste, make sure that you use a heavy-bottomed pan or use a double boiler over a slow, steady heat, and watch the time carefully.

Keeping Blood Sugar Steady

Another benefit of oats is that they appear to help keep the body's blood sugar levels in balance. This is important for the estimated 21 million Americans with impaired glucose tolerance, a condition that is similar to diabetes and that increases the risks of heart disease and strokes.

In people with this condition, blood sugar levels are higher than they should be, but not so high that the people are actually diabetic. Yet even slightly elevated blood sugar levels may be cause for concern because they cause the body to pump out larger amounts of insulin to bring them down.

The soluble fiber in oats lays down a protective gummy layer in the intestine. This slows the rate at which carbohydrates are absorbed by the body, which in turn helps keep blood sugar levels stable. In addition, soluble fiber appears to reduce the output of hormones in the digestive tract, which indirectly lowers the body's production of insulin.

Here's an additional benefit of the soluble fiber in oats. Because this type of fiber soaks up lots of water, it creates a feeling of fullness. This means that when you eat oats, you feel satisfied longer and so are more likely to eat less, which is good news for anyone who's trying to lose weight.

In one study by the New York Obesity Research Center at St. Luke's–Roosevelt Hospital in New York City, 60 people who ate oatmeal for breakfast instead of cornflakes had 30 percent fewer calories at lunch.

Help for HIV

Although the evidence is still preliminary, the saponins in oats may be effective in disabling HIV, the virus that causes AIDS.

It's long been a puzzling fact that while some people infected with HIV develop AIDS relatively quickly, others don't become sick for years. Scientists are working to discover what makes HIV stronger, or more virulent, in some people.

It could be that various compounds found in food, including the saponins in oats, may play a role in squelching HIV. "Although this research is in its very early stages, it certainly is something to pursue," says Dr. Rao.

GETTING THE MOST

Look for 3 grams or more. Cereal and bread that contain oats are considered a good source of fiber if they have at least 3 grams per serving, so check the nutrition label to make sure you're getting the best health benefit from your food. An excellent source of fiber contains 5 grams or more a serving.

Eat for convenience. Unlike many foods, in which the processed versions are often the least nutritious, oats retain their goodness in different forms. So when time is an issue, go ahead and enjoy quick oats. They provide just as many vitamins and minerals as the traditional, slower-cooking kind. Keep in mind, however, that quick oats do contain more sodium than their slower-cooking kin.

For protein, take your pick. Both rolled oats and oat bran are good sources of protein. One cup of cooked oat bran contains 7 grams, or 14 percent of the Daily Value (DV), while a serving of rolled oats has 6 grams, or 12 percent of the DV.

Cut calories with bran. When you're trying to eat lean, oat bran is often a better choice than oatmeal. A 1-cup serving of cooked oat bran contains 87 calories, whereas the same amount of oatmeal has 145.

Oatmeal-Apricot Cookies

- ⅔ cup dried apricots, coarsely chopped
- ⅓ cup boiling water
- 1 cup packed light brown sugar
- ¼ cup unsalted butter, at room temperature
- ¼ cup fat-free egg substitute
- 1½ teaspoons vanilla extract
- ½ cup all-purpose flour
- 1 teaspoon ground cinnamon
- 1 teaspoon baking soda
- ¼ teaspoon salt
- 2½ cups quick-cooking rolled oats

Preheat the oven to 350°F. Coat two baking sheets with cooking spray.

In a food processor, combine the apricots and water and process until well blended (some small chunks may remain).

Transfer to a large bowl. Add the brown sugar and butter. Beat with an electric mixer until well blended. Add the egg substitute and vanilla extract. Beat to mix.

Add the flour, cinnamon, baking soda, and salt. Beat just until well mixed. Sprinkle with the oats. Stir with a large spoon to mix.

Drop by tablespoonfuls onto the prepared baking sheets. Bake one sheet at a time until the cookies are golden, about 10 to 12 minutes. Transfer the cookies to a wire rack to cool. Store in a cookie jar or other covered container that's not airtight.

Makes 28 cookies

PER COOKIE

Calories: 78	Cholesterol: 4 mg
Total fat: 2.1 g	Sodium: 70 mg
Saturated fat: 1.1 g	Dietary fiber: 1 g

Olive Oil

AN ELIXIR FOR YOUR HEART

Researchers were amazed more than 40 years ago when they first started studying Greeks living on the island of Crete. Even though the traditional Greek diet is very high in fat, people had exceptionally low rates of heart disease. "They have to be doing something right, and olive oil seems to play a critical role," says Dimitrios Trichopoulos, MD, professor of epidemiology and cancer prevention at the Harvard School of Public Health.

We would do well to follow their example. Olive oil, which is made from crushed olives, not only appears to lower the risk of heart disease, it may reduce the risk of breast cancer as well.

A Better Fat

All fats, from butter and margarine to olive oil, contain almost the same number of calories. But they behave quite differently inside the body. Saturated fats, for example, which are found mainly in meats and dairy foods, are incredibly destructive because they make it difficult for the body to rid itself of harmful low-density lipoprotein (LDL) cholesterol, the kind that blocks arteries and raises the risk of heart disease.

Olive oil, however, is a monounsaturated fat. With no more than 2 grams of saturated fat per tablespoon, olive oil is recommended by the American Heart Association for your food preparation. Replacing saturated fats in the diet with olive oil lowers levels of LDL cholesterol while leaving the beneficial high-density lipoprotein (HDL) cholesterol alone.

Compared with butter, olive oil also seems to make us more satisfied, which means we won't overeat later. Researchers at the University of Illinois at Urbana-Champaign gave 341 restaurant diners bread and either olive oil or butter. Those who dipped their bread in olive oil tended to put 26 percent more fat on each bread slice, but those who had butter ate more bread, which added up to 17 percent more calories overall.

The olive oil–loving Greeks eat very little butter or margarine, Dr. Trichopoulos adds. What's more, their main meals usually consist of vegetables or legumes instead of meats. So even though they use a lot of olive oil, they get very little saturated fat.

One scientific project, called the Seven Countries Study, found that while 46 percent of deaths among middle-aged American men were due to heart disease, the number in Crete was a mere 4 percent—more than 10 times lower.

In addition to offering protection from heart disease, olive oil may help prevent many cancers by protecting cells in the body from oxidation. In a 2006 Denmark study, 182 European men included ¼ cup of olive oil in their diets every day. After 2 weeks, their DNA cells showed less oxidation, and, therefore, had more cancer protection.

Extra-virgin olive oil may also help lower the risk of rheumatoid arthritis, according to a Greek study published in the *American Journal of Clinical Nutrition*. The study authors examined the diets of 145 people with rheumatoid arthritis and 188 control subjects. They found that those who took in the lowest amount of extra-virgin olive oil over their lifetime were 2½ times more likely to develop rheumatoid arthritis than those who had the highest intake of the oil. Experts believe extra-virgin olive oil reduces the risk of rheumatoid arthritis because of its anti-inflammatory effects. One study found that the oil was similar to ibuprofen in reducing inflammation.

Chemicals for the Heart

It's not only the monounsaturated fat that makes olive oil good for the heart. It also contains other disease-fighting compounds that can prevent damage in the arteries before it starts.

In the Kitchen

Some olive oils are quite rare and exquisitely flavored—and exquisitely priced. Others are much more affordable and, of course, the flavors reflect that. Many cooks keep two (or more) kinds of olive oil in the kitchen—a gourmet oil for drizzling on salads or pastas and a heartier oil to use for cooking.

Extra-virgin is the Cadillac of olive oils. It's usually used as a flavoring oil and not for cooking. When buying extra-virgin olive oil,

look at the color. The deeper the color, the more intense the olive flavor.

Pure (also called virgin) olive oil is paler than extra-virgin and has a milder flavor. It's usually used for low- to medium-heat frying.

Light olive oil is often used by people who want the heart-healthy benefits of monounsaturated fats but don't want the strong olive taste. It stands up to heat well, so you can use it for high-heat frying.

Here's why. The body naturally produces harmful oxygen molecules called free radicals. These molecules damage LDL cholesterol in the bloodstream, making it more likely to stick to the linings of artery walls. But several of the compounds in olive oil, such as polyphenols, are powerful antioxidants. This means that they're able to disable free radicals before they do damage, Dr. Trichopoulos explains. As a result, getting more olive oil in your diet can help keep your arteries clear.

But it doesn't have to be a lot. Getting just 2 table-spoons of olive oil every day has been associated with a lower risk for heart disease in studies.

GETTING THE MOST

Look for extra-virgin. All olive oils are high in monounsaturated fats, but they don't contain equal amounts of disease-fighting polyphenols. To get the most of these compounds, look for olive oil labeled "extra-virgin." This type of oil is made from the first pressing of perfectly ripe olives, which leaves the polyphenols in and the bitter acids out.

Although it's a little more expensive, studies have shown that it's worth your money to buy extra-virgin olive oil. Researchers in Spain asked 24 men to use refined olive oil for 3 months and extra-virgin olive oil for 3 months. They found that the antioxidants in the extra-virgin olive oil kept their LDL, or bad, cholesterol from oxidizing and slowed the formation of plaque in the arteries, while the refined oil didn't offer the protection.

Keep it cold. Because people don't always use a lot of olive oil, it tends to go bad on the shelf, giving up both its good taste and its protective compounds. To keep olive oil fresh, store it in the refrigerator or another dark, cool place. Bringing it to room temperature will quickly restore its pourable nature. Or look for an olive oil that comes in a dark bottle to keep the light from adversely affecting it.

Buy only what you need now. Unless you'll finish the bottle of olive oil within 2 months, buy a smaller size. Oxygen fills the container when it empties, which begins to deteriorate the oil and cause it to taste stale.

Lemon-Rosemary Dressing

1 **sprig fresh rosemary**

1 **small clove garlic**

1 **strip lemon zest (1 × 3½ inches)**

¾ **cup extra-virgin olive oil**

¼ **cup fresh lemon juice**

Place the rosemary and garlic on a cutting board. Lightly crush both with the side of a heavy knife.

Place the rosemary, garlic, and lemon zest in a bottle or jar with a tight-fitting cap. Pour in the oil and lemon juice. Cap the bottle and shake well. Refrigerate if not using right away. Shake again before serving.

Makes 1 cup

Cook's Notes: *The dressing can be stored in the refrigerator for up to 1 week. Drizzle over steamed vegetables, fish, or seafood. Or use as a dressing for pastas, potato salads, or other salads.*

PER TABLESPOON

Calories: 90	Cholesterol: 0 mg
Total fat: 10.1 g	Sodium: 0 mg
Saturated fat: 1.4 g	Dietary fiber: 0 g

Onion Family

ROOTS OF GOOD HEALTH

Scene: The Civil War, 1864. The Union soldiers are ailing with dysentery. General Ulysses S. Grant wires a directive to the War Department to save his troops.

"I will not move my army without onions!"

Three trainloads are shipped the next day. The rest, as they say, is history.

It's a stretch to say that onions won the war between the states. And scientists haven't proven that onions can stave off dysentery. But onions and other members of the allium family—such as leeks, shallots, and scallions—contain dozens of compounds that provide protection from other conditions, including cancer, high blood pressure, heart disease, high cholesterol, and asthma.

So grab an onion, a sharp knife, and a hanky, and start chopping your way to better health.

Onion Rings and Heart Strings

Don't be offended the next time your honey suggests you "go Dutch" when you go out to dinner. He may be suggesting you take a cue from a group of heart-healthy men who ate their fill of onion-laden delights as part of a groundbreaking study in the Netherlands.

In this much-acclaimed study, researchers found that men who ate ¼ cup of onions a day, along with an apple and 4 cups of tea, had one-third the risk of dying from heart attacks compared with those who ate the least amounts of these foods.

What's so important about onions? Wrapped beneath their papery skins are dozens of compounds that help lower cholesterol, thin the blood, and prevent hardening of the arteries—all of which can go a long way toward preventing heart disease.

The first family of heart-healthy compounds in onions is the flavonoids. These are substances in plants that have potent antioxidant powers, meaning that they help prevent disease by sweeping up harmful, cell-damaging oxygen molecules called free radicals, which accumulate naturally in your body.

One particular onion-dwelling flavonoid called quercetin has been shown to help prevent heart disease in two ways. One, it helps keep the dangerous low-density lipoprotein (LDL) form of cholesterol from oxidizing, which is the process that makes it stick to the lining of artery walls. Two, it helps prevent platelets in the blood from sticking together and forming harmful clots.

A second group of protective compounds in onions are the same ones that make you cry—the sulfur compounds. Experts say that these compounds can raise your levels of beneficial high-density lipoprotein (HDL) cholesterol, which helps keep plaque from sticking to artery walls. At the same time, they can lower levels of dangerous blood fats called triglycerides, which helps make blood thinner, keeping your blood pressure in the safety zone.

You don't need a lot of onions to keep your pump primed with protective compounds. In fact, studies show that you can reap the benefits by eating just one medium onion, raw or cooked, a day.

Cancer Protection

You can hold the pickles if you like, but when you're looking for cancer protection, don't skimp on the onions. They may be a key player in cancer prevention, especially cancers of the gastrointestinal tract, say experts.

"The primary flavonoid found in onions—quercetin—actually halts the progression of tumors in the colons of animals," says Michael J. Wargovich, PhD, professor of pathology and microbiology at the University of South Carolina School of Medicine and director of the chemoprevention program at the South Carolina Cancer

Center, both in Columbia. This means that onions do double duty in suppressing tumors, because the sulfur compounds also fight cancer, he adds.

In a large study in the Netherlands, researchers looked at the diets of nearly 121,000 adults. The more odoriferous bulbs these onion-loving Hollanders included in their daily diets, the lower their risks of stomach cancer.

Scientists suspect that onions prevent cancer not only by putting the brakes on tumor development but also by stomping out harmful bacteria that may get stomach cancer started.

Onions have been shown to protect against other forms of cancer as well. After studying a group of 471 men in China, researchers found that the men who ate the largest number of onions had a much lower risk of prostate cancer than those who ate the least amount of onions.

In addition, eating onions has been found to reduce the risk of cancers of the oral cavity and pharynx, esophageal cancer, colorectal cancer, laryngeal cancer, prostate cancer, and renal cell cancer in southern Europe.

The sulfur in onions helps protect against cancer by damaging cancer cells and slowing their growth, according to the National Cancer Institute. Researchers at Cornell University have discovered that four types of onion—shallots, western yellow, pungent yellow, and northern red—are filled with more anticancer chemicals than other varieties.

A Good Kind of Onion Breath

Putting a few layers of raw onions on your turkey burger can give you industrial-strength breath, but those very same onions also may give people with asthma or other respiratory ailments clearer airways.

"There are sulfur compounds in onions that inhibit the allergic, inflammatory response like that seen in asthma," says Eric Block, PhD, professor of chemistry at the State University of New York at Albany.

Although more research needs to be done on onions' asthma-attacking abilities, you can see the anti-inflammatory effect for yourself. The next time you have an insect bite or other type of minor inflammation on your skin, rub a cut onion on it. This should help reduce the inflammation, says Dr. Block.

You only need to eat a few servings of onions a day to keep your breathing passages free and clear. "Unlike some foods, where it's just not conceivable that you could eat enough to produce a significant effect, you can with onions," says Dr. Block. "If you like onions, you can consume them in pretty large quantities. And there's good evidence that you should."

Combined Benefits

Whether you're eating for health or good taste, there's no reason to limit yourself to onions. Scallions, shallots, and other allium vegetables not only pack the same sulfur compounds and flavonoids as their bigger brothers, but they also have a few of their own nutrients that can help fight disease and boost immunity.

Scallions, also called spring or green onions, are actually just young, underdeveloped onions. But they are higher in nutrients, particularly in the B vitamin folate and vitamin C, than their adult counterparts.

A half-cup of chopped raw scallions provides 32 micrograms, or 8 percent of the Daily Value (DV) of folate, a nutrient that's essential for normal tissue growth and that may protect against cancer, heart disease, and birth defects. In that half-cup, you'll also get more than 9 milligrams (almost 16 percent of the DV) of vitamin C, an immunity-boosting antioxidant nutrient that helps vacuum up tissue-damaging oxygen molecules in the body.

Shallots, another miniature member of the allium family, have their own benefits. Just 1 tablespoon of chopped shallots contains 600 IU of vitamin A, or 12 percent of the DV. This essential nutrient helps keep immunity strong and also guards against vision problems associated with aging, like cataracts and night blindness.

> ## Doctor's Top Tip
>
> A wonderful way to enjoy onions is to put them on the grill. The Mayo Clinic in Rochester, Minnesota, recommends putting chunks of sweet onions on a skewer along with other vegetables, such as eggplant and squash, and grilling until they're lightly browned and tender. Brush the onions and veggies with heart-healthy olive oil before adding to the grill.

GETTING THE MOST

Add some color. To get the most nutrients from your daily dose of onions, eat several different kinds. Red and yellow onions and shallots have the highest flavonoid content, while white onions have the least.

Save your breath. If the fear of having horrific halitosis is keeping you from enjoying the health benefits of onions, here's a freshening tip. Eat a sprig of fresh parsley. This will help neutralize the sulfur compounds before they turn into offending breath. A breath freshener made with parsley seed oil can also help.

Keep your eyes peeled. Even if you like onions, you may not love them enough to eat a half-cup or so a day. That's why scientists are trying to develop new onion strains with high concentrations of flavonoids like quercetin. Experts aren't sure when these new onions will be on the market, but keep your eyes open for special displays at your supermarket.

Stuffed Vidalia Onions

4 **Vidalia onions**

½ **teaspoon olive oil**

3 **medium zucchini, shredded**

3 **cloves garlic, minced**

1 **teaspoon dried basil**

1 **teaspoon dried thyme**

3 **tablespoons unseasoned dried bread crumbs**

1 **tablespoon plus ½ teaspoon chopped toasted pine nuts**

3 **teaspoons grated Parmesan cheese**

Salt and freshly ground black pepper

Preheat the oven to 400°F. Line a baking sheet with foil.

Leaving the peels on, cut about ½ inch off the top of each onion. Slightly trim the bottoms so the onions stand upright. Place the onions, cut side up, on the baking sheet, and coat each onion lightly with cooking spray. Bake for 1 hour, or until soft. Set aside for 15 minutes, or until cool enough to handle.

Reduce the oven temperature to 350°F.

Remove and discard the onion peels. With a spoon, scoop out the onion centers, leaving a ½-inch shell. Chop the centers, and reserve 1 cup for the stuffing; save the remainder for another use.

In a large nonstick skillet, heat the oil over medium heat. Add the zucchini, garlic, basil, thyme, and chopped onion. Cook until the zucchini is softened and most of the liquid has evaporated, about 6 minutes.

Remove from the heat, and stir in the bread crumbs, pine nuts, and Parmesan. Season with salt and pepper to taste. Mix well. Divide the filling among the onion shells.

Coat the baking sheet with cooking spray. Place the onions on the baking sheet, and bake until golden, about 20 minutes.

Makes 4 servings

PER SERVING

Calories: 144
Total fat: 4 g
Saturated fat: 1 g

Cholesterol: 3 mg
Sodium: 267 mg
Dietary fiber: 5 g

Overweight
EATING AWAY THE POUNDS

Lose a pound a day—without dieting!" "Burn fat—while you sleep!" Yeah, right. When it comes to diets, most of us have swallowed enough snake oil to float a tanker. The only miracle about so-called miracle diets is that we keep trying them.

Losing weight and keeping it off doesn't take a miracle. It rests on one simple premise: "Energy in equals energy out," says Simone French, PhD, professor of epidemiology at the University of Minnesota in Minneapolis. "If you take in more energy than you expend, you gain weight. If you take in less energy than you expend, you lose weight." In other words, calories count. The number of calories you take in has to be less than the number of calories you burn. Exercise also counts because it helps you burn more calories.

Moreover, researchers are finding that what you eat is just as important as how much of it you eat. For example, the body doesn't process the calories in a high-fat chocolate-chip cookie the same way it does the calories in a potato or in a plate of carbohydrate-loaded pasta. Further, studies show that while some foods fuel the impulse to eat, others seem to "switch off" the appetite.

So the real miracle may be that certain foods can actually help, rather than hinder, your efforts to lose weight. Most people trying to lose weight can count calories in their sleep. But calories, while important, are just part of the weight-loss equation. Intriguing weight-loss research from major universities is revealing that when you pack a reduced-calorie diet with high-satisfaction foods, you can lose weight more easily. The magic foods: fruits, veggies, whole grains, lean protein, and good fats.

The High-Satisfaction Solution

Green beans and fresh-from-the vine tomatoes; juicy peaches and luxurious raspberries; stick-to-your-ribs whole grains. These nutrient-dense foods form the backbone of the most effective healthy-eating plans that control your weight. Why? They satisfy. All that fiber means food digests slowly, warding off hunger pangs and crazy food cravings by keeping your blood sugar low and under control—something refined carbs like white bread, white rice, and pasta just can't deliver.

Today, many overweight Americans are insulin-resistant—meaning that their cells "ignore" signals from the hormone insulin to absorb blood sugar. Insulin levels

SATISFACTION GUARANTEED

Controlling appetite is perhaps the key to successfully losing weight, according to a study at the University of Sydney in Australia. Researchers there have identified a number of "high-satisfaction" foods that help keep you feeling full longer. In the accompanying table, anything with a rating of 100 or better (the score given to white bread) is considered satisfying. Foods that scored less than 100 tend not to stick around, so you'll probably wind up eating more of them—and gaining weight.

Food Rating

Potatoes: 323	Bran cereal: 151	Jelly beans: 118
Fish: 225	Eggs: 150	French fries: 116
Oatmeal: 209	Cheese: 146	White bread: 100
Oranges: 202	White rice: 138	Ice cream: 96
Apples: 197	Lentils: 133	Potato chips: 91
Whole-wheat pasta: 188	Brown rice: 132	Yogurt: 88
Steak: 176	Crackers: 127	Peanuts: 84
Baked beans: 168	Cookies: 120	Candy bar: 70
Grapes: 162	White pasta: 119	Doughnut: 68
Grain bread: 154	Bananas: 118	Cake: 65
Popcorn: 154	Cornflakes: 118	Croissant: 47

rise extra high after meals if you're insulin-resistant. It's your body's way of forcing blood sugar into cells. So, if you've just eaten lots of refined carbs, your body's got a huge dose of blood sugar to dispose of. Insulin resistance throws up an extra weight-loss obstacle as well: Researchers think high insulin levels keep fat "locked" in fat cells, where it cannot be burned as readily. When you eat foods that keep your blood sugar low and steady, however, your body pumps out less insulin, and this doesn't happen.

Studies back this up. In a Tufts University–New England Medical Center study of 39 overweight adults, those with high insulin levels lost an average of 22 pounds in 6 months on the "steady blood sugar" plan—compared with 13 pounds on a diet with more refined carbs. Other research suggests that this eating strategy keeps your metabolism from downshifting dramatically, as happens on most weight-loss diets. Researchers from Children's Hospital Boston found that adult dieters who ate low-glycemic index (GI) foods burned 80 more calories per day than those on a higher-GI, lower-fat diet. They also felt more energetic.

Don't Be Afraid of Protein . . . or Fat

Two scrambled eggs for breakfast. Chicken salad (made with a smidgeon of canola oil mayo) on whole-wheat bread for lunch. A grilled tenderloin steak for dinner. We bet you're feeling satisfied just reading about these healthy weight-loss-friendly entrées!

It used to be that dieters were told to steer clear of liquid fats (no salad dressings, no cooking in oil) and fatty protein (watch out for those well-marbled steaks). After all, conventional wisdom said, fat's got 9 calories per gram, more than twice what you'd find in carbs like bread or a low-fat cookie. Fat on your plate . . . fat on your hips . . . was the mantra. But researchers now say that we actually need good mono- and polyunsaturated fats, like those found in seafood, olive oil, and canola oil, to maintain a healthy cardiovascular system and nervous system. And it's now been shown that good fats and good protein both have the unique power to satisfy hunger as well.

Protein makes you feel full after eating and keeps you feeling full for hours. In a Danish study of 25 adults, those who ate a bit more protein lost 10 percent more belly fat than those on a higher-carb plan—and what they lost was dangerous fat tucked around internal organs that raises risk for diabetes and heart disease.

A moderate amount of good fat—the kind in nuts and nut butters, olive and canola oils, and oily, cold-water fish—has weight-loss advantages, too. When 65 overweight adults followed a 1,000-calorie-a-day diet for 24 weeks, those who ate almonds at snack time lost 18 percent of their body weight, while those whose treats were carbohydrate-based (such as wheat crackers or baked potatoes) lost just 11 percent. The nut eaters whittled their waists 14 percent; the carb snackers, 9 percent. Other research shows that eating a moderate amount of peanut butter every day also aids weight loss.

High-Satisfaction Foods

If your idea of a weight-loss plan is to "eat light," you may want to consider doing just the opposite. Research suggests that controlling appetite and weight gain may be as simple as choosing "high-satisfaction" foods.

Researchers at the University of Sydney in Australia had volunteers eat 240-calorie portions of a variety of foods, including fruits, baked goods, snack foods,

> ### Doctor's Top Tip
>
> Filling your plate with high-fiber fruits, veggies, and whole grains plus generous portions of lean protein may be the smartest weight-control strategy ever, says Donald K. Layman, PhD, professor of nutrition in the department of food science and human nutrition at the University of Illinois at Urbana-Champaign.
>
> Protein foods like eggs and lean meat contain an amino acid that seems to protect muscle, Dr. Layman says. Studies show that people who eat more protein and fewer refined carbs when dieting tend to lose more body fat and less muscle.

high-carbohydrate foods, high-protein foods, and cereal. After eating, the participants rated their feelings of hunger every 15 minutes. The goal was to see which
foods kept them feeling satisfied the longest.

White bread was assigned an automatic score of 100 points, and all other foods
were measured against that. Here's how the menu lined up. A potato topped the list,
receiving a score of 323 and making it more than three times as satisfying as white
bread. It was followed by fish (with a score of 225), oatmeal (209), oranges (202),
apples (197), and whole-wheat pasta (188). Surprisingly, baked goods got the least
satisfactory ratings. Even more surprising, the more fat a food contained, the less
likely it was to rank high on the scale. A croissant, for example, received a score of
47, which meant that it was less than half as satisfying as a piece of white bread. Foods
containing more protein, fiber, and water received higher scores.

To put the results of this study to work, always select satisfying foods like vegetables and fruits over their higher-fat, lower-fiber counterparts, recommends Barbara
Rolls, PhD, professor in the nutrition department at Pennsylvania State University.
For example, choose a baked potato over a serving of french fries. Between meals,
snack on a cup or two of air-popped popcorn, which is more likely to satisfy you
than the same amount of potato chips. Better yet, grab an apple or an orange. The
idea is to satisfy your hunger immediately and help control your appetite for the next
few hours, without loading you up with unwanted calories.

Pectin

STAY WELL WITH GEL

The next time you sit down to breakfast, spread a little jam on a piece of toast. Then take a bite from a succulent pear. Even though their tastes and textures are totally different, these foods actually have something in common, and that something is very good for your health.

Jellies and jams, along with legumes, fruits, vegetables, and a variety of grains, contain pectin, a type of dietary fiber that acts as a natural thickener. Food manufacturers often use pectin as a binding agent in jellies and jams. Nature, as it turns out, uses pectin in much the same way.

Because pectin is a water-soluble fiber, it dissolves in the body, creating a sticky gel inside the intestine. The gel binds to potentially harmful substances, preventing them from being absorbed. At the same time, it causes nutrients to be absorbed a little more slowly. Both of these factors make pectin a key player in preventing a number of conditions, from heart disease and diabetes to weight gain.

Protection from Heart Disease, Diabetes . . . and Cancer, Too

The biggest health threat that Americans face is heart disease, and one of the leading causes of heart disease is high cholesterol. The danger from cholesterol is so great, in fact, that doctors estimate that for every 1 percent that you lower your cholesterol, you reduce the risk of heart disease by 2 percent.

Getting more pectin in your diet is an excellent strategy for lowering cholesterol, says nutrition researcher Beth Kunkel, PhD, RD, professor of food and nutrition at Clemson University in South Carolina. Because pectin dissolves into a gel, molecules of fat and cholesterol get trapped before they make it into your bloodstream. And because pectin itself isn't absorbed, it goes out of the body in the stool, taking the fat and cholesterol with it.

Pectin helps lower cholesterol in yet another way. Because it isn't digested, bacteria in the intestine start gobbling it up. In the process, they release chemicals that travel to the liver, interrupting the production of cholesterol, says cardiologist Michael H. Davidson, MD, executive medical director of Radiant Research in Chicago. In fact, research has shown that people who get about 6 grams of pectin a day—approximately the amount in 3 cups of grapefruit sections—can lower their cholesterol by at least 5 percent. While grapefruit is a good source of pectin, with 1 gram in a 4-ounce serving of sections, it's not the only one. Apples, bananas, and peaches are good sources, as are beans.

Pectin also helps lower insulin resistance—a serious health threat often linked with obesity—say nutrition researchers from the University of Kuopio in Finland. Less insulin resistance means your cells easily "obey" signals from the hormone insulin to absorb blood sugar—lowering sugar levels and reducing your body's need to produce extra insulin. Less sugar and less insulin cut your risk for diabetes and for cardiovascular disease.

Getting more pectin can be especially important for people with diabetes, who must do everything they can to keep their blood sugar levels steady. Since pectin slows the rate at which sugars are absorbed, it can prevent the sudden surges of glucose (blood sugar) that can damage the nerves, eyes, and organs in people with diabetes.

There's emerging evidence that pectin fights cancer, too. Researchers at Taiwan's Taipei Medical University say pectin seems to protect cells from damage that can lead to cancer, and it can also slow the proliferation of cancer cells. It may work by cooling off damaging inflammation in the body.

Smoother Digestion

People who are trying to lose weight are often advised to eat more fruits, legumes, and other pectin-rich foods. There's a good reason for this. When pectin dissolves in the stomach, it gradually expands, taking up more room. At the same time, it slows the absorption of sugars and nutrients into the bloodstream. This helps you feel more satisfied even when you haven't had a lot to eat.

"Pectin helps to give you that feeling of fullness, so you don't need to eat as much," says researcher Barbara F. Harland, PhD, professor of nutrition at Howard University in Washington, D.C. "One of the most important things for losing weight and keeping it off is getting more fiber, including pectin."

In the Kitchen

Pectin, whether it comes in a plastic package or ready-wrapped in nature's own fruit, is what makes it possible for jellies, jams, and preserves to gel. An easy, fun, and fast way to watch pectin at work is to make your own cranberry sauce for Thanksgiving. Simply heat a cup of water and a cup of sugar to a boil, then dump in a bag of cranberries. Bring back to a boil, then simmer. Within minutes, the berries begin to break down, releasing pectin and causing the mixture to rapidly thicken.

Here are a few pectin pointers for the next time you're making your own jam, jelly, or sauce.

- Some fruits, like apples and gooseberries, are naturally high in pectin and will gel without the addition of commercial pectin.
- Blueberries and peaches contain very little pectin. To help them gel, you'll probably need to add liquid or powdered pectin.
- Another way to promote gelling is to combine low-pectin fruits with those that are higher in pectin. Apples are a common addition to jams, not just for their flavor but also because of their high pectin content.

Potatoes

OUR SUPER STAPLE

Early in the history of the New World, in the Andes Mountains of Peru and Bolivia, people had a thousand names for the potato. It was that important.

In the 4,000 or so years since, the starchy tuber's reputation has peaked and dipped. The Spanish conquistadors thought the new root captivating enough to take back to the Old World. (Within a few years, potatoes became standard fare on Spanish ships because they prevented scurvy.) Once the potato arrived in Europe, though, its fortunes sagged, not because of any shortcomings of its own but because of its kinship with the deadly nightshade family, plants that had the reputation for being toxic. Potatoes were feared rather than appreciated.

Eventually, though, both botanists and diners alike learned the whole story. Potatoes aren't remotely dangerous. Plus, they're a super food staple, making them the world's number one vegetable crop.

"The potato has a little bit of almost everything," says Mark Kestin, PhD, professor of nutrition at Bastyr University and affiliate assistant professor of epidemiology at the University of Washington, both in Seattle. "You could get many of your nutritional needs met from potatoes, if you had to," he adds. Indeed. One large baked potato with the skin provides 48 percent of the Daily Value (DV) for vitamin C, about 40 percent of the DV for vitamin B_6, about 30 percent of the DV for copper, manganese, and potassium, as well as 7 grams of fiber.

Peel Power

A potato's healing abilities start in the peel, which contains an anticarcinogenic compound called chlorogenic acid, says Mary Ellen Camire, PhD, professor in the department of food science and human nutrition at the University of Maine in Orono. In laboratory studies, this particular acid has been shown to help the fiber in potatoes absorb benzo(a)pyrene, a potential carcinogen found in smoked foods such as grilled hamburgers. "The acid in the food reacts with the carcinogen by basically binding it up and making too big a molecule for the body to absorb," she explains. "In our study, it prevented the carcinogen from being absorbed almost completely."

In the Kitchen

Potatoes aren't all created equal. Some taste better baked, while others are good for soups or salads. A third type, the all-purpose potato, has been "designed" both for baking and steaming. Here's what to look for when considering potatoes:

Waxy potatoes. Known as round whites or round reds, waxy potatoes are low in starch and have a high moisture content. These potatoes keep their shape well during cook-ing, making them a good choice for soups, stews, and salads.

Starchy potatoes. The russet potato is a common type of starchy spud. It has a mealy, floury interior, which works well for mashing or baking.

All-purpose potatoes. Spuds like long whites are great to keep on the shelf because they can be prepared any way—baked, boiled, or steamed.

Slashing the Pressure

We don't normally think of potatoes as being high in potassium, but in fact, a baked 7-ounce spud contains more than twice the potassium of one medium-size banana. One baked potato with the skin will give you about 1,137 milligrams of potassium, almost a third of the DV for this mineral.

Potassium is important because it seems to calm the spiking effect that salt has on blood pressure. For some people, increasing potassium in their diets by eating pota-toes could reduce the need for blood pressure medication, notes pharmacist Earl Mindell, RPh, PhD, professor emeritus of nutrition at Pacific Western University in Los Angeles and author of *Earl Mindell's Food as Medicine*. In one study of 54 people with high blood pressures, half added potassium-rich foods like potatoes to their diets, while the other half continued to eat their normal fare. By the end of the study, Dr. Mindell says, 81 percent of the potato eaters were able to control their blood pressures with less than half the medication they had used previously.

Recently, British scientists stumbled upon another compound inside potatoes that may help explain this veggie's extraordinary ability to help you control your blood pressure. Called kukoamines, these compounds have previously only been documented in some Chinese herbal remedies, say scientists from England's Insti-tute of Food Research. "Potatoes have been cultivated for thousands of years, and we thought traditional crops were pretty well understood," says food scientist Fred Mellon, PhD, from the Norwich-based institute. "But this surprise finding shows that even the most familiar of foods might conceal a hoard of health-promoting chemicals."

Blood Sugar Bad Guy?

White potatoes have gotten a lot of bad press in the past few years. This veggie has been vilified by nutrition researchers who say it can send blood sugar soaring, and by nutritionists who warn that, too often, potatoes are just a vehicle for oil, butter, sour cream, and/or salt (think french fries, scalloped potatoes, and baked potatoes with the works).

But you don't have to give up spuds. Truth is, eaten in moderate quantities, with the peel on, potatoes remain a satisfying, nutritionally valuable food. In fact, the glycemic load (a measure of how much a regular serving of a food really raises your blood sugar) of a baked potato is on par with that of healthy grain foods such as barley and whole-wheat spaghetti, say blood sugar researchers from the University of Sydney, Australia. The danger? Eating potatoes every night (fried . . . or with butter) instead of choosing a variety of different veggies. (Plenty of us do just that. Potato consumption has doubled in the United States since 1970, and Americans eat more spuds than any other veggie.)

The humble spud also packs a surprising nutritional bonus—a healthy dose of vitamin C. We don't think of vitamin C as affecting our blood sugar, but there's emerging evidence that this powerful antioxidant vitamin, well-known for helping prevent heart disease, may be of help to people with diabetes. On top of this, vitamin C may also be effective in diminishing the damage to proteins caused by free radicals, dangerous oxygen molecules that damage tissues in the body.

In one study, researchers in the Netherlands found that men eating healthy diets, which were high not only in potatoes but also in fish, vegetables, and legumes, appeared to have a lower risk for diabetes. It's not yet clear what the protective mechanism is, but researchers speculate that antioxidants, including vitamin C, may play a role in keeping excess sugar out of the bloodstream.

Because potatoes are high in complex carbohydrates, they're also good for people who already have diabetes. Complex carbohydrates must be broken down into simple sugars before they're absorbed into the bloodstream. This means that the sugars enter the bloodstream in a leisurely fashion rather than pouring in all at once. This, in turn, helps keep blood sugar levels stable, which is a critical part of controlling the disease.

Further, potatoes can be key players in helping people with diabetes keep their weight down, an important benefit because being overweight makes it more difficult for the body to produce enough insulin, the hormone that helps transport sugars out of the bloodstream and into individual cells. At the same time, being overweight makes the insulin that the body does produce work less efficiently. What potatoes do is keep you full so that you're less likely to be hungry later on.

In a study of 41 hungry students at the University of Sydney in Australia, researchers found that spuds filled them up more than other foods, while at the same time delivering fewer calories. On a satiety scale that measured white bread at 100, oatmeal at 209, and fish at 225, potatoes were way ahead at 323.

GETTING THE MOST

Keep the peel. To take advantage of potatoes' cancer-fighting abilities, you really have to eat the peel, says Dr. Camire. This can be particularly important when eating grilled foods, which leave small amounts of cancer-causing substances on the food. It would be nice if you could get a fast-food burger on a potato-peel bun, says Dr. Camire. "That would help absorb the carcinogens from the grilling," she says.

A more practical solution is simply to add a baked potato or potato salad (with the peel) to your plate whenever you eat a grilled hamburger, a hot dog, or other smoky foods.

Cook them carefully. Although boiling is one of the most popular cooking methods for potatoes, it's perhaps the worst choice for preserving nutrients, since vitamin C and some B vitamins are pulled out of the potatoes and into the cooking water. In fact, boiling potatoes can result in losing about half the vitamin C, a quarter of the folate (a B vitamin), and 40 percent of the potassium, says Marilyn A. Swanson, PhD, RD, adjunct associate professor of pediatrics at Baylor College of Medicine in Houston, Texas.

If you do boil potatoes, you can recapture some of the nutrients by saving the cooking water and adding it to other foods such as soups and stews.

Baking and steaming do a good job of tenderizing potatoes, while at the same time preserving more of their nutrients. "Microwaving is your first choice," says Susan Thom, RD, a nutrition consultant in Brecksville, Ohio.

Prepare them late. Busy cooks have traditionally peeled and sliced potatoes ahead of time, then submerged them in water to keep them from darkening. This may keep potatoes looking fresh, but it also strips valuable nutrients. "You lose some of the soluble vitamins in the water," says dietitian Mona Sutnick, RD, a nutrition consultant in Philadelphia.

> ## Doctor's Top Tip
>
> Get a nutritional boost with Technicolor taters. Potatoes with gold, red, purple, and blue skin—and even some with gold, red, blue, orange, and purple flesh—are turning up at farmers' markets and in the produce section of supermarkets, too. They look pretty on your plate—and offer an extra dose of disease-fighting phytochemicals such as beta-carotene, lutein, and zeaxanthin, say nutrition experts from the University of California, Berkeley.

Barbecue Oven Fries

4 **medium baking potatoes**

2½ **tablespoons ketchup**

4 **teaspoons canola oil**

2 **teaspoons cider vinegar**

2 **teaspoons Worcestershire sauce**

⅛ **teaspoon salt**

Preheat the oven to 425°F. Coat a baking sheet with cooking spray.

Scrub the potatoes and pat dry with paper towels. Cut each potato lengthwise into 5 or 6 slices, then stack the slices and cut at ¼-inch intervals to make french fries.

In a large bowl, combine the ketchup, oil, vinegar, Worcestershire sauce, and salt. Add the potatoes and toss to coat.

Spread the potatoes evenly on the baking sheet. Bake for 20 minutes, then turn and bake for 10 to 15 minutes longer, or until tender and golden. Test for doneness by inserting the tip of a sharp knife into a fry.

Makes 4 servings

PER SERVING

Calories: 185
Total fat: 4.7 g
Saturated fat: 0.3 g

Cholesterol: 0 mg
Sodium: 218 mg
Dietary fiber: 3 g

Poultry

BIRDS FOR STRONG BLOOD

Americans have long considered poultry to be a sign of prosperity. During the Depression, Franklin Delano Roosevelt promised a chicken in every pot. And every Thanksgiving we gather around a dressed turkey and show appreciation for our blessings.

A bird on the table is more than just a symbol, however. Properly prepared, poultry is an important part of a healthful diet. Without the skin, it not only is a low-fat alternative to fattier meats like beef and pork but also provides a host of disease-fighting, energy-boosting vitamins and minerals that are difficult to get from plant foods alone.

Of course, there is one caveat: That healthful piece of poultry may become a permanent part of your waistline unless you remove the skin before taking a bite. This is particularly true when buying fast food or chicken with the skin on, doused in gravy, at popular chain restaurants. For example, researchers found that a half-chicken platter at Boston Market rivaled a Big Mac, served with large fries and a chocolate milk shake, in fat, sodium, and calories.

A B-Vitamin Boost

Most of us understand the importance of getting our daily fill of the vitamin all-stars, like vitamins C and E and beta-carotene. But ask someone what the B vitamins are good for, and you'll likely get a blank stare. That's because these unsung heroes of the vitamin world don't directly prevent major health problems like heart disease and cancer—though they certainly may lend a helping hand. Mostly, they're maintenance workers; in a lot of little ways, they keep our minds and bodies working smoothly. Take away the B vitamins, and you'd find yourself fumbling through life, depressed, confused, anemic, and nervous—or worse.

Luckily, poultry is bursting with three essential B vitamins: niacin, vitamin B_6, and vitamin B_{12}.

Depending on the part of the bird you pick, chicken and turkey provide between 16 and 62 percent of the Daily Value (DV) of 20 milligrams for niacin. (Chicken

In the Kitchen

Chefs agree that the trick to making perfect poultry is to cook the bird in the skin. The melting fat from skin acts like a natural baste, keeping the meat flavorful and moist during the long cooking process.

"Poultry can be horribly dry when you cook it without the skin," says Susan Kleiner, PhD, RD, owner of High Performance Nutrition in Mercer Island, Washington. "And studies show that as long as you remove the skin when it's done cooking, the fat content of the poultry is about the same as if you had removed it beforehand."

In a hurry? Grab a rotisserie bird at the supermarket. The National Chicken Council estimates that 700 million rotisserie chickens were sold to hungry Americans in 2006 alone. True, they're higher in fat and salt than a home-cooked chicken could be, but if you remove the skin and discard the drippings, 3 ounces of white meat has just 102 calories and 2 grams of fat. And it's versatile. Dress it up by chopping the breast meat and mixing it with corn, black beans, and salsa in a microwaveable casserole dish. Top with shredded cheese and reheat for a few minutes. Or create quick curried chicken salad: Toss chunked breast meat with canola oil mayo, curry powder, sliced almonds, pineapple chunks, chopped mango, and raisins.

---

breast is at the high end of the scale, and turkey dark meat is at the low end.) Studies show that it may reduce cholesterol and cut the risk for heart attacks.

Poultry also contains 0.3 microgram of vitamin B_{12}, or 5 percent of the DV. Vitamin B_{12}, which is found almost solely in animal foods, is essential for healthy brain function. Get too little B_{12}, and you may find yourself feeling fatigued and experiencing memory loss and other neurological problems.

Another B vitamin, B_6, is critical for maintaining immunity. It's also necessary for making red blood cells and maintaining a healthy nervous system. Poultry provides between 0.2 and 0.5 milligram of vitamin B_6, or 10 to 25 percent of the DV.

Metal for Your Mettle

When knights went into battle, they donned suits of armor to make them stronger. Though none of us are jousting these days, we still need iron for the everyday battles of life. We just need to eat it, not wear it.

Iron is one of the most important nutrients for maximum energy and vitality. Yet many of us fall short of the 15 milligrams needed each day, says Susan M. Kleiner, PhD, RD, owner of High Performance Nutrition in Mercer Island, Washington, and author of *The Good Mood Diet* and *Power Eating: Build Muscle, Increase Energy, Cut Fat.*

Although iron abounds in fortified cereals, tofu, beans, and other nonmeat foods,

it's not always easy for the body to absorb. By contrast, the iron in poultry (called heme iron) is easily absorbed, says Dr. Kleiner. Your body can absorb up to 15 percent more heme iron than nonheme iron, she explains. Plus, when you eat heme iron, it helps your body absorb nonheme iron. That way, you get the most iron from all your food, says Dr. Kleiner.

In the Pink with Zinc

In order to stay in the pink—free from infections, colds, and other health problems that keep us home in bed watching bad daytime TV—we need strong immune systems. Getting enough zinc in the diet is critical for immunity because

---

TAKE FLIGHT ON THE WILD SIDE

Have you eaten so much chicken that you're starting to resemble Frank Purdue? Maybe it's time to leave that poultry behind and take flight with some birds of a different feather. Although they tend to be higher-priced, birds like pheasant and quail add variety to your diet while providing the same nutritional benefits as chicken or turkey.

Here's how two of the less common varieties of poultry add up. All nutritional information is based on 3-ounce servings, and the percentages of the DV or, in the case of iron, the RDA, are given.

Pheasant

Calories: 113

Fat: 3 grams

Calories from fat: 25 percent

Iron: 1 milligram (10 percent of RDA for men and 7 percent for women)

Niacin: 6 milligrams (30 percent of DV)

Vitamin B_6: 0.6 milligram (30 percent of DV)

Vitamin B_{12}: 0.7 microgram (12 percent of DV)

Zinc: 0.8 milligram (5 percent of DV)

Riboflavin: 0.1 milligram (8 percent of DV)

Vitamin C: 5 milligrams (6 percent of DV)

Quail

Calories: 123

Fat: 4 grams

Calories from fat: 31 percent

Iron: 4 milligrams (40 percent of RDA for men and 27 percent for women)

Niacin: 8 milligrams (40 percent of DV)

Vitamin B_6: 0.5 milligram (25 percent of DV)

Thiamin: 0.3 milligram (20 percent of DV)

Zinc: 3 milligrams (20 percent of DV)

Riboflavin: 0.3 milligram (18 percent of DV)

Vitamin C: 7 milligrams (12 percent of DV)

The New Safety Rules

Consumer Reports magazine shocked the nation in December 2006, when it announced that 83 percent of the chicken sold in supermarkets may contain bacteria that cause food-borne illness. They found bacteria in brand-name birds, store-brand birds, and organic chickens alike. "We think it's really startling," said Jean Halloran, a policy director for Consumers Union, which publishes *Consumer Reports*. "It's a very significant deterioration in food safety."

While the USDA disputed the findings as "junk science" (government studies have found that 26 to 60 percent of chickens harbor bacteria), no one disputes the fact that raw poultry is a playground for salmonella, campylobacter, and other organisms that can cause diarrhea, tummy cramps, and fever. There's no way to eliminate bacteria entirely, but these updated rules can help you keep your poultry safe and healthy:

When you buy: Choose packages that feel cool and have no tears or punctures. (Skip poultry stuffed at the store, it's too vulnerable to bacterial growth.) Put each pack in a plastic bag, so that poultry juices can't contaminate other foods. Buy poultry last; store in an ice chest if you won't be home to refrigerate it within an hour; and when you get home, unload and fridge it first.

Storage: Use or freeze poultry within 2 days. Whole birds and parts will keep, frozen, for 6 to 9 months. Ground poultry and giblets, for 3 to 4 months. (Never thaw poultry at room temperature—place it in fridge to thaw or microwave.)

Prep: Don't wash poultry—this just splashes germy juices around your kitchen (and on you). Cooking heat kills any bacteria. But do scrub tools, cutting boards, and your work area thoroughly with hot, soapy water after preparing raw chicken to prevent bacteria from multiplying. Wash your own hands frequently and dry with paper towels. Marinate birds in the fridge and toss the marinade afterward—it's a swimming pool packed with bacteria.

Cooking: Find—or buy—a food thermometer. Checking the internal temperature of poultry is the only way to ensure that it's fully cooked (going by color, texture, or juice color is unreliable, according to the USDA). Target temperatures: All poultry should be cooked to a minimum internal temperature of 165°F throughout. For whole chicken and turkey, you should check the internal temperature on the innermost part of the thigh and the thickest part of the breast.

our infection-fighting cells require adequate stores of this trace mineral to do their job.

In addition, studies show that getting enough zinc can help slow the progression of a prevalent eye disorder called macular degeneration, which can cause irreversible vision loss, especially among the elderly.

As with iron, zinc is found in foods besides meat, like whole grains and wheat germ—but again, your body has a harder time absorbing it from plant foods than from meats, says Dr. Kleiner.

Eating poultry will help keep your zinc supply at the necessary levels, Dr. Kleiner says. Most poultry provides 6 to 25 percent of the 15 milligrams of zinc you need each day.

GETTING THE MOST

Grab a drumstick. Lots of people pick around the dark meat of poultry because it's higher in fat. And that's true, concedes Dr. Kleiner, but it's also a lot higher in minerals and worth digging into occasionally.

"If you've removed the skin, you've removed the mother lode of fat anyway," she says, "and a lot of the iron and zinc are in the dark meat."

Read chicken labels carefully. Think "free-range" chicken means a friendly flock of hens pecking in the farmyard—and getting natural food, air, and sunshine that make the meat healthier? Think again. The USDA poultry labeling standards allow any bird that has outdoor access for a few minutes a day to be labeled free range. And the words "natural" and "hormone free" aren't really guarantees that a chicken was raised organically and without unnecessary medications. (The USDA already prohibits the use of hormones in the raising of chickens for home consumption.) Your best bet for finding a chemical-free bird? Look for labels that say "USDA organic," which means the chicken was raised without hormones, antibiotics, or feed grown with synthetic pesticides or fertilizers. If you'd like a happy chicken raised on grass, not a concrete-floored coop, look for labels that say "Certified Humane Raised and Handled"—a claim that's verified by a third-party group before poultry farmers can use it on the label.

Doctor's Top Tip

Hectic day? When the only sane meal option is the drive-thru, order grilled chicken sandwiches—not the nuggets—all around, says the American Institute for Cancer Research. "Chicken nuggets can include not just the chicken meat itself but also the skin, with several types of flour, starches, and oils," the group notes. "That makes nuggets higher in calories with about half the protein compared to an equal portion of plain cooked skinless chicken." Nuggets have four times the saturated fat and trans fats, too.

Turkey Cutlets with Oregano-Lemon Sauce

1 pound turkey breast cutlets

3 tablespoons all-purpose flour

¾ teaspoon dried oregano

⅛ teaspoon salt

1 tablespoon olive oil

2 cloves garlic, minced

¼ cup defatted reduced-sodium chicken broth

3 tablespoons fresh lemon juice

Rinse the turkey and pat dry.

On a plate, combine the flour, ½ teaspoon of the oregano, and salt. Mix with a fork. Place the turkey cutlets in the flour mixture, turning to dust both sides evenly. Shake off any excess.

In a large nonstick skillet, heat the oil over medium-high heat. Add the cutlets in a single layer, and cook for 2 to 3 minutes per side, or until golden and cooked through. Check for doneness by inserting the tip of a sharp knife into a cutlet. Remove the turkey to a plate.

Add the garlic to the skillet, and cook for 10 to 12 seconds, or until fragrant. Add the broth, lemon juice, and the remaining ¼ teaspoon oregano. Cook, stirring, for 2 to 3 minutes, or until hot. Pour the sauce over the turkey.

Makes 4 servings

PER SERVING

Calories: 184	Cholesterol: 77 mg
Total fat: 4.6 g	Sodium: 124 mg
Saturated fat: 0.8 g	Dietary fiber: 0.3 g

Prunes

NATURE'S LAXATIVE

Would you rather have prunes . . . or dried plums? We bet you'd pick the latter. So did the California Prune Board, which officially petitioned the FDA to change the name of this sweet, chewy fruit from stodgy old "prune" to the sophisticated "dried plum" in 1999. The change drew a lot of laughs—dried plums made an appearance on *The Tonight Show* with Jay Leno and became the focus of a series of Millard Fillmore comic strips. The spiffy new moniker also boosted flagging sales by 11 percent in just 3 months, reports the renamed California Dried Plum Board.

And that's a good thing. By any name, this chewy, slightly sticky, densely sweet treat is a unique fruity package full of vitamin A, potassium, and a very special, useful fiber.

Nature's Laxative

Pharmacies stock dozens of medications for preventing and relieving constipation. But most of the time they really aren't necessary if you get in the habit of adding prunes to your daily diet. Prunes contain not just one but three different ingredients that work together to help keep your digestive system on track.

For starters, prunes are high in insoluble fiber, which is perhaps the key to preventing constipation. Since insoluble fiber isn't absorbed by your body, it stays in the digestive tract. And because it's incredibly absorbent, it soaks up large amounts of water, making stools larger and easier to pass. (Prunes also contain soluble fiber, the type that helps lower cholesterol and with it the risk of heart disease.) Just five prunes contain almost 3 grams of fiber, or about 12 percent of the Daily Value (DV).

In addition, prunes contain a natural sugar called sorbitol. Like fiber, sorbitol soaks up water wherever it can find it, says Mary Ellen Camire, PhD, professor in the department of food science and human nutrition at the University of Maine in Orono. Most fruits contain small amounts (usually less than 1 percent) of sorbitol. Prunes, however, are about 15 percent sorbitol, which explains why they're such a potent bulking agent and are often recommended for relieving constipation.

Finally, prunes contain a compound called dihydroxyphenyl isatin, which stimulates the intestine, causing it to contract. This process is essential for having regular bowel movements.

You don't need a lot of prunes to get the benefits. One daily serving—about five prunes—is all most people need to help themselves stay regular.

All-Around Protection

As with most fruits, prunes contain generous amounts of a variety of vitamins, minerals, and other healthful compounds. In fact, they're a concentrated source of energy because they lose water during the drying process. This means that you get a lot of value in a very small package.

One of the most healthful compounds in prunes is beta-carotene. Like vitamins C and E, beta-carotene is an antioxidant, meaning that it helps neutralize harmful oxygen molecules in the body. Prunes also contain generous amounts of potassium, a mineral that's essential for keeping blood pressure down. Studies have shown that when potassium levels decline, even for short periods of time, blood pressure rises.

Prunes are a very good source of potassium, with five prunes containing 313 milligrams, which is about 9 percent of the DV. In fact, when Harvard School of Public Health researchers tracked 41,000 nurses for 4 years, they found that those who ate the most prunes, apples, oranges, and grapes had the lowest blood pressure levels.

GETTING THE MOST

For vitamins, drink the juice. Although prune juice has less fiber than the whole fruit, it's a more concentrated source of vitamins. For example, five whole prunes contain more than 1 milligram of vitamin C, while a 6-ounce glass of juice contains almost 8 milligrams. (And by the way, it's still called prune juice—not dried-plum juice.)

For regularity, eat the fruit. Since fiber is such an important part of digestive health, doctors recommend eating whole prunes, either fresh or canned, when you're trying to stay regular. While prune juice has also been used to help relieve constipation, it's somewhat less effective than the whole fruit.

Cook outside the box. Try adding whirled prunes to burgers. Texas A&M

University researchers have found that adding prune purée to hamburger meat creates a mix that's moister when cooked. Try making prune purée (use pitted prunes) in a food processor, then adding some to lean ground beef before shaping the burgers for the grill.

Baked Chicken with Prunes

1 pound skinless, boneless chicken breast halves

16 pitted prunes

¼ cup red wine

1 teaspoon minced fresh rosemary

¼ teaspoon salt

Freshly ground black pepper

Preheat the oven to 350°F.

Coat a 12- × 8-inch baking dish with cooking spray. Arrange the chicken in the dish in a single layer.

In a small microwaveable bowl, combine the prunes and wine. Microwave on high power for 1 minute, or until the wine boils. Pour the mixture over the chicken. Sprinkle with the rosemary.

Bake for 30 minutes, or until the chicken is no longer pink in the center. Test for doneness by inserting the tip of a sharp knife in the center of a breast half. Sprinkle with the salt and season with pepper to taste. Remove the chicken to 4 plates. Stir the pan juices to combine the spices, and spoon over the chicken.

Makes 4 servings

PER SERVING

Calories: 215	Cholesterol: 63 mg
Total fat: 2.9 g	Sodium: 190 mg
Saturated fat: 0.8 g	Dietary fiber: 3.3 g

Shellfish

HEALTH ON THE HALF SHELL

For most folks, shellfish like lobster, shrimp, scallops, and oysters are luxuries—foods to be reserved for special occasions. For one thing, shellfish are expensive, often costing twice as much (or more) as other fish. Shellfish also have a reputation for containing boatloads of cholesterol and a sea of sodium, both of which health-conscious diners usually try to avoid.

While it's true that shellfish are high in cholesterol and sodium, these aren't the health threats that scientists once thought they were, says Robert M. Grodner, PhD, professor emeritus in the department of food science at Louisiana State University in Baton Rouge. In addition, shellfish contain good amounts of vitamins, minerals, and other healthful compounds that more than offset their slight nutritional downside.

Good for the Heart

People who eat a lot of seafood fare even better than vegetarians when it comes to heart health. In one study, seafood eaters with high concentrations of omega-3s in their blood had significantly lower blood pressure and lower levels of cholesterol and triglycerides—blood fats that in large amounts can increase the risk of heart disease—than vegetarians who didn't eat shellfish. Although many of the studies on omega-3s have focused on fish like salmon and mackerel, all fish, including shellfish, contain some omega-3s. In fact, eating six medium oysters five to seven times a month will provide all the omega-3s your heart needs.

Omega-3s love your heart and blood vessels. These fatty acids improve the electrical stability of the heart, guarding against deadly out-of-rhythm heartbeats, notes researcher Dariush Mozaffarian, MD, DrPH, a cardiologist at Harvard Medical School and the author of a recent study finding that people who eat just two fish meals per week cut their risk of heart disease death by a respectable 36 percent. Omega-3s also make the linings of blood vessels function better and may improve the way cells respond to insulin, the hormone that tells cells to absorb blood sugar. Insulin problems raise the risk for diabetes and heart disease.

Scallops, as well as other shellfish, give your cardiovascular system a boost of

In the Kitchen

Shellfish are extremely perishable. Even when properly stored, they stay fresh for only a day or two. In addition, they cook very quickly. The difference between "just right" and "yuck" is often measured in minutes—or less. Here are a few tips for having the freshest catch every time:

Buy them live. Since shellfish go bad so quickly, it's best to buy them live and cook them the same day. To keep them fresh after bringing them home from the store, be sure to store them in the refrigerator until you're ready to start cooking.

Check for doneness. Few foods are less appetizing than undercooked shellfish. Lobsters and crabs turn bright red when they're done, usually in about 15 to 20 minutes. Clams, mussels, and oysters are nearly done when the shells open. Letting them cook for another 5 minutes will finish the job.

---

vitamin B_{12}—one serving of scallops packs a third of your daily needs. In its heart-protecting role, vitamin B_{12} helps your body deactivate the amino acid homocysteine before it can harm the thin inner lining of artery walls and set the stage for a buildup of artery-clogging plaque.

What about cholesterol? Shrimp's quirky cholesterol count—about 200 milligrams in 12 large ones, which is about the same as the cholesterol in one large egg—could make you pass up this low-cal delicacy. But for most of us, shrimp should get the green light: In a definitive Rockefeller University study, shrimp raised bad low-density lipoprotein (LDL) cholesterol by 7 percent, but also boosted good high-density lipoprotein (HDL) cholesterol even higher and decreased heart-threatening blood fats called triglycerides by 13 percent. Researchers concluded that when they took all of shrimp's effects on blood fats into consideration, the bottom line is that shrimp's a heart-smart treat. In contrast, eating two eggs raised LDL levels 10 percent but didn't have the same positive effects on other blood fats.

And don't be deterred by the sodium in shellfish, either. As you would expect of creatures from the sea, shellfish contain quite a bit—about 150 to 900 milligrams in a 3-ounce serving, depending on the type. But unless your doctor has suggested that you reduce the sodium in your diet, shellfish shouldn't be a problem. One serving of shellfish is well within the Daily Value (DV) of 2,400 milligrams of sodium.

Multivitamins in a Shell

Aside from their role in protecting the heart, shellfish are incredibly rich sources of a variety of essential (and hard-to-find) vitamins and minerals. The large amounts of vitamin B_{12} in shellfish are important to your health for other reasons. The body uses this nutrient to keep nerves healthy and make red blood cells. When levels of vitamin B_{12} slip, the body (and mind) can literally short-circuit, causing memory loss, confusion, slow reflexes, and fatigue. In fact, what's thought to be senility in older people is sometimes nothing more than a lack of vitamin B_{12}.

Three ounces of crab contains 10 micrograms of vitamin B_{12}, or 167 percent of the DV. Clams are even better, with 3 ounces—about nine small steamed clams—providing 1,400 percent of the DV.

With the exception of shrimp, shellfish also contain a lot of zinc, which is essential for keeping the immune system strong. Oysters are the best source, with six oysters containing about 27 milligrams, or almost 181 percent of the DV.

It's sometimes hard to get enough iron from foods, which is why about 20 percent of Americans are low in this important mineral. But if you can muster up enough muscle to lift a mussel to your mouth, you'll get much of the iron you need to help prevent iron-deficiency anemia. Three ounces of mussels provides about 6 milligrams of iron, or 60 percent of the Recommended Dietary Allowance (RDA) for men.

Finally, many shellfish are good sources of magnesium, potassium, and vitamin C. The vitamin C is a great bonus because it helps the body absorb more of the iron found in these foods.

FOOD ALERT

Hazards on the Half Shell

Shellfish are nutritious and delicious. But unless they're prepared with care, they can also be dangerous.

In order to eat and breathe, shellfish such as clams and oysters filter 15 to 20 gallons of water a day through their shells. When the water contains bacteria, like the potentially harmful *Vibrio vulnificus*, the shellfish become contaminated and have the ability to make you sick.

This doesn't mean that you can't eat shellfish safely. Since the bacteria are readily killed by heat, cooking your catch will prevent potential problems. While this is bad news for lovers of oysters on the half-shell, there may be an alternative, at least in the future. Laboratory studies suggest that dousing raw oysters with hot sauce will kill the bacteria. Until further research is done, however, it's best to be safe and eat your shellfish cooked.

Brain Food That's Fun to Eat

Your brain's got one of the highest concentrations of omega-3 fatty acids in your entire body. These long chains of fat molecules are woven into the membranes of brain cells, helping to send and receive the electrical and hormonal signals that translate into thoughts and feelings. "Researchers who look at problems like schizophrenia and depression are finding associations between lower levels of seafood intake and a greater likelihood of problems," notes researcher Susan E. Carlson, PhD, professor of dietetics and nutrition at the University of Kansas Medical Center in Kansas City. "And lab studies are showing that when you change the composition of brain cell membranes, so that there's less good fat in the mix, the membranes don't send and receive signals as well."

Doctor's Top Tip

For low-pollution, eco-friendly shellfish, go for these varieties: farmed scallops, blue or New Zealand green mussels, butter or Pacific littleneck clams, Northern shrimp, and spotted prawns. Eat with confidence! These shellfish are low in contaminants and raised with environmentally friendly methods that don't pollute surrounding waters or endanger other sea creatures, advises Bill Chameides, PhD, chief scientist for the Environmental Defense Fund. Dungeness and stone crabs are also recommended.

GETTING THE MOST

Eat them with vitamin C. Since your body is better able to absorb the iron in foods when you eat them with vitamin C, include vitamin C–rich foods such as broccoli or peppers on the shellfish menu.

Mix and match. Because shellfish are usually considered a luxury item, most people eat only a handful or two at a time. An easy way to include more of them in your diet is to toss them together in one big, briny stew, says Dr. Grodner. "It can be a mighty healthful meal," he says.

Seafood Stew

2 tablespoons olive oil

1½ cups chopped onions

1 tablespoon minced garlic

1 can (28 ounces) plum tomatoes with basil (with juice)

2½ cups water

1 cup reduced-sodium vegetable juice

¼ cup no-salt-added tomato paste

1 teaspoon dried oregano

8 ounces Dungeness or blue crabmeat

9 ounces medium shrimp, peeled and deveined

8 ounces chopped clams (with juice)

1 tablespoon chopped parsley

In a Dutch oven, heat the oil over medium heat. Add the onions and garlic. Cook, stirring frequently, until the onions soften, about 5 minutes. Add the tomatoes (with juice), breaking up the tomatoes with the back of a spoon.

Add the water, vegetable juice, tomato paste, and oregano. Stir to mix. Bring to a boil, then reduce the heat to low. Cover and cook for 30 minutes.

Meanwhile, pick over the crabmeat, and discard any bits of shell. Place the crabmeat in a fine strainer. Rinse with cold water and drain.

Add the crabmeat, shrimp, and clams to the pot. Increase the heat to medium-high. As soon as the stew returns to a boil, remove it from the heat. Set aside, covered, until the shrimp are opaque in the center, about 5 minutes. Test by cutting a shrimp in half.

Sprinkle with the parsley.

Makes 6 servings

Cook's Note: *Serve the stew with plenty of whole-grain bread for dipping in the sauce.*

PER SERVING

Calories: 227
Total fat: 6.6 g
Saturated fat: 0.9 g

Cholesterol: 108 mg
Sodium: 481 mg
Dietary fiber: 2.7 g

Smoking
OUTSMARTING THE EVIL WEED

Apparently there aren't a lot of smokers thumping melons or scrutinizing tomatoes at the local supermarket. Experts aren't sure why, but smokers don't eat as many fruits and vegetables as nonsmokers do. But the more fruits and vegetables you eat, studies show, the better your odds of escaping the ravages of the smoker's "big three"—heart disease, stroke, and cancer.

You don't have to eat boatloads of bananas or bushels of Brussels sprouts to get the benefits. Eating just one fruit or a serving of vegetables a day may slightly cut your risk of lung cancer, and having nine or more servings a day can have a significant impact.

There are two reasons that fruits and vegetables should get top billing on a smoker's plate. First, they're packed with antioxidants, powerful nutrients that protect against smoking-related diseases like heart disease and cancer. Plus, produce is loaded with phytonutrients, compounds found in plants that show promise for preventing or even treating these diseases. Just how powerful are the antioxidants in produce? In a Chinese study of 63,257 adults, those who ate the most fruits and vegetables loaded with the antioxidant beta-cryptoxanthin had a 27 percent reduction in lung cancer risk. But smokers in the study who ate the most foods containing this carotenoid cut their risk by 37 percent.

Understanding the Danger

Bananas turn brown. Cooking oils turn rancid. Our bodies eventually decay. Yech—it's not a pretty image. In all these cases, the damage is caused by the same thing: highly reactive, dangerous molecules called free radicals.

Although free radicals occur naturally, their numbers are greatly increased by such things as pollution and exposure to cigarette smoke—either as a smoker or as someone who breathes in secondhand smoke on a regular basis. The result? Damage caused by free radicals contributes to a host of age-related maladies like heart disease, cancer, and a type of vision loss called age-related macular degeneration.

The danger's not just for smokers. It's for anyone exposed to cigarette smoke. Secondhand smoke—which includes both the smoke exhaled by smokers and "sidestream smoke" from the end of a lit cigarette, pipe, or cigar—contains over 4,000

THE BEST PROTECTION

The USDA recommends that we eat at least five servings of fruits and vegetables a day. But because tobacco smoke depletes valuable nutrients from the body, smokers "ought to eat at least twice that amount," says James Scala, PhD, a nutritionist and author of *If You Can't/Won't Stop Smoking*.

While it's always best to eat a wide variety of fruits and vegetables, some foods have been found to be especially protective.

Citrus fruit. Smoking one cigarette destroys between 25 and 100 milligrams of vitamin C, says pharmacist Earl Mindell, RPh, PhD, professor emeritus of nutrition at Pacific Western University in Los Angeles and author of *Earl Mindell's Food as Medicine*. "It would be a good idea to eat a fruit or vegetable that's rich in vitamin C for every cigarette you smoke," he says.

Cruciferous vegetables. Broccoli, cauliflower, watercress, and other members of this vegetable family contain compounds called indoles and isothiocyanates, which in laboratory studies have been shown to slow the growth of cancers.

Soy foods. Tofu, tempeh, and other soy foods contain a number of cancer-fighting substances, including genistein and protease inhibitors. In Japan (where people eat large amounts of soy), more than 60 percent of men over age 20 smoke, yet the incidence of lung cancer is much lower than it is here, says Dr. Mindell.

Strawberries, grapes, and cherries. These fruits are rich in ellagic acid, a phytochemical that has been shown to destroy hydrocarbons, potentially cancer-causing chemicals in cigarette smoke.

Tomatoes. Inside tomatoes is a substance called lycopene, which has powerful antioxidant abilities. In fact, tomatoes appear to provide more cancer protection than other fruits or green vegetables.

---

chemical compounds, including 60 known or suspected to cause cancer. Breathing this stuff in causes an estimated 46,000 deaths from heart disease in nonsmokers who live with smokers and about 3,400 lung cancer deaths in nonsmoking adults.

It would seem logical that taking an antioxidant supplement would offer all the protection you'd need. But a famous and tragic study of 29,133 male smokers from Finland proves dramatically that getting your antioxidants from food is the way to go. The men took high-dose supplements of beta-carotene, alpha-tocopherol, both, or nothing for several years. Men taking the supplements had an 18 percent increased risk for lung cancer. Another beta-carotene supplementation study for smokers was cut short when researchers found an increased risk of lung cancer for smokers. Experts can't fully explain why, but they suspect that antioxidants like beta-carotene work when they're in their original, natural package—and come with hundreds of other phytonutrients. In other words, a carrot is better for you than a capsule. Since these two earlier studies were done, more recent studies of smaller doses of vitamins A, C, and E have found no advantage to taking them as separate supplements and, in some cases, found increased risk of death, though researchers could not pinpoint the cause.

"People who eat more fruits and vegetables get half the lung cancer per given amount of smoking compared with the people who eat less. So there's clearly some big interaction. Plus smoking depletes all your antioxidants. It's well known that it's an oxidative stress," notes Bruce Ames, PhD, professor of biochemistry and molecular biology and director of the National Institute of Environmental Health Sciences Center at the University of California, Berkeley.

The Main Players

While supplements may not be a smart way to get extra antioxidants, plenty of research shows that a diet rich in fruits, vegetables, whole grains, and nuts—all top sources of a wide range of antioxidant compounds—certainly is. If you smoke, you need these foods even more than a nonsmoker does. The body pulls antioxidants out of the blood and into the lungs in a valiant attempt to neutralize free-radical damage, says Gary E. Hatch, PhD, a research pharmacologist and branch chief of the pulmonary toxicology branch of the Environmental Protection Agency. "The cells in the lungs of a smoker are loaded with a lot more antioxidants than those of a nonsmoker," he explains. "The antioxidants are trying to protect the airways from the onslaught of these noxious chemicals."

Those antioxidants that have been linked with lower cancer rates include beta-carotene (which the body converts to vitamin A), vitamins C and E, and the mineral selenium.

Beta-carotene. Abundant in orange and yellow fruits and vegetables such as apricots, cantaloupes, carrots, pumpkins, and squash, beta-carotene from foods seems to protect against "smokers' cancers"—those of the colon, kidneys, skin, and lungs, says James Scala, PhD, a nutritionist and author of *If You Can't/Won't Stop Smoking*. Study after study shows that low levels of beta-carotene are associated with a greater cancer risk, including the risk of lung cancer.

Vitamin C. Found in strawberries, papaya, citrus fruits, and many other foods, vitamin C has been found to protect against a variety of cancers as well as heart disease and stroke, says pharmacist Earl Mindell, RPh, PhD, professor emeritus of nutrition at Pacific Western University in Los Angeles and author of *Earl Mindell's Food as Medicine*.

Vitamin E. Concentrated in wheat germ and wheat germ oil, vitamin E helps keep cell walls intact so it's harder for marauding free radicals to push their way in. More important, it also neutralizes free radicals, says Dr. Scala.

Selenium. Found in most fruits and vegetables, especially garlic, onions, and other bulb vegetables, selenium works with vitamin E to neutralize free radicals.

The Case for Produce

The evidence is strong (and getting stronger) that people who eat lots of fresh fruits and vegetables have a lower risk of developing lung and other cancers than people who eat less produce.

In a Japanese study, for example, researchers found that men who ate raw vegetables every day slashed their lung cancer risk by about 36 percent. Those who ate fruit every day reduced their risk of lung cancer by 55 percent.

Even the men who were smokers benefited. Smokers who ate fruit, raw vegetables, and green vegetables every day reduced their lung cancer risk by 59 percent, 44 percent, and 52 percent, respectively.

The benefits of produce aren't only in relation to lung cancer either. A high intake of fruits and vegetables has been linked to lower risks of just about every type of cancer.

Secondhand Protection

It's not only smokers who need extra dietary protection. Research has shown that secondhand smoke can be dangerous for people who live or work with those who light up. According to a study led by Susan Taylor Mayne, PhD, professor of chronic disease epidemiology at the Yale School of Public Health, eating 1½ additional servings of raw fresh fruits or vegetables a day may slash the risk of lung cancer from secondhand smoke by as much as 60 percent.

"Eating fruits and vegetables is associated with a decrease in risk, regardless of the amount of passive smoke that nonsmokers are exposed to," says Dr. Mayne. Particularly good choices are cantaloupes, carrots, and broccoli, which are loaded with beta-carotene.

Spices
PROTECTIVE FLAVORINGS

In biblical times, mustard seeds were thought to cure everything from toothaches to epilepsy. (Some people even sniffed ground mustard seeds because sneezing was thought to purge the brain.) Saffron, black pepper, fenugreek, and many other spices were also prized for their healing powers.

As it turns out, the ancients had an uncanny sense of which spices were most likely to be effective. "Researchers have identified many substances in spices that offer health benefits," says Melanie Polk, RD, director of nutrition education at the American Institute for Cancer Research. In fact, researchers are studying the healing potential of many kitchen spices, including black pepper, cumin, cloves, cinnamon, nutmeg, fenugreek, and turmeric.

The National Institute of Nutrition in India, for example, has found that turmeric contains compounds that may help prevent cancer. The research is so promising, in fact, that India's National Cancer Institute has proposed a public education campaign to promote greater use of this aromatic spice. (Read more on turmeric below.)

Unlike herbs, which come from the leaves of plants, spices are made from the buds, bark, fruits, roots, or seeds. The drying process doesn't appear to diminish their healing powers. When properly stored, spices can retain their active ingredients for months or even years.

Research into the world of spices is very new, Polk says, so scientists are only beginning to understand their healing potential. But what has been discovered so far is impressive.

Defense against Cancer

Spices contain an abundance of compounds called phytochemicals, or phytonutrients, many of which may help prevent normal, healthy cells from turning into cancer. And the ways in which these compounds work are as varied as the spices themselves.

Many spices, for example, contain antioxidants, substances that block the effects of free radicals in the body. Free radicals are harmful oxygen molecules that punch holes in healthy cells, sometimes causing genetic damage that can lead to cancer.

> **HEALING POWER**
> **Can Help:**
>
> Protect against cataracts
>
> Prevent cancer
>
> Lower cholesterol and triglycerides
>
> Prevent excessive blood clotting

Turmeric is a very rich source of antioxidants, including a compound called curcumin. In animal studies, curcumin has been shown to reduce the risk of colon cancer by 58 percent. Other research suggests that it may work against skin cancer as well.

What's more, some spices have the ability to help neutralize harmful substances in the body, taking away their cancer-causing potential. Nutmeg, ginger, cumin, black pepper, and coriander, for example, have been shown to help block the effects of aflatoxin, a mold that can cause liver cancer.

Finally, some spices appear to be capable of killing cancer cells outright. In laboratory studies, for example, compounds from saffron were placed on human cancer cells, including cells that cause leukemia. Not only did the dangerous cells stop growing, but the compounds appeared to have no effect on normal, healthy cells.

Since the research is still very new, researchers can't predict which spices or how much of different spices you might need to reduce your risk of getting cancer. "The best advice for now," Polk says, "is to use a variety of spices, especially for replacing salt and fat in your food."

Keeping Arteries Clear

There is good evidence that getting more spices in your diet can help cut your risk for heart disease. Some of the same compounds in spices that prevent free radicals from damaging healthy cells also prevent them from damaging cholesterol. This is important, because when cholesterol is damaged, it's much more likely to stick to artery walls.

In the Kitchen

Despite their robust appearance, spices don't last forever. And even when they're fresh, they're often reluctant to give up their full range of flavors. Here are a few ways to get the best tastes every time:

Stock up often. If you haven't bought spices since the last time you moved, it's probably time to throw out the old ones and start fresh. Ground spices lose their flavor quickly, usually in about 6 months. Whole spices, however, will keep their flavors for a year or two. Fresher is better, of course, but spices retain their health-promoting properties for several months or longer.

Store them carefully. Exposure to light, moisture, and air will quickly rob your spices of their delicious flavors. To keep them fresh, store them in airtight containers in a cool, dry place, preferably kept away from direct light.

Boost the flavor. To make a spice's natural flavors stand out even more, toast it briefly in a dry skillet until it's slightly brown and aromatic.

Cloves, for example, contain the powerful antioxidants kaempferol and rhamnetin. The curcumin in turmeric can also protect the arteries. Turmeric, incidentally, may provide double protection because it not only blocks free radicals but also has been shown to lower levels of triglycerides—dangerous blood fats that, in large amounts, appear to raise the risk of heart disease.

Yet another way in which certain spices keep cholesterol levels down is by trapping cholesterol-containing substances in the intestine. Fenugreek, for example, contains compounds called saponins, which bind to cholesterol and cause it to be excreted from the body. In one study, for example, scientists found that animals given fenugreek had drops in cholesterol of at least 18 percent.

It's not only high cholesterol that can raise the risk for heart disease. Another potential problem is platelets—small, cell-like components in blood that aid in clotting. While platelets are essential for stopping bleeding, sometimes they get too active and begin forming excessive clots in the bloodstream. If a clot gets large enough to block an artery, the result can be a heart attack or even a stroke.

At least five spices—turmeric, fenugreek, cloves, red chile peppers, and ginger—have been shown to help prevent platelets from clumping. In fact, a compound in ginger called gingerol has a chemical structure somewhat similar to aspirin's, which is a proven clot-busting drug.

Cutting Diabetes Risk

Cinnamon improves your body's ability to obey insulin and take up glucose (blood sugar), report researchers at the USDA's Beltsville Human Nutrition Research Center in Maryland. It also cuts heart-threatening triglycerides and bad low-density lipoprotein (LDL) cholesterol. At work is a compound in this spice called methylhydroxy chalcone polymer, which makes cells absorb glucose faster and convert it more easily into energy. When 30 men and 30 women with type 2 diabetes received either cinnamon or a placebo capsule (dummy pill) every day for 40 days, researchers found that the cinnamon group's blood sugar levels had fallen by 18 to 29 percent, their LDL cholesterol dropped 7 to 17 percent, their triglycerides fell 23 to 30 percent, and their good high-density lipoprotein (HDL) cholesterol rose slightly.

A Promising Future

Since spices contain a large number of compounds, researchers have just begun mapping their healing powers. But research from around the globe indicates that the list of benefits will only keep growing.

Researchers at the National Cancer Institute, for example, have found that the curcumin in turmeric can help prevent HIV, the virus that causes AIDS, from multiplying. Research has shown, in fact, that when people with AIDS were given curcumin, the illness progressed at a slower rate.

Curcumin has also been shown to protect the eyes from free radicals, which are one of the leading causes of cataracts. In fact, a laboratory study found that curcumin was able to reduce free-radical damage to the eyes by 52 percent. Other studies have found that curcumin supplements could ease the pain and inflammation of rheumatoid arthritis.

There's growing evidence that ginger, too, could help quell the inflammation associated with some forms of arthritis. In several studies, adults with osteoarthritis and rheumatoid arthritis who took ginger extracts experienced a significant reduction in pain and as a result, needed less of their pain medications and anti-inflammatory drugs. (A reality check: They still rated ibuprofen as a better pain reliever than ginger!) Lab studies confirm that compounds in ginger inhibit inflammation, suggesting it could help cut risk for health problems like heart disease, cancer, and Alzheimer's disease, as well as arthritis.

The gingerol in ginger relaxes blood vessels. This spice has a long history of use easing stomach upsets. Now, researchers at the University of Michigan are studying whether ginger can help ease nausea for cancer patients undergoing chemotherapy. "Ginger has been shown to be effective in a number of clinical trials against nausea and vomiting associated with motion sickness, pregnancy, and postoperative recovery," says lead investigator Suzanna Zick, ND, MPH. "With this trial, we hope to determine its efficacy and safety for chemotherapy-induced nausea and vomiting. "We hope ginger will be effective for patients who continue to experience delayed nausea and vomiting despite treatment with other antinausea drugs," Dr. Zick adds.

On another front, spicy, red-hot paprika shows promise for cutting cancer risk, due to the anti-inflammatory and antioxidant properties of the compound capsaicin.

And a powerful, inflammation-fighting, numbing compound in cloves called eugenol has made it a top choice in products used by dentists during root canal surgery. It may even help cut risk for digestive system cancers.

Finally, researchers at the University of Wales College of Medicine discovered that a strain of black pepper called West African black pepper appears to produce changes in the brains of mice that can reduce the severity of seizures.

"We only have information on a few spices so far," Polk says. "But no doubt, we'll be uncovering similarly exciting information about many others in the future."

Indian-Style Spice Mix

8 **teaspoons dry mustard**

4 **teaspoons ground fenugreek**

4 **teaspoons ground cumin**

2 **teaspoons ground cloves**

2 **teaspoons ground coriander**

2 **teaspoons ground ginger**

2 **teaspoons ground turmeric**

½ **teaspoon ground cinnamon**

In a small bowl, combine the mustard, fenugreek, cumin, cloves, coriander, ginger, turmeric, and cinnamon. Mix well to blend. Store in a small, airtight jar in a cool, dark cupboard or the refrigerator.

Makes ½ cup

Cook's Notes: *Ground fenugreek is available in Indian groceries, some specialty food shops, and health food stores.*

You could easily double this recipe. The spice mixture is delicious enough—and versatile enough—to keep on hand in the kitchen. It's excellent as a rub for broiled or pan-cooked meats, fish, and poultry (rub the mixture over the food generously before cooking). Or use it as a flavoring for steamed cauliflower, carrots, and other vegetables. To bring out the flavor, toast the spice mix briefly in a dry skillet just before using.

Spiced Potato Cakes

3 **large baking potatoes**

2 **teaspoons canola oil**

1 **cup chopped onions**

4 **teaspoons Indian-Style Spice Mix (page 219)**

¾ **cup fat-free plain yogurt**

¼ **cup fat-free egg substitute**

2 **teaspoons unsalted butter**

¼ **teaspoon salt**

Scrub the potatoes and pat dry with paper towels. With a fork, pierce each potato in 3 or 4 places. Arrange the potatoes, spoke fashion, in a microwave oven on top of a paper towel. Microwave on high power for 10 minutes. Turn the potatoes, and rotate from the front to the back of the microwave. Microwave for 8 to 10 minutes, or until the potatoes are tender. Test for doneness by inserting the tip of a small, sharp knife into a potato. Let the potatoes stand for 5 minutes.

Halve the potatoes lengthwise. Use a large spoon to scrape all the flesh into a medium bowl; discard the skins. Mash with a fork and set aside.

In a large nonstick skillet, heat the oil over medium-high heat. Add the onions and cook, stirring frequently, until they start to turn golden, about 5 minutes. Add the spice mix, and cook for 30 seconds, or until fragrant.

Remove from the heat and transfer to a large bowl. Add the yogurt, egg substitute, butter, and salt. Stir to combine. Add the potatoes. Mix well.

Wipe the skillet with a paper towel, and coat with cooking spray. Heat over medium-high heat. Drop the potato mixture into the skillet in 4 mounds, patting the mixture with a spatula to make thick cakes. Cook until golden on the bottom, about 5 minutes. Turn and cook until golden on the second side, about 3 minutes.

Makes 4 servings

PER SERVING

Calories: 243	Cholesterol: 5 mg
Total fat: 4.9 g	Sodium: 171 mg
Saturated fat: 1.4 g	Dietary fiber: 3.9 g

Stomach Upset
CALMING THE QUEASIES

One of life's ironies is that many of the foods we like best, like creamy chocolate éclairs or a feast of roast turkey, stuffing, and gravy, are the same ones that our stomachs like least, at least when we overindulge. And overindulge we do—with family, friends, and co-workers—more than a few times a year. This is why our festive feasts sometimes end not with a glass of wine but with a spoonful of Pepto-Bismol or a glass of bubbly Alka-Seltzer (instead of champagne!).

Getting too much food in your system at one time is a common cause of stomach upset because your body has trouble handling the sudden increase in volume, says William Ruderman, MD, a gastroenterologist in private practice in Orlando, Florida. Eating too much fat at once can also be a problem because it may trip the nausea sensor in your brain, which sends those miserable, queasy sensations down to your stomach.

High-fat foods are bad in yet another way. They temporarily weaken a small muscle at the base of the esophagus, the tube leading from the mouth to the stomach. This allows digestive juices, which normally stay in the stomach, to surge upstream, causing heartburn or nausea, says Marie Borum, MD, professor of medicine and director of the division of gastroenterology at George Washington University Medical Center in Washington, D.C. The combination of heartburn and that too-full feeling can take the cheerful bloom off any social evening.

Two of the best ways to keep your stomach calm are to eat a little bit less at meals and to cut back on your intake of fatty foods, especially fried meats, says Dr. Borum. But if your stomach's already upset, what you really need is something that will take the queasiness away fast. As it turns out, foods, especially bland foods, can do that, too.

"I recommend starting with water, then moving on to toast, broth, bland soup, or soft-boiled eggs," says Dr. Borum. "Naturally, you also want to avoid the hard-to-digest foods like ice cream or fried chicken."

When even bland foods are hard to get down, don't even try to eat, Dr. Borum adds. There's nothing wrong with going without food for 4 to 6 hours. Many people are reluctant to skip meals, but a temporary fast can actually be very soothing. In fact, that may be just the right thing to help your stomach recover.

MERRY, MERRY, QUITE CONTRARY

Good food, good drink, and good company—who doesn't like a good party? But making too many trips to the punch bowl can leave your stomach wishing you'd spent the night playing solitaire.

While there's no real cure for "morning-after stomach," there are a few foods that will help ease the discomfort of a hangover. Here are some examples that you can try in a pinch.

Keep it plain. Having a slice of plain bread—without butter, peanut butter, or cream cheese—will help buffer acids in the stomach that can lead to nausea, according to Marie Borum, MD, professor of medicine and director of the division of gastroenterology at George Washington University Medical Center in Washington, D.C. In addition, bland foods like bread and pasta are very easy to digest, which can help keep an upset stomach calm.

Drink like a fish. Getting more water into your system can help relieve the nausea and dehydration that may be caused by excessive drinking. If you've been drinking alcohol, in fact, it's a good idea to have plenty of water before going to bed at night because it can help prevent some of the discomfort you might experience the next morning.

One of the most popular remedies for an upset stomach is also one of the oldest. Studies show that ginger can sometimes work better than over-the-counter drugs to settle a somersaulting stomach. "Ginger is the one herbal treatment that's pretty widely accepted as effective," says Marvin Schuster, MD, founder of the Marvin M. Schuster Digestive and Motility Disorders Center at Johns Hopkins Bayview Medical Center in Baltimore.

While fresh ginger is effective, it's really too spicy to use to get the amounts that are necessary for healing. An easier strategy, says Dr. Schuster, is to brew a cup of ginger tea. Grate 2 teaspoons of fresh ginger, and let it steep in hot water for 10 minutes. Strain the tea, then drink it until you feel better. For many people, just 1 cup is enough to do the trick.

Another beverage that may help settle your stomach is Coca-Cola. The ingredients in Coke are top secret, so no one really knows why so many people reach for the "real thing" when their stomachs are flip-flopping. Still, drinking Coke does seem to be helpful, says Dr. Borum. "Coke is also high in sugar, which is important if you've already been sick and need hydration," she adds.

One problem with having an upset stomach is that it's often difficult even to drink water without feeling sicker. To keep yourself from getting dehydrated, try keeping a small piece of ice in your mouth, Dr. Borum suggests. This will allow some water to enter your system, but not so much that it will upset your stomach even more. Sometimes sipping extremely cold liquids may do the trick. Or take small, frequent sips every 15 to 30 minutes (this is easier on an upset tummy and promotes absorption).

Dieting and have stomach upset? Don't soothe your tummy with "sugar-free" foods. These sweets and drinks are often made with sugar alcohols like sorbitol, xylitol, mannitol, and maltitol, which can cause gas and bloating—and even act as a laxative.

And if your stomach is queasy, be sure to skip nonsteroidal anti-inflammatory drugs (NSAIDs). Ibuprofen (including Advil and Motrin) and aspirin can further upset your tummy. Use acetaminophen if you need a pain reliever.

Doctor's Top Tip

If you're not just nauseous, but also vomiting, make an effort to stay hydrated. Drink small, steady amounts of clear liquids, suggests the National Institutes of Health. If you've been sick for several hours, switch to diluted fruit juice, a sports drink like Gatorade, or broth. Your body may be depleted of fluids and also short on electrolytes like potassium and sodium, which help cells function and communicate. You can create your own rehydration drink by mixing together ¾ teaspoon of table salt, 1 teaspoon of baking powder, 4 tablespoons of white sugar, 1 cup of orange juice, and 1 quart of water. Take small, frequent sips.

Stress

GETTING EASE WITH Bs

Late for work—grab a doughnut. The report's due—pour another cup of coffee. Stress is all around us, and food often provides a welcome, if momentary, break. Unfortunately, the foods we often turn to in times of stress, like coffee and sweets, have a way of making us feel even more frazzled later on.

It doesn't have to be this way. Research has shown that eating more of some foods and less of others can cause stress hormones in the body to decline. Making slight changes in your diet will produce physical changes in the brain that can make the world's problems just a little bit easier to handle.

Calming Carbohydrates

Mashed potatoes. Fresh-baked bread. A steaming plate of pasta. These are just a few of the "comfort foods" that many of us instinctively turn to in times of stress. As it turns out, our instincts are dead-on. Researchers have found that foods high in carbohydrates produce changes in the brain that can take the edge off stress.

During emotionally trying times, the brain quickly uses up its supply of serotonin, a chemical that imparts feelings of well-being. When serotonin levels fall, negative feelings tend to rise, says Joe Tecce, PhD, a neuropsychologist and associate professor of psychology at Boston College in Chestnut Hill, Massachusetts.

Eating foods that are high in carbohydrates, like pasta, bagels, or baked potatoes, can quickly raise low serotonin levels, making you feel less stressed and more relaxed, says Dr. Tecce. And here's a little carbohydrate bonus: As serotonin levels rise, appetite usually decreases, which means that you're less likely to eat your way through hard times.

A Zoo Story

Next time you visit the monkey house, take a moment to admire our swinging cousins. They turn somersaults, hang from trees, and generally appear to be having a great time. They don't have to deal with carpools or bills, which could explain their lack of stress. Then again, maybe it's all the bananas they've been eating.

Research suggests that foods high in vitamin B_6, such as bananas, potatoes, and prunes, can relieve irritability and stress, making people (and maybe monkeys) feel just a little bit better. In one study, Dr. Tecce and his colleagues at the Jean Mayer USDA Human Nutrition Research Center on Aging at Tufts University in Boston lowered vitamin B$_6$ levels in a group of volunteers. The people became increasingly irritable and tense.

Vitamin B$_6$ improves mood by raising levels of dopamine, a chemical in the brain that is related to feeling good. When you don't get enough vitamin B$_6$ in your diet, dopamine levels fall, and you can experience negative feelings. In addition, people who don't get enough vitamin B$_6$ may produce too little serotonin, which will make them feel even worse.

It's not yet clear how much vitamin B$_6$ you might need to help keep stress levels down, says Dr. Tecce. It seems likely, however, that the Daily Value (DV) of 2 milligrams is probably enough. It's very easy to get this much vitamin B$_6$ in your diet. One banana, for example, has 0.7 milligram, or 35 percent of the DV; a half-cup of chickpeas has 0.6 milligram, or 30 percent of the DV; and a baked potato has 0.4 milligram, or 20 percent of the DV.

The Caffeine Crash

Just about anywhere there are people hard at work, there will also be a coffeepot. And the more stress these people feel, the more likely they are to hit the joe. In a study of almost 300 people, for example, researchers at the University of Minnesota in Morris found that half of them drank more coffee or caffeine-containing soft drinks during high-pressure times.

Caffeine produces a quick zing that can momentarily make you feel more relaxed and confident. Fairly quickly, however, it stimulates the production of cortisol, a stress hormone that raises blood pressure and heart rate. This can make you feel more stressed than you did before, says William Lovallo, PhD, professor of psychiatry and behavioral sciences at the University of Oklahoma Health Sciences Center in Oklahoma City.

It doesn't take potfuls of coffee to rev up your stress levels, Dr. Lovallo adds. In a study of 48 men, Dr. Lovallo and his colleagues found that those drinking just 2 to 3 cups had a significant increase in blood pressure.

This doesn't mean that you have to give up your favorite drinks, Dr. Lovallo adds. But when the pressure's on, switching to drinks without caffeine will help keep you calmer and more in control.

And while you're filling your cup, put the lid back on the sugar. Within minutes after eating sweets, blood sugar levels start to fall. "When your blood sugar is going up and down, you are more susceptible to moodiness and irritability," says Peter Miller, PhD, professor of psychiatry and behavioral sciences at the Medical

University of South Carolina in Charleston and former executive director of the Hilton Head Health Institute in Hilton Head Island, South Carolina.

The Stress-Cookie Connection

There's a good reason we head for the cookies, chocolate, or (fill in your favorite stress-busting food) when we are under pressure. Eating sugar- and fat-rich foods helps blunt the effects of our physiological response to chronic stress.

During chronic stress, levels of glucocorticoid hormones increase. Researchers at the University of California, San Francisco, found that rats with elevated glucocorticoid levels engage in pleasure-seeking activities such as eating fat and sugar. When they do so, they gain abdominal fat.

Eating comfort foods puts the brakes on a key element of chronic stress. In the short term, it may be worth gaining a couple of pounds to calm down. In the long term, however, fixing the source of the stress or finding alternatives such as yoga or meditation are healthier.

The other problem with the stress/carb connection: roller-coaster cravings. First, blood sugar soars (and you feel great). Then your pancreas pumps out a big dose of insulin, which pushes all that sugar into your cells, and blood sugar plummets. You feel cranky again . . . so you reach for more cookies. The result? More crankiness . . . and finally difficulty fitting into your favorite jeans.

Stroke

A HEALTHY-BRAIN DIET

The most frightening thing about stroke is how suddenly it can strike. People who have had a stroke say there's often no discernible warning, no sign—just a split-second sense that something has suddenly gone wrong.

But even though the stroke itself comes out of the blue, the problems that cause it can be years in the making. Stroke occurs when blood, and the oxygen and nutrients it contains, stop reaching parts of the brain—thanks usually to a blood clot blocking a tiny artery in your brain or, less often, when an artery ruptures and blood is lost.

High blood pressure, high cholesterol, diabetes, and a dangerous prediabetic condition called metabolic syndrome all raise your risk—and they're all factors that can be reduced significantly by choosing the right foods. "Your diet plays a critical role in preventing stroke," says Thomas A. Pearson, MD, PhD, professor of epidemiology and chairman of the department of community and preventive medicine at the University of Rochester in New York.

These six eating strategies offer powerful protection:

Calm high blood pressure with dairy and potassium. High blood pressure (135/85 or higher) doubles your risk for a stroke. Here's why. Pummeled by high-speed bloodflow, arteries in the brain thicken and can ultimately squeeze shut. Under pressure, small arteries may rupture. High blood pressure also ups the risk for developing clot-producing plaque in artery walls. If everyone with high blood pressure in the United States brought it under control, more than 300,000 strokes annually could be prevented.

Your food plan? Include low-fat dairy products and plenty of potassium-rich foods in your diet. Not only does potassium fight high blood pressure (something 50 million of us suffer from), it also appears to make blood less likely to clot, which can reduce the risk of stroke even more. Not sure what foods are good sources of potassium? Fat-free and 1% milk, low-fat yogurt, vegetable juice cocktail, baby limas, kidney beans, and lentils are all rich in potassium. So are baked potatoes, prune juice, dried peaches, and Swiss chard.

Milk is another beverage that appears to play a role in reducing the risk of stroke. In one large study, researchers from the Honolulu Heart Program found that men who did not drink milk were twice as likely to have a stroke as those who drank at least 16 ounces daily. When reaching for the carton, however, be sure that it contains low-fat or fat-free milk, since the saturated fat that's in whole milk may offset its benefits.

Reverse metabolic syndrome with smart meal combos. Metabolic syndrome is a combination of prediabetic conditions including insulin resistance—which occurs when your cells stop responding quickly to insulin's command to absorb blood sugar—plus slightly high blood pressure, blood sugar, and triglyceride levels, plus low levels of good high-density lipoprotein (HDL) cholesterol. Nearly everyone who has this condition—and there are at least 40 million Americans who are at risk for metabolic syndrome—is overweight. Having metabolic syndrome doubles stroke risk.

What fights it? Eating high-fiber, low-sugar foods, lean protein, good fats such as nuts, oily cold-water fish (or fish oil capsules), and flaxseed. Eating fruits, vegetables, and grain products low on the glycemic index (a ranking system based on how foods affect your blood sugar levels) also keeps blood sugar and insulin levels lower. This can cut cravings and help you lose weight and can almost instantly make cells throughout your body more sensitive to insulin's signals. Foods to avoid: doughnuts, sugary soft drinks, and white bread, all of which send sugar levels soaring, fast. Foods to embrace: most whole grains, beans, fruits, and vegetables, which digest more slowly in the gut and so release sugar into the bloodstream at a leisurely rate. You can also slow the rise in blood sugar after a meal by combining a high-fiber or high-protein food with a refined carbohydrate—for example, have some navy beans with instant rice.

Lose weight. Not only what you eat but how much you eat can play a role in controlling stroke. Being overweight is perhaps the leading cause of high blood pressure, which vastly increases stroke risk. In fact, people with high blood pressure are five times more likely to have a stroke than those whose blood pressures are normal. In addition, being overweight makes you more likely to develop diabetes, which also increases the risk of stroke.

Get serious about treating diabetes with slow carbs. Keep diabetes under control by choosing "good," "slow," complex carbohydrates like fruits, vegetables, and whole grains. These keep your blood sugar lower and steadier and also help to control levels of insulin in your body. Experts suspect that the surges of insulin after a meal that is heavy in refined carbs contribute to biochemical changes in the body that promote high blood pressure and blood clot formation—which are two big stroke risks.

Rebalance your cholesterol profile with better fats. High levels of bad low-density lipoprotein (LDL) cholesterol and low levels of good HDL cholesterol both raise stroke risk. A lack of good HDL leaves your body unable to haul away the bad-guy LDL, giving it free rein to lodge inside the lining of artery walls and start the process that leads to clogged arteries.

For lower LDL and higher HDL levels, eat less saturated fat and more good fats. Choosing olive or canola oil over other kinds of fats for cooking, and snacking on a small handful of walnuts can help maintain healthy HDL levels. (Add exercise to really give 'em a boost.)

Doctor's Top Tip

Dropping just a few pounds can cut stroke risk. You don't have to be super-thin to stay healthy, says Thomas A. Pearson, MD, PhD, of the University of Rochester. Losing 10 to 20 pounds is often enough to lower blood pressure and with it, the risk of having a stroke.

At the same time, skip full-fat milk, cheese, sour cream, and ice cream . . . and turn down that fat-marbled prime rib. What you don't eat can be just as important as what you do, adds Dr. Pearson. Research has shown, for example, that people getting the most fat in their diets—especially the saturated fat found in meats and other animal foods—are much more likely to have a stroke than those who are eating more healthful foods. This is because a diet that's high in saturated fat raises cholesterol levels. Cholesterol, which is notorious for clogging arteries in the heart, can also block blood vessels in and leading to the brain.

"Reducing saturated fat intake is the most powerful dietary maneuver you can make to lower cholesterol levels," says John R. Crouse, MD, professor of medicine and public health sciences and currently associate director of the Wake Forest University School of Medicine General Clinical Research Center.

For most people, limiting meat servings to 3 or 4 ounces a day, using little (or no) butter, switching to low-fat dairy foods, and avoiding high-fat snacks is all it takes to keep cholesterol at healthy levels.

And choose lots of produce, too. When researchers from the well-known Framingham Heart Study group scrutinized the diets of more than 830 men, they found that for every three servings of fruits and vegetables people ate every day, their risk of stroke declined 22 percent.

There are several reasons that fruits and vegetables are so beneficial for preventing stroke. For one thing, they're high in fiber, which has been shown to lower cholesterol. And according to epidemiologist Michael Hertog, PhD, of the National Institute of Public Health and Environmental Protection in the Netherlands, these foods also contain powerful antioxidants, which help prevent the harmful LDL cholesterol from sticking to artery walls and blocking bloodflow to the brain. Foods especially high in antioxidants include garlic, onions, kale, carrots, Brussels sprouts, broccoli, blueberries, plums, cherries, oranges, and red grapes.

It doesn't take a lot of antioxidant-rich foods to get the benefits. Even one large carrot (which contains as little as 15 milligrams of beta-carotene) can reduce the risk of stroke.

Along with fruits and vegetables, tea (both the green and black varieties) is an excellent source of flavonoids. When Dr. Hertog studied more than 550 men ages 50 to 69, he found that those who got most of their flavonoids from tea were able to reduce their risk of stroke by 73 percent, compared with those who got the least of these healthful compounds. He found that those who drink at least 5 cups of tea daily can reduce their stroke risk by more than two-thirds, compared with those who drink less than 3 cups a day.

Sweet Peppers

PICK A PECK FOR HEALTH

Due to the growing interest in ethnic cuisines, sweet peppers, which range in color from dark green to fire engine red, depending on how long they're left on the vine, aren't found only in salad bars anymore. They're also being used in soups, sauces, stir-fries, purées, and pasta dishes. Peppers do more than add a sweet high note to recipes. They're also filled with nutrients that have been shown in studies to battle cataracts and heart disease. And unlike their fiery-tempered siblings, the chile peppers, sweet peppers are mild enough to eat in large amounts, so you can easily reap their health benefits.

Stuffed with Antioxidants

Even though sweet peppers such as bell peppers, pimientos, and frying peppers don't get as much attention as broccoli, cauliflower, and other powerhouse foods, they're among the most nutrient-dense vegetables you can buy, especially when it comes to vitamin C and beta-carotene. (As a rule, the redder the pepper, the more healthful beta-carotene it contains.)

Bite for bite, few vegetables contain as much beta-carotene (which is converted to vitamin A in the body) as the sweet red pepper. This is important because beta-carotene plays a key role in keeping the immune system healthy. It's also a potent antioxidant, meaning that it fights tissue-damaging oxygen molecules known as free radicals, which scientists believe contribute to major health foes like heart disease and cataracts.

Sweet red peppers are such a good source of beta-carotene, in fact, that a group of German researchers has classified them as a "must-eat" food for people trying to get more of this antioxidant. One pepper has 4 milligrams of beta-carotene, or 40 to 66 percent of the recommended daily amount of 6 to 10 milligrams.

Both sweet red and green peppers also contain generous amounts of vitamin C, another powerful antioxidant. A half-cup of chopped green pepper (about half a pepper) contains 45 milligrams of vitamin C, or 74 percent of the Daily Value (DV). Sweet red peppers are even better, with the same-size serving providing 142 milligrams of

In the Kitchen

Some like it hot—and some don't. If you prefer peppers that are sweet to those that make you sweat, here are a few varieties you may want to try:

- **Bell peppers**, which are now available in almost every color of the rainbow, can be eaten raw, grilled, baked, or stir-fried.
- **Frying peppers** have a mild, sweet taste, and their thin walls make them perfect for sautéing and using as a topping for toasted Italian bread.
- **Hungarian yellow wax (banana) peppers**, which resemble the fruit both in color and shape, have a mild, sweet taste, and are often used in salads and sandwiches.
- **Paprika peppers**, which are dried to make the spice, can also be fried, stuffed, or eaten raw.
- **Pimientos** are squat, heart-shaped peppers that aficionados claim are the best-tasting peppers you can buy. While they're often used commercially for stuffing olives, you can buy them fresh in some specialty produce markets from late summer to fall.

vitamin C, or 236 percent of the DV. That's more than twice the amount that you'd get from a medium-size orange.

The combination of vitamin C and beta-carotene can provide potent protection. These two compounds work together in your body to disarm free radicals. In a study of more than 900 people, Italian researchers found that those who ate sweet peppers and other foods rich in beta-carotene regularly were significantly less likely to have cataracts than those who did not.

Some limited studies appear to indicate that eating a diet high in antioxidants may also reduce the risk of developing age-related macular degeneration, a leading cause of blindness in the United States. More research is needed, but it's not too soon to eat more fruits and vegetables high in the eye-protecting antioxidants lutein and zeaxanthin, including red, green, and yellow/orange bell peppers.

Another antioxidant found in abundance in red peppers is beta-cryptoxanthin, an orange-red carotenoid that can significantly cut risk for lung cancer.

GETTING THE MOST

Cook them lightly. Since vitamin C is fragile, it's readily destroyed during cooking. Eating peppers raw will provide the most of this nutrient. Beta-carotene, on the other hand, needs a little heat to release it from the pepper's fiber cells. To get the most of both nutrients, it's a good idea to steam, sauté, or microwave peppers until they're softened but still have a little crunch.

Add some fat. In order for beta-carotene to be absorbed into the bloodstream, it needs to be accompanied by a little fat. Drizzling peppers with a touch of olive oil, before or after cooking, will help you get the most of this important compound. If you're eating raw peppers, dunking them in a bit of dip will also help the beta-carotene be absorbed.

Mix 'em up. Even though peppers are one of the healthiest vegetables going, few people eat enough of them to get the full benefit. The easiest way to get more peppers in your diet is to use them as an ingredient in various recipes. You can use peppers to add a sweet punch to pasta dishes and meat loaf, for example.

Layer in a salad or a main dish. Eating a broad range of fruits and vegetables and whole grains packed with a wide variety of cancer-fighting antioxidants is a smart health strategy promoted by the American Institute for Cancer Research. Creating layered salads and entrées that include peppers is a smart way to put this plan on your plate. For example, create triple-tiered salads with a bed of mixed greens, topped with your favorite beans, topped with thinly sliced red bell peppers. Make a casserole that includes a layer of sautéed mixed peppers with onions.

Raise a glassful. Another way to get more peppers in your diet is to make them into juice. The juice from two green bell peppers contains 132 milligrams of vitamin C, three times the amount you'd get from the usual half-cup serving of chopped green pepper. Although pepper juice isn't very appetizing on its own, it adds a sweet zip to other juices, such as carrot juice. Try mixing four or five carrots with two green bell peppers in a juicer for a supercharged antioxidant cocktail.

> ## Doctor's Top Tip
>
> Roasting red bell peppers gives them a rich, full, extra-sweet, and slightly smoky flavor. Mayo Clinic dietitians suggest creating this culinary treat at home by placing washed, seeded bell peppers on a baking sheet lined with aluminum foil. Broil in the oven, turning frequently with tongs, until the skin blackens all over, about 10 minutes. Transfer the peppers to a bowl, cover, and let steam until the skin loosens, about 10 minutes. Peel and refrigerate, covered, until needed.

Sautéed Bell Peppers

1   green bell pepper

1   red bell pepper

1   yellow bell pepper

2   teaspoons olive oil

1   tablespoon balsamic vinegar

⅛   teaspoon salt

   Freshly ground black pepper

Cut the green, red, and yellow peppers in half lengthwise. Remove and discard the ribs and seeds. Cut the peppers lengthwise into ¼-inch-wide strips.

In a large skillet, heat the oil over medium-high heat. Add the peppers, and cook until they just begin to soften, 2 to 3 minutes. Remove from the heat, and sprinkle with the vinegar and salt. Season to taste with pepper. Toss and serve warm.

Makes 4 servings

PER SERVING ———————————————————

Calories: 44

Total fat: 2.4 g

Saturated fat: 0.3 g

Cholesterol: 0 mg

Sodium: 77 mg

Dietary fiber: 1.5 g

Sweet Potatoes

PACKED WITH ANTIOXIDANTS

Have you ever wondered how Scarlett O'Hara maintained her 19-inch waist? One secret may have been sweet potatoes. Before Scarlett went to a barbecue, her nanny dished up sweet potatoes to keep her from filling up on fattening party fare. We can almost hear Scarlett's gentle protest—"Why, I can't eat a thing!"—as she pushed away temptation, filled up as she was by those sweetly nutritious, oddly shaped little tubers.

Sweet potatoes are more than just a filling food, of course. A member of the morning glory family (except in name, they're not related to white potatoes), they contain a trio of powerful antioxidants: beta-carotene and vitamins C and E. This means that they can play a role in preventing cancer and heart disease. And because sweet potatoes are rich in complex carbohydrates and low in calories— there are 117 calories in a 4-ounce serving—experts recommend them for controlling weight and weight-related conditions like diabetes.

A Package of Protection

Experts often recommend sweet potatoes for their high amounts of beta-carotene. A 4-ounce serving will provide more than 14 milligrams of beta-carotene. They are an easy way to get the heart-health and cancer-fighting benefits into your diet, says Pamela Savage-Marr, RD, a health education specialist at Oakwood Health Care System in Dearborn, Michigan.

As do vitamins C and E and other antioxidants, beta-carotene helps protect the body from harmful oxygen molecules known as free radicals, says Dexter L. Morris, MD, PhD, associate professor in the department of emergency medicine at the University of North Carolina School of Medicine at Chapel Hill. Eating sweet potatoes and other foods that are rich in beta-carotene helps neutralize these molecules before they damage various parts of the body, such as the blood vessels or certain parts of the eye.

In a study of almost 1,900 men, Dr. Morris and his colleagues found that men who had the most carotenoids in their blood—not just beta-carotene but also such phytonutrients as lutein and zeaxanthin—had 72 percent fewer heart attacks than

In the Kitchen

Is that thing really a sweet potato? Sweet potatoes come in all shapes and sizes, so don't be surprised if the veggie touted by that name at your supermarket looks a little different from month to month. Sweet potatoes can have skin that's white, yellow, orange, red, or even purple. Inside, the flesh may be yellow or deep orange. But don't call it a yam—true yams are grown in South America, the Caribbean, and Africa. They have brown or black outer skin and flesh that's off-white, purple, or red and tastes sweeter than that of a sweet potato. Most "yams" sold in US supermarkets are really sweet potatoes.

Because they are cured (meaning that they are kept in high humidity and temperatures for about a week and a half) by growers before they are shipped to market, sweet potatoes are excellent keepers and will stay fresh for about a month after you bring them home from the store. It's important, however, to store them carefully to prevent them from going bad.

Keep them cool. Sweet potatoes should be stored in cellars, pantries, or basements, where temperatures stay around 45° to 55°F.

(Don't put them in the refrigerator, since this shortens their shelf life.) When sweet potatoes are stored at room temperature, they'll keep for about a week.

Store them dry. Sweet potatoes will spoil once they get wet. That's why it's best to store them dry, then wash them only when you're ready to start cooking.

Treat them gently. Sweet potatoes spoil quickly when they get cut or bruised, so don't buy them if they look damaged. At home, treating them gently will help ensure their longevity.

Bake a big batch. Baked sweet potatoes will keep in the refrigerator for 7 to 10 days. To bake, scrub the potatoes, dry them, and pierce the skins in several places. Place them on a baking sheet covered with aluminum foil (to catch dripping juices) and bake at 350°F for about 1 hour. Any leftovers can be reheated in a microwave oven or mashed with trans-fat-free margarine (buy a brand that's low in saturated fat, too) and a dab of brown sugar for a quick side dish later in the week.

those with the lowest levels. Even smokers, who need all the protection they can get, showed the benefits: Those who got the most of these protective compounds had 25 percent fewer heart attacks than those who got the least.

Sweet potatoes are also a rich source of vitamin C, with a 4-ounce serving providing 28 milligrams, or nearly half the Daily Value (DV). In addition, the same-size serving provides 6 IU of vitamin E, or 20 percent of the DV. "That's a very difficult nutrient to get from natural sources," says Paul Lachance, PhD, executive director of the Nutraceuticals Institute at Rutgers University in New Brunswick, New Jersey.

Controlling Blood Sugar

Since sweet potatoes are a good source of fiber, they're a very healthful food for people with diabetes. The fiber indirectly helps lower blood sugar levels by slowing the rate at which food is converted into glucose and absorbed into the bloodstream. And because sweet potatoes are high in complex carbohydrates, they can help people control their weight, which also helps keep diabetes under control.

The connection between weight and blood sugar levels is not a casual one. About 85 percent of people with type 2 (non-insulin-dependent) diabetes are overweight. Since sweet potatoes are so satisfying, you're less likely to reach for other, fattier foods.

The resulting weight loss can cause a dramatic improvement. In fact, losing even 5 to 10 pounds will help some people maintain normal blood sugar levels, says internist Stanley Mirsky, MD, associate clinical professor of metabolic diseases at Mount Sinai School of Medicine in New York City and author of *Controlling Diabetes the Easy Way*.

> ### Doctor's Top Tip
>
> Choose sweet potatoes over white potatoes. Harvard School of Public Health nutritionists say it's always smart to choose a more colorful vegetable over a less colorful one. That alone would make sweet a better choice than white when it comes to potatoes. The sweet potato's orange flesh is a richer source of beta-carotene and vitamins. But there's a new reason: Sweet potatoes are better for your blood sugar. Despite their name, and a flavor so divine it makes a good dessert, sweet potatoes don't raise your blood sugar as high, or as fast, as white potatoes do.

Good for the Mind

In addition to fiber and antioxidant vitamins, sweet potatoes also contain the B vitamins folate and B_6. These are the vitamins that may give the brain a boost in performing some of its functions, which can diminish as we age.

In a study at the Jean Mayer USDA Human Nutrition Research Center on Aging at Tufts University in Boston, researchers looked at the levels of folate and vitamins B_6 and B_{12} in the blood of 70 men ages 54 to 81. Men with low levels of folate and B_{12} had higher levels of an amino acid called homocysteine. High levels of homocysteine were linked to poorer performances on spatial tests such as copying a cube or a circle or identifying patterns.

GETTING THE MOST

Shop for color. When buying sweet potatoes, always choose those with the most intense, lush orange color. The richer the color, the greater the jolt of beta-carotene, says Mark Kestin, PhD, professor of nutrition at Bastyr University and affiliate assistant professor of epidemiology at the University of Washington, both in Seattle.

Have a little fat. While some vitamins dissolve in water, beta-carotene requires the presence of fat to get through the intestinal wall, says John Erdman, PhD, a beta-carotene expert and professor of food science and human nutrition at the University of Illinois in Urbana-Champaign. In most cases, you'll get the necessary amount of fat, usually 5 to 7 grams, in other foods you'll be having with your meal, he explains.

Sesame Sweet Potatoes

2 **pounds sweet potatoes**

2 **teaspoons sesame seeds**

1 **bunch scallions, chopped**

1 **tablespoon olive oil**

2 **cloves garlic, minced**

1 **tablespoon reduced-sodium soy sauce**

1 **tablespoon packed light brown sugar**

1 **teaspoon dark sesame oil**

Scrub the sweet potatoes and pat dry with paper towels. With a fork, pierce each potato in 3 or 4 places. Place the potatoes, in spoke fashion and with the thinner ends pointing toward the center, on a paper towel in a microwave oven. Microwave on high power for 5 minutes. Turn the potatoes.

Microwave for 5 to 8 minutes more, or until the potatoes can easily be pierced with the tip of a sharp knife but are still firm. Set aside until cool enough to handle. Peel, then cut into thick slices.

Place the sesame seeds in a large nonstick skillet. Stir over medium heat for 30 seconds, or until golden. Stir in the scallions, olive oil, and garlic. Cook for 30 seconds longer, or until fragrant. Add the soy sauce, brown sugar, and sesame oil. Cook until the sugar melts, about 10 seconds. Add the sweet potatoes to the pan, and toss to coat. Cook for 1 minute to heat through.

Makes 6 servings

PER SERVING

Calories: 208
Total fat: 5.6 g
Saturated fat: 0.8 g

Cholesterol: 0 mg
Sodium: 275 mg
Dietary fiber: 4.7 g

Tea

A CUP OF GOOD HEALTH

What would you think if a man in a string tie and a long, black coat came up to you and said, "Psss-ss-st. Wanna buy a drink that stops cancer of the skin, lung, stomach, colon, liver, esophagus, and pancreas? And cancer of the small intestine? And heart disease and stroke? And cavities—did I say cavities?"

"Snake oil salesman": That's what you'd think.

Well, Mister Snake Oil would be more right than wrong. Laboratory studies have shown that tea has indeed stopped tumors from forming. The risk of stroke and heart disease tumbles when you drink tea. And tea does have clout against cavities.

Tea contains hundreds of compounds called polyphenols. These compounds act like antioxidants—that is, they help neutralize harmful oxygen molecules in the body known as free radicals, which have been linked to cancer, heart disease, and a number of less serious problems, such as wrinkles.

"In general, polyphenols are very, very good antioxidants. But the best polyphenols are in tea, which has a lot of them," says Joe A. Vinson, PhD, professor of analytical chemistry at the University of Scranton in Pennsylvania. "They make up nearly 30 percent of tea's dry weight."

This may help explain why tea is the most popular beverage in the world.

Arterial Protection

Blocked arteries (and the heart attacks, high blood pressure, and strokes they can lead to) don't happen all at once. They're typically preceded by years of steadily increasing damage, in which the body's dangerous low-density lipoprotein (LDL) cholesterol oxidizes and gradually makes arteries stiff and narrow.

That's where tea can help. In studies, Dr. Vinson found that the polyphenols in tea were extremely effective in preventing cholesterol from oxidizing and fouling blood vessels. In fact, one of the polyphenols in tea, epigallocatechin gallate (EGCG), was able to neutralize five times as much LDL cholesterol as vitamin C, the strongest of the antioxidant vitamins.

One reason that tea's polyphenols are so effective is that they can work in two places at once, blocking the harmful effects of oxidized LDL cholesterol both in the bloodstream and at the artery walls, "where LDL really produces atherosclerosis," says Dr. Vinson.

In a Dutch study of 800 men, researchers found that those who ate the most flavonoids, a large phytochemical family that includes tea's polyphenols, had a 58 percent lower risk of dying from heart disease than those who ate the least. When the results were further analyzed, it was revealed that the healthiest men were those getting more than half their flavonoids from black tea, with onions and apples contributing most of the rest.

You don't need to drink rivers of tea to get the benefits. In the Dutch study, the healthiest men drank about 4 cups of tea a day.

Just as tea helps protect arteries leading from the heart, it has a similar effect on those in or leading to the brain, says Dr. Vinson.

In another large study, Dutch researchers looked at the diets of 550 men ages 50 to 69. As in the heart study, the men who had the highest flavonoid levels—those who drank almost 5 cups of black tea a day or more—were 69 percent less likely to have a stroke than the men who drank less than 3 cups of black tea a day. This finding is backed up by a new Japanese study finding that people who drank at least 5 cups of green tea daily had a whopping 62 percent lower risk of dying from clot-caused strokes. Experts think that the antioxidants in green tea help keep platelets—sticky cells that clump together to form clots—sliding safely past each other. No clots, no stroke.

Help against Cancer

Every time you grill a hamburger, compounds called heterocyclic amines form on the surface of the food. In the body, these chemicals turn into more dangerous forms, which can cause cancer, says John H. Weisburger, MD, PhD, vice president for research and director of the Naylor Dana Institute for Disease Prevention at the American Health Foundation in Valhalla, New York.

Enter the tea polyphenols. Inside the body, these compounds help prevent the formation of potential carcinogens, Dr. Weisburger says. In other words, they help stop cancer before it starts.

Cancer researcher Hasan Mukhtar, PhD, of the department of dermatology at the University of Wisconsin in Madison, has seen tea stop cancer at each stage of its life cycle, arresting both its growth and spread. And where cancerous tumors have already formed, he has seen tea shrink them.

Studying the effects of green tea on sunburned skin in laboratory animals, Dr.

THE COLOR OF TEA

Green tea. Black tea. Vanilla maple tea. French vanilla tea. Raspberry tea. Black currant tea. Apricot tea. Which tea has the most healing polyphenols?

It doesn't matter. As long as it's real tea and not herbal tea, which doesn't contain leaves from *Camellia sinensis*, the tea plant, there's very little difference among them, says tea researcher Joe A. Vinson, PhD, of the University of Scranton in Pennsylvania. After all, they all contain leaves from the same plant.

They're not identical, however. The lightest leaves, green and white, are minimally processed and, in general, retain more disease-protective polyphenols and other antioxidants. But darker teas contain healthy theaflavins, which form when their polyphenols ferment and turn orange-red. Here's a brief look at the various "real" teas:

Black. The color refers to the leaves; the beverage is deep amber. Black tea varieties include Darjeeling and Earl Grey; flavors range from spicy to flowery. Black tea may lower the risk of heart disease and colon cancer; it can also inhibit bacteria that cause cavities and bad breath.

Green. If you find the flavor too "grassy," try jewel green matcha or Japanese sencha. Green tea has been shown in numerous studies to help prevent many kinds of cancer, lower cholesterol, and boost immunity.

Oolong. Midway between green and black tea in color, flavor, and antioxidant action, oolong has a fresh floral or fruity aroma. Drinking 3 cups a day may help relieve itchy skin rashes.

Pu-ehr (poo-air). This dark red tea has an earthy flavor reminiscent of coffee and tobacco. It's considered a delicacy in China (you can purchase it online), where its processing is a highly guarded secret. The most oxidized of teas, pu-ehr is said to mellow and improve with age, like wine. It may help reduce cholesterol.

White. Rare and somewhat expensive, this least-processed tea has an extremely subtle flavor. But it does contain more antioxidants than other teas. Test tube studies show that it can block DNA mutations (which trigger tumor formation). A study on rats discovered it prevented precancerous colon tumors.

Mukhtar found that the animals given tea developed one-tenth as many tumors as those given water. (Even when the tea-treated animals developed tumors, they were often benign, not cancerous.) What's more, tea was equally effective whether given as a drink or applied to the skin. Some cosmetics companies have started adding green tea to skin products for its potential protective benefits.

Good for the Teeth

Having a toothache generally isn't a big deal, unless it's *your* toothache. Tea can help prevent the pain, since it contains numerous compounds, polyphenols as well as tannin, that act as antibiotics. In other words, tea is great for mopping up the bacteria that promote tooth decay.

Tea also contains fluoride, which provides further dental protection. When researchers at Forsyth Dental Center in Boston tested a variety of foods for their antibacterial qualities, they found that tea was far and away the most protective.

Japanese researchers at Kyushu University in Fukuoka, Japan, have identified four components in tea—tannin, catechin, caffeine, and tocopherol (a vitamin E–like substance)—that help increase the acid resistance of tooth enamel. This quartet of compounds was made even more effective with the addition of extra fluoride. The extra oomph made tooth enamel 98 percent impervious to the action of acids on the teeth.

GETTING THE MOST

Steep three and see. When you brew tea, it takes 3 minutes for it to release the health-promoting compounds. That's also the amount of time researchers use in their studies on tea. Although longer steeping causes more compounds to be released, "those compounds are bitter. And a bigger dose doesn't necessarily put twice as much of them in the body," says Dr. Vinson.

Bag it. Tea aficionados always use loose tea. No easy tea bags for them. But the pulverized contents of tea bags actually release more polyphenols than the larger loose leaves. That's because the tiny particles in the bag yield more surface area for polyphenols to dissolve into hot water.

Pick your flavors. Although green tea has been more thoroughly researched than the black variety (mainly because the first studies were done in China and Japan, where green tea is the preferred brew), both kinds show equally salutary effects, says Dr. Vinson.

If you prefer decaffeinated tea, by all means drink up. The removal of caffeine has little effect on tea's polyphenol content, so little is lost in the translation, Dr. Vinson says.

The same goes for bottled teas, iced tea, and teas made from mixes, Dr. Vinson adds. In fact, some soft drink and juice companies have been so impressed with tea's benefits that they've begun fortifying their beverages with green tea. Check out your health food store for new products.

Hold the milk—at least for now. One preliminary study in Italy found that adding milk to tea, as the British do at tea time, blocked tea's antioxidant benefits. "There is some evidence that milk protein binds to some of the tea compounds and blocks their absorption. But those compounds could get unbound in the stomach. So we're not so sure milk is bad," says Dr. Vinson.

Keep it fresh. If you make your own iced tea, drink it within a few days, suggests Dr. Vinson. "And make sure you cover it to keep it fresh when you refrigerate it," he advises. "My experience tells me not to keep iced tea for more than a week because the concentration of compounds falls off. You get to the point where about 10 percent has been lost or changed."

Have tea with meat. Since tea's polyphenol compounds help to block the formation of cancer-causing chemicals, it's a good idea to enjoy a tea party after eating fried or charred meat.

Drink it iced, too. Many bottled and powdered iced teas retain spectacular antioxidant levels. In one magazine analysis of antioxidants in various commercial iced teas, even the lowest-scoring convenience iced teas contained at least as many antioxidants as fruits and vegetables, such as strawberries and spinach! But highest honors went to homemade iced tea—cold-brewed refrigerator tea and classic hot-brewed tea that was then chilled came in almost dead even with each other for antioxidant levels. (One tip: Shake cold-brewed tea before removing tea bags, it seems to knock more antioxidants into the liquid.)

Tomatoes

PROTECTION FOR THE PROSTATE

If it weren't for Colonel Robert Gibbon Johnson, America might never have tasted the tomato.

For centuries, tomatoes, which are members of the deadly nightshade family, were thought to be toxic, capable of causing appendicitis, cancer, and "brain fever." But Colonel Johnson, an admittedly eccentric gentleman, thought otherwise. After a trip overseas in the early 1800s, he returned to Salem, New Jersey, with tomatoes and a plan to liberate this lush, red fruit from its fearsome reputation.

Never one to miss a dramatic opportunity, Johnson announced to the townsfolk that on September 26, 1820, he would eat not just one but an entire basket of tomatoes. Public excitement was high, and some 2,000 spectators arrived to watch Johnson commit what they were certain would be suicide.

He lived, of course, and tomatoes went on to become our favorite fruit. Better yet, tomatoes contain compounds that may help prevent a number of serious conditions, from heart disease and cancer to cataracts.

Cellular Protection

Tomatoes contain a red pigment called lycopene. This compound appears to act as an antioxidant—that is, it helps neutralize cell-damaging oxygen molecules called free radicals before they cause damage. Almost no one reaps more benefits from tomatoes than Italians, who eat them in one form or another virtually every day. While cooked tomatoes with a touch of oil have the highest levels of lycopene, even raw tomatoes offer powerful protection. Researchers in Italy found that people who ate seven or more servings of fresh, uncooked tomatoes a week had a 60 percent lower chance of developing stomach, colon, or rectal cancers than folks who ate two servings or less.

In one large US study of nearly 48,000 men, Harvard researchers found that men who ate at least 10 servings a week of tomatoes, whether raw, cooked, or in sauce, were able to cut their risk of developing prostate cancer by 45 percent. Ten servings sounds like a lot, but when they're spread out over an entire week, it's probably not

Trouble on the Vine

As nutritious as tomatoes are, for some people they're simply too hard to handle.

They're a common cause of allergies, causing symptoms such as hives, asthma, and headaches, says Richard Podell, MD, clinical professor in the department of family medicine at Robert Wood Johnson Medical School in New Providence, New Jersey. For some people, the problem with tomatoes is simply their acidity; eating them may make their stomachs upset or cause mouth irritation.

It's particularly important to avoid tomatoes if you're allergic to aspirin—at least until you get your doctor's okay. This is because tomatoes contain chemicals called salicylates, which are the active ingredients in aspirin. While most aspirin-sensitive people do not react to the salicylates in foods, you could be the exception, and allergic reactions can be quite serious, or even fatal, says Dr. Podell.

much more than you're getting now. A single serving, after all, is only a half-cup of tomato sauce, which is about the amount of sauce on a slice of pizza.

"Lycopene is a very strong antioxidant," says Meir Stampfer, MD, coauthor of the study and professor of epidemiology and nutrition at the Harvard School of Public Health. "For some reason, lycopene concentrates in the prostate. Men with high levels of lycopene in their blood are at lower risk for prostate cancer."

Lycopene may help cut risk by inhibiting the growth and replication of cancer cells. New lab research from the University of Illinois at Urbana-Champaign suggests lycopene may also shift the balance of male hormones that can fuel prostate cancer. It may also stop cancer before it starts by protecting genes from damage caused by free radicals. But recent studies don't agree on how protective lycopene really is. One landmark National Cancer Institute study that tracked the health and diets of 29,361 men for 4 years found only a 17 percent reduction in prostate cancer risk for those who ate pizza once a week compared with those who ate pizza less than twice a month. Of note: Among the men with a family history of prostate cancer, risk dropped if they ate more tomato products that come with a smidge of fat, such as spaghetti sauce or foods containing tomato sauce such as lasagna or pizza.

Reality check: Lycopene, tomatoes, and sauce aren't magic bullets. Recently, the FDA allowed food manufacturers to print only watered-down health claims on tomato products—claims so mild that experts expect they may never show up on the label of your favorite brand of spaghetti sauce. According to a 2-year-long government analysis, there's only limited evidence that eating a half-cup to a full cup of tomatoes or sauce a week cuts prostate risk. The FDA also concluded that it's highly unlikely or uncertain that tomatoes and sauce could prevent gastric or pancreatic cancer.

The bottom line? No single nutrient or food is so powerful that it can single-handedly stop big health threats. But don't give up on salads and order another cheeseburger. A new line of research suggests there's actually strength in numbers: Serious health benefits come when you eat a rainbow-hued diet rich in a variety of fruits, vegetables, and whole grains. In an intriguing new lab study from the Netherlands, lycopene plus vitamin E—a combination you'd get from tomato sauce and whole-wheat pasta—inhibited the growth of prostate cancer cells.

New Discoveries

In the not-too-distant future, doctors may be recommending tomatoes as a way of preventing lung cancer. Tomatoes contain two powerful compounds, coumaric acid and chlorogenic acid, that may help block the effects of nitrosamines, which are

In the Kitchen

Come February, the juiciest, vine-ripe tomatoes are but a wistful summer memory. Cheer up. Even when fresh tomatoes are out of season, sun-dried tomatoes are a great way to get the delicious taste all year and are a nice change of pace from the Roma, grape, and cherry tomatoes you can find just about year-round in the supermarket.

Unfortunately, sun-dried tomatoes can be expensive. To enjoy their rich taste without paying an exorbitant price at the supermarket, you may want to take advantage of the abundance of vine-ripened tomatoes available in summer, at a low price, and dry some yourself. Here's how:

1. Choose ripe, unbruised tomatoes. Wash thoroughly and cut off the stems and butt ends.

2. Place each tomato on its side, and cut into ¼-inch slices.

3. Put the slices on a baking sheet, and place in a 120° to 140°F oven for about 24 hours. The tomatoes are done when they're leathery, yet still pliable.

4. Pack the dried tomatoes into small jars, plastic freezer bags, or plastic containers, and refrigerate or freeze until you're ready to use them. If you're using glass jars, make sure they're at room temperature before putting them in the freezer to prevent them from breaking.

Be sure to discard any tomatoes that develop black, yellow, or white spots, which could be mold that sometimes develops during the drying process.

cancer-causing compounds that form naturally in the body and "are the most potent carcinogen in tobacco smoke," says Joseph Hotchkiss, PhD, professor of food chemistry and toxicology at Cornell University in Ithaca, New York.

Until recently, scientists believed that it was the vitamin C in fruits and vegetables that helped neutralize these dangerous compounds. But a study conducted by Dr. Hotchkiss and his colleagues revealed that tomatoes blocked the formation of nitrosamines even after the vitamin C was removed from the fruit.

The protective coumaric and chlorogenic acids found in tomatoes are also found in other fruits and vegetables, like carrots, green peppers, pineapples, and strawberries. Dr. Hotchkiss speculates that these compounds may be one of the reasons that people who eat more fruits and vegetables have a lower risk of developing cancer.

Additional Protection

Lemons and limes are not the only fruits that are high in vitamin C. Tomatoes also contain loads of this powerful vitamin, which has been shown to help relieve conditions ranging from cataracts and cancer to heart disease. One medium-size tomato provides almost 24 milligrams, or 40 percent of the Daily Value (DV) for this vitamin.

Tomatoes are also a good source of vitamin A, which has been shown to boost immunity and help prevent cancer. One medium tomato provides 766 IU of vitamin A, or 15 percent of the DV.

In addition, a tomato provides 273 milligrams of potassium, or 8 percent of the DV for this mineral. Each tomato also contains about 1 gram of iron, or 10 percent of the Recommended Dietary Allowance (RDA) for men. While the amount of iron is relatively small, your body is able to absorb it very efficiently when it's taken with the abundant vitamin C that's also in the tomatoes.

GETTING THE MOST

Shop for color. When buying fresh tomatoes, look for a brilliant shade of red. Ripe red tomatoes can have four times more beta-carotene than green, immature ones.

Shop for convenience. You don't have to buy fresh tomatoes—or those pale impostors that hit the supermarket come February—to get the healing benefits. Lycopene can withstand the high heats used in processing, so canned tomatoes and tomato sauce both contain their full complement of this helpful compound.

Get four-season fresh tomatoes (that taste good). Check out the cherry, grape, and Roma tomatoes that are for sale 12 months of the year in the produce section of your supermarket. They taste great, are juicy, and make great snacks. They taste like summer, even when vine-ripened local tomatoes are months away.

Have a little fat. "If you eat a tomato with a little bit of fat, like olive oil, you'll absorb the lycopene better," says Dr. Stampfer.

Classic Tomato Sauce

2 teaspoons olive oil

1 cup chopped onions

2 cloves garlic, minced

1 can (28 ounces) crushed tomatoes in purée

2 tablespoons no-salt-added tomato paste

1½ teaspoons dried basil

½ teaspoon dried thyme

In a Dutch oven, heat the oil over medium-low heat. Add the onions and garlic. Cook, stirring occasionally, until the onions soften, about 8 minutes. Add the tomatoes, tomato paste, basil, and thyme. Partially cover, and cook over medium heat until the tomatoes are softened, about 30 minutes.

Makes about 4 cups

Cook's Note: *This sauce is perfect served over whole-wheat pasta, couscous, quinoa, brown rice, or baked potatoes.*

PER CUP

Calories: 111	Cholesterol: 0 mg
Total fat: 2.4 g	Sodium: 495 mg
Saturated fat: 0.3 g	Dietary fiber: 4.4 g

Tropical Fruits
EXOTIC HEALING

The next time you're pushing your shopping cart past the pineapples, pause for a moment to check out their tropical neighbors. From October to January, you'll find perfect pomegranates. Guavas, masquerading as oversized lemons and limes, make their appearance in summer and again in winter. And all year long, you'll find papayas, which look like pears on steroids, as well as mangoes in hues ranging from a rather unripe green to a ripe, rosy orange. Despite their unfamiliar appearance, tropical fruits offer many of the same benefits as their homegrown kin—and then some. Not only are they high in fiber, but they also contain an array of powerful compounds that can help fight heart disease and even cancer.

While dozens of tropical fruits are grown worldwide, the ones you're most likely to find in this country are mangoes, papayas, guavas, and pomegranates.

Mango Magic

You don't really chew a mango—you slurp it up. But even though this exceedingly juicy fruit, which tastes like peach and pineapple mixed together, only sweeter, is messy to eat, it's well worth the effort.

Mangoes, like many fruits, contain large amounts of vitamin C. What makes them really special is that they also contain a lot of beta-carotene. Both vitamin C and beta-carotene are antioxidants—meaning they can block the effects of harmful oxygen molecules called free radicals. This is important because free radicals can damage healthy tissues throughout the body. What's more, they also damage the body's low-density lipoprotein (LDL) cholesterol, making it more likely to stick to the lining of artery walls and increase the risk of heart disease.

One mango contains almost 5 milligrams of beta-carotene, or 50 to 83 percent of the recommended amount of 6 to 10 milligrams, and 57 milligrams of vitamin C, or 95 percent of the Daily Value (DV). It's a very healthful mix. In an Australian study, people were given juice containing both beta-carotene and vitamin C every day for 3 weeks. Researchers found that the LDL cholesterol in the juice drinkers suffered less damage than before they started drinking up.

In a recent University of Florida study, mango extracts inhibited the growth of cancer cells in test tubes. "We can't say these compounds from mangoes are going to prevent cancer in humans because those studies haven't been done," says Susan Percival, PhD, a University of Florida nutrition and immunity specialist. "But what we can say about the mango is that it contains potent antioxidants, and it would be a good part of a healthy diet."

It's not only antioxidants that make mangoes good for the heart. They're also high in fiber, with one mango supplying almost 6 grams of fiber—more than you'd get in 1 cup of cooked oat bran. What's more, nearly half of the fiber in mangoes is the soluble kind. Study after study has shown that getting more soluble fiber in the diet can help lower cholesterol and reduce the risk of heart disease, high blood pressure, and stroke. The insoluble fiber in mangoes is also important, because it causes stools—and any harmful substances they contain—to move through the body more quickly. This means that eating more mangoes can play a role in reducing the risk of colon cancer.

The Power of Papayas

On the outside, they look like yellow or orange avocados. On the inside, you'll find beautiful yellow-orange flesh that hints at the healing power within.

In the Kitchen

The one problem with tropical fruits, at least for American shoppers, is knowing how to pick the best ones. Here's how to get the best taste every time:

Take a sniff. Tropical fruits should smell sweet and fragrant, even before they're cut. So put your nose to work before putting them in your cart. If the smell is weak, the taste will be disappointing, too.

Keep them cool, not cold. When tropical fruits need a little time to ripen, it's best to store them in a cool, dry place. But don't put them in the refrigerator, since cold literally kills the flavor.

Find the right combination. Fruit salads, yes; gelatin salads, no. It's not a good idea to combine raw papaya or pineapple with gelatin. The enzymes in the raw fruit will break down the protein in the gelatin and keep it from setting.

Avoid pomegranate stains. Rather than wrestle with the fruit itself, keep the mess to a minimum by slicing off the crown of the fruit, then cutting the remaining pomegranate into sections, says the California-based Pomegranate Council. Put the sections into a bowl of water. Roll the juice-filled arils out of the submerged sections with your fingers. Discard the fibers and skin, drain off the water, and enjoy this ancient treat.

Papayas are packed with carotenoids, natural plant pigments that give many fruits and vegetables their beautiful hues. But carotenoids do much more than pretty up a plate. They can, quite literally, save your life.

The carotenoids in papayas are extremely powerful antioxidants. Studies have shown that people who eat the most carotenoid-rich foods like papayas have a significantly lower risk of dying from heart disease and cancer.

Many fruits and vegetables contain carotenoids, but papayas are way ahead of the pack. In one study, German researchers rated 39 foods according to their carotenoid content. Papayas came out on top, with half a fruit providing almost 3.8 milligrams of carotenoids. By contrast, grapefruits (which came in second) have 3.6 milligrams, and apricots have 2.6 milligrams.

Papaya also contains a number of protease enzymes, such as papain, which are very similar to enzymes produced naturally in the stomach. Eating raw papaya during or after a meal makes it easier for the body to digest proteins, which can help ease an upset stomach. Papaya may play a role in preventing ulcers as well. In a laboratory study, animals given high doses of stomach-churning drugs were less likely to get ulcers when they were fed papaya for several days beforehand. While similar research hasn't been done in people, it seems likely that having a little papaya each day could help counteract the irritating effects of aspirin and other anti-inflammatory drugs.

In another new study, Russian researchers have found that papaya extracts speed wound healing. They speculate that papaya's antioxidant action may protect tissue from ongoing damage during the healing process.

Great Guavas

It's not always easy to find guavas in the supermarket, but these pink or yellow, lemon-size fruits, which are often available in gourmet, Hispanic, or Indian markets, are definitely worth the search.

What makes guavas so special is a carotenoid called lycopene. For a long time, lycopene took a backseat to a related compound called beta-carotene. But studies now suggest that lycopene may be even more powerful than its more-famous kin. In fact, lycopene is one of the strongest antioxidants, says Paul Lachance, PhD, professor of nutrition and executive director of the Nutraceuticals Institute at Rutgers University in New Brunswick, New Jersey.

In laboratory studies, Israeli scientists found that lycopene was able to quickly block the growth of lung cancer cells. And in a large study of almost 48,000 men, Harvard researchers found that men who got the most lycopene in their diets had a 45 percent lower risk of developing prostate cancer than those getting the least. While tomatoes have long been admired for their high lycopene content, and studies on its effects often produce conflicting results, guavas are a far better source, with at least 50 percent more lycopene in a single fruit. When researchers at the USDA's Citrus and Subtropical Products Laboratory in Winter Haven, Florida, compared the antioxidant content of 14 South Florida tropical fruits, red guava came out on top.

Finally, when it comes to dietary fiber, guava is truly a superstar, containing about 9 grams per cup. That's more fiber than you'd get in an apple, apricot, banana, and nectarine combined. This has drawn the attention of heart researchers, since getting more fiber in the diet is one of the best ways to lower cholesterol.

In a study of 120 men, Indian researchers found that those who ate five to nine guavas a day for 3 months had a drop in total cholesterol of almost 10 percent. Better yet, their levels of healthful, high-density lipoprotein cholesterol actually rose 8 percent.

Popular Pomegranates

Exotic and a tad mysterious (how do you eat one without making a huge mess?), pomegranates originated in tropical Asia and have been grown for thousands of years throughout the Mediterranean and the Middle East. Popular at Thanksgiving and Christmas, fresh pomegranates have a leathery exterior; inside are hundreds of magenta "arils"—sacs full of this fruit's distinctive sweet-tart-earthy juice. Bottled, the juice is available year-round.

Rich in antioxidants, pomegranate phytochemicals may help guard against heart-threatening atherosclerosis. When researchers at Rambam Medical Center in Haifa, Israel, tested compounds from pomegranates in lab studies, they found that these flavonoids protected particles of bad LDL cholesterol against oxidation—the first step in the development of gunky plaque that builds up in artery walls.

Moreover, a daily glass of pomegranate juice slowed the rise of cancer markers called prostate-specific antigens (PSAs) to one-quarter their usual rate in a 3-year University of California, Los Angeles, study of 50 men who had undergone surgery or radiation for prostate cancer. When prostate cancer is present, PSA levels normally double every 15 months; for juice drinkers, it took 54 months. Researchers announced they had also seen a slowdown in PSA–doubling rates for men with early-stage prostate cancer who had chosen a "watchful waiting" strategy rather than surgery, radiation, or hormone treatment. Antioxidants in the juice may protect healthy cells while isoflavones may trigger the death of cancerous cells, experts suspect.

GETTING THE MOST

Add a little fat. The lycopene in guavas is absorbed more efficiently when it's eaten with a little fat. Spooning yogurt on sliced guava, for example, will help you get the most lycopene, while adding a hint of richness to this tangy fruit.

Keep the heat down. Tropical fruits are often used as ingredients in recipes such as sauces for meat dishes. Unfortunately, the heat used in cooking destroys some of the vitamin C, says Donald V. Schlimme, PhD, professor emeritus of nutrition and food science at the University of Maryland in College Park. To get the most vitamins, he recommends eating tropical fruits raw—the way nature intended.

Store them carefully. Tropical fruits that are exposed to air and sunlight will quickly give up their vitamin C. Keeping the fruits in a cool, dark place will help keep them fresh while preserving this vital nutrient.

Ulcers

EATING FOR RELIEF

Gone are the days when doctors treated ulcers by putting people on a bland diet consisting of milk, cream, and eggs. The idea was that this bland fare would somehow neutralize excess stomach acid, which was caused, it was thought, by stress or frequent meals of three-alarm chili, and allow the ulcers to heal.

As it turns out, most ulcers are caused by a nasty bacterium called *Helicobacter pylori*—a tummy-damaging foe that can't be vanquished with a bland diet. Still, if you have an ulcer, what you eat and drink does affect how you feel, says Isadore Rosenfeld, MD, clinical professor of medicine at New York Hospital–Cornell Medical Center in New York City, and author of *Doctor, What Should I Eat?* Some foods, like coffee (including decaf), stimulate the secretion of stomach acid, which can delay healing and make the pain of ulcers worse. On the other hand, a number of foods may help protect the stomach's protective lining from attack. And choosing the right foods during ulcer treatment can make you more comfortable and even help ulcers heal faster.

The Head Healer

Cabbage is one of the oldest folk remedies for ulcers, dating back to Roman times. In 1949, a group of researchers at Stanford University School of Medicine decided to put this virtuous vegetable to the test. In the study, 13 people with ulcers drank 1 liter (about a quart) of raw cabbage juice every day. They healed six times faster than people whose only treatment was the standard bland diet.

Cabbage contains glutamine, an amino acid that increases bloodflow to the stomach and helps strengthen its protective lining.

It's an extremely effective ulcer treatment, says Michael T. Murray, ND, a naturopathic doctor, professor at Bastyr University in Seattle, and author of *Natural Alternatives to Over-the-Counter and Prescription Drugs*. The healing usually takes place in less than 1 week, he adds.

During an ulcer flare-up, Dr. Murray says, you should drink the juice from half a head (about 2 cups) of cabbage each day. If you prefer to chew your medicine, eating the same amount of raw cabbage is equally effective. Don't cook the cabbage, however, since heat destroys its anti-ulcer abilities.

Produce Protection

Your body produces extremely powerful acids to digest the food you eat. While the lining of your stomach and duodenum—the top of your small intestine—can usually protect itself from these acids, *H. pylori* can weaken it so that acids reach and erode the stomach or intestinal wall. Two-thirds of all ulcers that develop in the stomach and upper intestinal tract are caused by *H. pylori*. Most of the others are the results of overuse of over-the-counter or prescription nonsteroidal anti-inflammatory drugs—NSAIDs—such as ibuprofen or aspirin.

Many people have *H. pylori* infections. But not everyone who has an infection will develop an ulcer. Fiber may tip the ulcer odds in your favor. When Harvard School of Public Health researchers tracked 47,806 men ages 40 to 75 for 6 years, they discovered that eating fruits and vegetables helped protect against the development of duodenal ulcers—ulcers in the delicate lining of the upper part of the small intestine.

How much? Men who ate seven servings of produce a day had a 33 percent lower risk for ulcers than guys who had less than three daily helpings of fruit and vegetables. Men who ate the most had a 45 percent lower risk compared to those whose diets were more focused on meat, fat, and refined carbohydrates. And those who ate the most soluble fiber—the kind that becomes gel-like in your gastrointestinal system—cut risk by 60 percent. And getting plenty of vitamin A—from fruits and vegetables, as well as supplements—slashed risk by 57 percent. Why would fiber protect the stomach lining? Even experts at the Institute of Medicine in Washington, D.C.—a medical group that advises the federal government—aren't quite sure, but they suspect it has something to do with fiber's ability to slow down the process of digestion. This may prevent stomach acids from rushing into your small intestine and damaging it.

A Sweet Solution

When ulcer pain hits, most people are more likely to reach for a bottle of antacid than a spoonful of honey. But a dose of honey goes down a lot easier than that chalky white stuff, and it may do more than a bit of good.

Honey has been used in folk medicine for all kinds of stomach troubles. Researchers at King Saudi University College of Medicine in Saudi Arabia found that raw, unprocessed honey strengthens the lining of the stomach. And a laboratory study at the University of Waikato in New Zealand found that a mild solution of honey made from the nectar of the manuka flower, native to New Zealand, was able to completely stop the growth of ulcer-causing bacteria. Some experts recommend using only raw, unpasteurized honey for easing an ulcer, since heat-processed honey doesn't contain any of the beneficial substances. Try taking 1 tablespoon of raw, unprocessed honey at bedtime on an empty stomach. You can do this every day to help the ulcer heal. Continue this sweet treatment indefinitely to help prevent ulcers from coming back, he adds.

Healing Cultures

Yogurt is one of the great healing foods. It has been used successfully for treating yeast infections, easing lactose intolerance, and boosting immunity. There's reason to believe that it may play a role in preventing ulcers as well.

Yogurt's healing ability stems from the living stowaways it contains—live, healthful bacteria in every creamy cupful. These are friendly bacteria that will compete with the bacteria that cause ulcers. The helpful bacteria in yogurt, such as *Lactobacillus bulgaricus* and *L. acidophilus*, hustle for elbow room inside the stomach. Get enough of these beneficial bacteria in your system, and the ulcer-causing bacteria will find themselves outnumbered and unwelcome.

In addition, a natural sugar in yogurt called lactose breaks down into lactic acid during digestion. This helps restore a healthful acidic environment in the intestines.

When you have an ulcer, try eating 1 cup of yogurt three or four times a day for a couple of weeks, recommends Dr. Rosenfeld. When you combine yogurt therapy with any medical treatment you may be using, you can expect to shorten the course of your ulcer by about a third.

Incidentally, when buying yogurt, look for brands labeled "live and active cultures," which contain the beneficial live bacteria.

A Whole-Diet Plan

Even though you can help heal an ulcer by eating specific, healing foods, there's really no substitute for an overall healthful diet—even when you're clearing up your ulcer with antibiotics that fight *H. pylori* or by switching your pain reliever to something that won't damage your gastrointestinal system.

For starters, help yourself to a plantain. This cousin to the banana contains an enzyme that stimulates mucus production in the stomach lining, strengthening its natural defenses. When buying plantains, look for those that are green and slightly unripe, because these are thought to contain more of the healing enzymes.

It's also a good idea to take advantage of fiber. Getting lots of fruits, whole grains, legumes, and vegetables in your diet can help prevent or even heal ulcers. This is because these foods contain generous amounts of dietary fiber, which encourages the growth of the stomach's protective mucous layer. Dr. Rosenfeld recommends getting at least 35 grams of fiber every day, although the Daily Value (DV) for fiber is 25 grams.

Even though doctors once recommended milk as the cornerstone of anti-ulcer diets, it was bad advice. Milk not only increases stomach acid production, but some people are allergic to it, and food allergies may cause ulcers, according to Dr. Murray.

While you're making basic changes in your diet, don't forget to look at some of the obvious problem areas. Even though the caffeine in coffee doesn't cause ulcers, it can make you more susceptible to getting them. Along with cigarettes and alcohol, it can also make existing ulcers worse, says Dr. Rosenfeld.

Wheat

THE E GRAIN

Forget corn, oats, rice, or rye. For Americans, wheat is by far the number one grain. The average American, in fact, eats 148 pounds of wheat, in the form of pasta, bread, bagels, and cereals, a year.

One reason that we eat so much wheat is that it's a remarkably versatile grain. Even if you don't care for bread, there are literally dozens, if not hundreds, of common recipes that call for wheat. It has a light flavor that works well in all kinds of foods, from the flakiest biscuits to the heartiest polentas.

It's our good fortune that wheat is nutritious as well as delicious. In fact, it's one of the most healthful foods you can buy. Like all grains, wheat is rich in vitamins, minerals, and complex carbohydrates.

But what makes wheat truly special is that it contains one thing that many foods do not: vitamin E. This is important because vitamin E is mainly found in cooking oils such as safflower and canola oils. As a result, getting the Daily Value (DV) of 30 IU of vitamin E can be tricky unless you choose your foods carefully, says Susan Finn, PhD, chairperson of the American Council for Fitness and Nutrition.

Eating more wheat makes it just a little bit easier. It's worth doing, Dr. Finn adds, because vitamin E may play a direct role both in lowering cholesterol and in preventing it from sticking to the lining of artery walls, which can help reduce the risk of heart disease.

A Vitamin for the Heart

Every day, the body produces an enormous number of free radicals, which are harmful oxygen molecules that have lost an electron. As a result, these molecules go zipping through the body, grabbing extra electrons wherever they can find them. In the process, they damage cholesterol in the bloodstream, making it sticky and more likely to cling to artery walls—the first step in causing heart disease.

Research has shown that eating more wheat can help stop this process from getting started. In a study of 31,000 people, for example, researchers found that those who ate the most whole-wheat bread had a much lower risk of heart disease than those who ate white bread.

Doctors speculate that the vitamin E in wheat causes the liver to produce less cholesterol, says Michael H. Davidson, MD, executive medical director of Radiant Research in Chicago. In one study, for example, people with high cholesterol were given 20 grams (about a quarter-cup) of wheat germ a day for 4 weeks. (Most of the vitamin E in wheat is concentrated in the germ layer.) Then, for 14 weeks after that, they upped the amount to 30 grams. At the end of the study, researchers found that their cholesterol levels had dropped an average of 7 percent.

Wheat germ is a very concentrated source of vitamin E, with a little less than 2 tablespoons providing 5 IU, or about 16 percent of the DV. Oat bran and whole-wheat breads and cereals also contain vitamin E, although in smaller amounts than the germ.

Body-Wide Benefits

If you remember the oat bran frenzy of a few years ago, you already know that this grain is prized for its high fiber content. But oats aren't the only way to get a lot of

In the Kitchen

Much of the wheat in our diets comes from bread and breakfast cereals, but there are many other kinds of wheat as well. To get the most of this nutritious, delicious grain, here are a few variations you may want to try:

- **Bulgur** is made from whole-wheat kernels that have been parboiled and dried. Used either whole or cracked, it makes a great side dish and is often used as a substitute for rice.
- **Cracked wheat**, like bulgur, is made from the entire grain. However, it's milled more thoroughly and is broken into small pieces, which allows it to cook more quickly. Cracked wheat is often used as a hot cereal. It can also be used to add a nutty crunch to other cereals or to casseroles.

- **Wheat germ** is the embryo, or the sprouting part, of the grain. It's a super source of both vitamin E and fiber. You can add wheat germ when baking breads or casseroles. Some people even use it as a topping for yogurt or ice cream. Because wheat germ contains a lot of oils, however, it spoils rapidly unless it's kept in the refrigerator.
- **Rolled wheat** is made by rolling the whole grains into flat little flakes. Rolled wheat is often used for making hot cereal or as an ingredient in baked goods.

Doctor's Top Tip

Food manufacturers sometimes make it difficult to tell if you've really got a whole-wheat product, or a look-alike, warn Harvard School of Public Health nutrition experts. Your whole-wheat bread, pasta, or cereal's the real thing if it meets one of these criteria: Whole wheat is the first ingredient; there are at least 3 grams of fiber per serving; the label's got this claim: "Diets rich in whole-grain foods and other plant foods and low in total fat, saturated fat, and cholesterol may reduce the risk for heart disease and certain cancers," which means it is at least 51 percent whole grain by weight.

fiber in your diet. Wheat bran, in fact, contains more than 1½ times the fiber of oat bran, and that's good news for your health.

The type of fiber that is in wheat, called insoluble fiber, absorbs lots of water as it passes through the intestine, causing stools to get larger and heavier. The larger stools pass through the body more quickly—which means that any harmful substances they contain have less time to damage cells in the colon, says Beth Kunkel, PhD, RD, professor of food and nutrition at Clemson University in South Carolina.

When researchers analyzed more than 13 international studies involving more than 15,000 people, they found that those who got the most fiber in their diets had a substantially lower risk of developing colon cancer. The researchers estimated that if people would increase the amount of fiber in their diets to 39 grams a day, their risk of colon cancer might drop as much as 31 percent.

One serving of a whole-grain cereal (look for the words "whole wheat" or "whole oats" as the first ingredient on the ingredients list) can have 4 to 7 grams of fiber per serving and also gives you a range of nutrients found only in whole grains: a dose of niacin, thiamin, riboflavin, magnesium, phosphorus, iron, and zinc, as well as protein and some good fat. Wheat germ is also a good fiber source, with a little less than 2 tablespoons providing more than 1 gram. Bulgur, whole-wheat pasta, and cracked wheat (which is used to make tabbouleh) are other good fiber finds, says Dr. Finn.

In other studies, whole grains such as whole wheat cut risk for type 2 diabetes. Just three servings a day reduced risk by 21 to 30 percent. Grains reduce insulin resistance—a prediabetic condition in which cells resist insulin's signals to absorb blood sugar. Eating more whole grains can improve your insulin sensitivity in just 6 weeks.

Whole wheat can help guard against cancer, too. Eating more whole grains can cut the risk of gastrointestinal tract cancers, including cancers of the mouth, throat, stomach, colon, and rectum. But by how much? One review of 40 studies has found that diets rich in whole grains slashed cancer risk 34 percent.

On a day-to-day basis, more whole wheat (and other whole grains) can make life more comfortable—preventing constipation by softening and bulking up stools. Diets rich in whole grains and fiber may also cut risk for diverticulosis—a condition in which small pouches form in the colon.

Whole Wheat Versus White

If you haven't given up the white bread habit yet, we've got even more reasons why you should make the switch. According to data collected by the USDA, whole wheat's got nearly five times more fiber, twice the calcium, seven times more magnesium, and about 10 percent more niacin than enriched bleached all-purpose white flour.

GETTING THE MOST

Buy it whole. To get the most vitamin E and fiber from wheat, it's important to buy foods containing wheat germ or whole wheat, which contain the outer, more-nutritious parts of the grain. Once wheat has been processed—when making white bread or "light" cereals, for example—most of the protective ingredients are lost, says Dr. Finn.

Find it in new places. Choose whole-wheat pasta, and bake with whole-wheat flour instead of white flour (or go half-and-half). Choose whole-wheat snack crackers, tortillas, and dinner rolls. And look for breakfast cereals like shredded wheat and wheat flakes, too.

Whole-Wheat Pancakes

1¼ cups whole-wheat flour
¼ cup toasted wheat germ
1½ teaspoons baking powder
½ teaspoon ground cinnamon
⅛ teaspoon salt
1½ cups fat-free milk
¼ cup fat-free egg substitute
1 tablespoon unsalted butter, melted

In a large bowl, combine the flour, wheat germ, baking powder, cinnamon, and salt. Mix well. Add the milk, egg substitute, and butter. Mix just until the ingredients are blended. Do not overmix.

Coat a large nonstick skillet with cooking spray. Heat over medium-high heat until a drop of water dropped into the skillet sizzles. Using a ¼-cup measuring cup as a ladle, scoop out slightly less than ¼ cup of batter for each pancake. Drop the batter into the pan, being careful not to crowd the pancakes.

Cook for 2 minutes, or until the edges begin to look dry. Flip and cook for 1 minute, or until browned on the bottom. Remove from the pan.

Take the skillet off the heat, and coat it with more cooking spray. Continue until all the batter is used.

Makes 4 servings (3 pancakes each)

Cook's Note: *Place the pancakes on a baking sheet in a 175°F oven to keep them warm until all are cooked. Serve with maple syrup or honey, if desired.*

PER SERVING

Calories: 221
Total fat: 4.5 g
Saturated fat: 2.1 g

Cholesterol: 10 mg
Sodium: 325 mg
Dietary fiber: 5.5 g

Calories: 221	Cholesterol: 10 mg
Total fat: 4.5 g	Sodium: 325 mg
Saturated fat: 2.1 g	Dietary fiber: 5.5 g

Wine

THE SECRET TO A HEALTHY HEART

Ever since man discovered the fruits of fermentation, wine has been a welcome guest, not just at the dinner table but also at weddings, religious rituals, and even doctors' offices.

Only recently, however, have scientists begun to investigate the actual health benefits of sipping Chianti with your ziti. And the findings they've uncorked are enough to make any wine lover raise his glass and say, "Salut!"

Used in moderation, wine, particularly the red varieties, can help lower cholesterol and fight hardening of the arteries and heart disease. In addition, studies suggest that it can kill the bacteria that cause food poisoning and traveler's diarrhea. Obviously, experts don't recommend that people start guzzling wine rather than sipping it or that people who don't drink should suddenly start. Rather, what the evidence suggests is that moderate drinking can be a helpful addition to a healthy diet.

HEALING POWER
Can Help:

Prevent heart disease and stroke

Control intestinal bacteria

Fruit of the Vein

For years, researchers looked with amazement across the Atlantic as their French allies indulged in cigarettes, buttery croissants, and fat-laden pâtés—and were still 2½ times less likely to develop heart disease than their supposedly healthier American counterparts.

Researchers are still investigating the so-called French paradox, but it appears likely that the French have healthier hearts at least partly because of their penchant for red wines. These wines are rich in compounds that help lower cholesterol and prevent harmful low-density lipoprotein (LDL) cholesterol from sticking to the lining of artery walls—the process that leads to heart disease. Red wines also help keep blood platelets from sticking together and forming dangerous clots.

Dual-Action Heart Protection

The ways in which red wine keeps your pump primed are complex. There is more than one chemical compound at work, and some of these compounds have more than one benefit, say researchers.

For starters, the alcohol in red wine may be beneficial. For example, people who drink small amounts of alcohol seem to have increased protection from heart disease, studies show.

The reason, say researchers, is that ethanol, or alcohol, in spirited drinks raises levels of good, heart-protecting high-density lipoprotein (HDL) cholesterol.

But if raising HDL cholesterol were the only benefit, drinking red wine wouldn't be any more effective than, say, quaffing a shot of scotch or a mug of beer. And while beer and other alcoholic drinks have some benefits, wine's the only one with health-promoting polyphenols.

The reason wine seems to offer superior protection is that it contains powerful flavonoids such as quercetin. Along with other potentially protective compounds like resveratrol, it apparently helps prevent the body's dangerous LDL cholesterol from oxidizing. This, in turn, makes bad LDL cholesterol less likely to stick to artery walls.

In lab studies, resveratrol has been shown to slow aging in mice, protect against weight gain, and boost endurance. How? Resveratrol seems to improve the functioning of mitochondria—tiny power plants inside every cell in your body.

"Flavonoids in red wine are more powerful than vitamin E, which everyone knows is an important antioxidant," says John D. Folts, PhD, professor of medicine and director of the coronary thrombosis laboratory at the University of Wisconsin Medical School in Madison.

Keeping LDL cholesterol in check is a good start against heart disease, but that's not all the quercetin in wine does, says Dr. Folts. It also helps prevent platelets in blood from sticking together. Indeed, a study led by Dr. Folts and his colleagues found that when red wine was given to laboratory animals, it eliminated potentially dangerous clots, which can cause heart attacks and stroke.

"Red wine performs double duty, giving you two major benefits in one place," says Dr. Folts.

Color Counts

When researchers talk about the healing benefits of wine, they're usually referring to red wine. When it comes to heart health, researchers say, light wines pale in comparison to their robust red brethren.

In a laboratory study at the University of California, Davis, for example, researchers found that red wines could prevent anywhere from 46 to 100 percent of LDL cholesterol from oxidizing, while white wines were not as protective. Similarly, laboratory studies suggest that white wine lacks the clot-blocking ability of red, says Dr. Folts.

THE BENEFITS WITHOUT THE BOOZE

For every connoisseur of fine bouquets and vintages, there's someone who would just as soon skip the sherry and sip something sans alcohol.

If nonalcoholic wine is your toast of choice, you're in luck. Except for the alcohol, which is extracted during processing, these beverages contain the same active ingredients as "real" wines, including quercetin and resveratrol, two compounds that show healing potential.

When drinking for health, experts say, pick nonalcoholic wines the same way you do their spirited counterparts, by the darkness of their hue. Many of the protective compounds are also the ones that give the beverage its crimson color.

Why is red wine so much superior to its paler counterpart? It's all in the making, say experts.

When vintners make wine, they throw everything in the vat—not just grapes but also the skins, seeds, and stems. They're all mashed up to create a chunky mixture called must, which is where the healthy flavonoids reside.

"The longer the must ferments in the alcohol, the more of these compounds release into the wine," says Dr. Folts. "With white wine, the must is taken out early so that the wine never darkens. With red wine, the must is kept in a long time, and the wine picks up a lot of flavonoids."

UC Davis researchers have found that some red wines are also rich in saponins, which lower heart disease risk by binding to cholesterol and preventing their absorption. Saponins may also cool bodywide inflammation, which could also lower heart disease and cancer risk.

Researcher Andrew Waterhouse, PhD, professor of enology (wine chemistry) at UC Davis found that red wines contain 3 to 10 times more saponins than whites. The richest source was red Zinfandel, followed by Syrah, Pinot Noir, and Cabernet Sauvignon. The two white varieties in the study, Sauvignon Blanc and Chardonnay, contained less.

The saponins may come from the waxy grape skins and seem to dissolve into the wine during fermentation. Wines with the highest alcohol content also had the most saponins.

In moderation, wine may help you maintain a healthy weight. When researchers at the Mayo Clinic tracked drinking behavior and weight in 8,200 adults, they found that those who enjoyed one to two alcoholic beverages a day were 54 percent less likely to be obese than teetotalers. Nondrinkers and ex-drinkers were twice as likely to be obese. "People who have a glass of wine or beer each day often have it with the evening meal, and it could be that a drink replaces a later, high-calorie evening snack," speculates study coauthor Jim Rohrer, PhD.

But more didn't translate into extra-slim physiques: Those who swallowed four or more drinks per day were about 50 percent more likely to be obese than nondrinkers.

Wine against Infection

When you were a kid, you probably ran into your share of bacteria that resulted in nasty bouts of the runs. At the same time, you probably spent a lot of time running away from your mother as she chased you with drippy pink spoonfuls of bismuth subsalicylate, better known as Pepto-Bismol.

Even today, experts advise taking a shot of the pink stuff while traveling to help prevent bacterial infections that can cause traveler's diarrhea. If only it didn't taste so bad! Wouldn't it be nice if you could exchange that chalky, neon liquid for something a bit more palatable—like a nice glass of Chardonnay?

You might be able to, say scientists from Tripler Army Medical Center in Honolulu. Intrigued by the use of wine as a digestive aid throughout history, the researchers tested red wine, white wine, and bismuth subsalicylate against some of the meanest intestinal germs, including shigella, salmonella, and *Escherichia coli*. They found that both red and white wine were more effective than the drug for wiping out harmful bacteria.

FOOD ALERT

The Grapes of Wrath

Everyone knows that having a glass too many of red wine can leave you wishing your head were attached to someone else's body.

But for some people with a tendency toward migraine headaches, even a little wine can cause a lot of headache. Red wine contains substances called amines, which cause blood vessels in the brain to constrict and then expand. In sensitive people, this can result in eye-popping headaches.

Although white wine contains fewer headache-producing amines than the red varieties, it doesn't contain as many healing compounds either. So if headaches are a problem for you, you may want to ask your doctor if a nonalcoholic wine will allow you to enjoy the great tastes without the pain.

More research is needed, but it appears likely that sipping a little wine with your vacation meals could help bolster your intestinal health so that you aren't slowed down by a case of the runs.

GETTING THE MOST

Know when to say when. The most important tip for getting the maximum health benefits from your wine cellar is knowing when to put your glass down, say the experts. The daily limit is two 5-ounce glasses a day for men. Experts agree, however, that if you're at risk for overindulging—or if you have a personal or family history of alcoholism—you're better off skipping alcohol entirely.

Go for the gusto. When you're scanning the shelves for the wine with the highest levels of heart-healthy compounds, go for the full-bodied, robust varieties, advises Dr. Waterhouse.

"There is a close relationship between the level of tannin, the substance that makes wine dry, and the level of healing compounds in red wines," says Dr. Waterhouse. Three of the most heart-healthy wines are Cabernet Sauvignon, Petite Sirah, and Merlot.

Doctor's Top Tip

Nibble a wine drinker's favorite foods. When researchers from Denmark's National Institute of Public Health analyzed 3.5 million sales at 98 Danish supermarkets, they discovered another reason why wine drinkers are healthier: The Danish wine drinkers bought more healthy foods such as olives, fruits, vegetables, poultry, veal, beef, milk, and low-fat cheese. In contrast, beer drinkers bought more prepared foods, cold cuts, sausages, pork, lamb, chips, sugar, butter, margarine, and soft drinks, says Morten Groenbaek, MD, PhD, deputy director of research at the institute.

Index

Underscored references indicate boxed text.